The Anxious Mind

The Anxious Mind

An Investigation into the Varieties and Virtues of Anxiety

Charlie Kurth

The MIT Press
Cambridge, Massachusetts
London, England

© 2018 Massachusetts Institute of Technology

All rights reserved. No part of this book may be reproduced in any form by any electronic or mechanical means (including photocopying, recording, or information storage and retrieval) without permission in writing from the publisher.

This book was set in ITC Stone by Jen Jackowitz. Printed and bound in the United States of America.

Library of Congress Cataloging-in-Publication Data is available.

ISBN: 978-0-262-03765-5

10 9 8 7 6 5 4 3 2 1

For Pippin

Contents

1 **Introduction: The Philosophical Significance of Anxiety** 1
    1.1 Life's Anxieties 2
    1.2 Anxiety as a Biocognitive Emotion 6
    1.3 Puzzles and Projects: A Preview of What's to Come 13

I **Unity, Diversity, and the Science of Anxiety** 19

2 **Kinds: Anxiety, Affect Programs, and the Biocognitive Model of Emotion** 21
    2.1 The Biocognitive Model and Two Causes for Concern 22
    2.2 A Way Forward: Predictive and Explanatory Power 29
    2.3 The Case for Anxiety as a Genuine Category 32
    2.4 What Kind of Thing Might Anxiety Be? 47
    2.5 Conclusion 59

3 **Diversity: Varieties of Anxiety and Vindication** 61
    3.1 Macroindividuation and the Anxiety Affect Program 62
    3.2 Microindividuation Part I: Specifying a Standard 66
    3.3 Microindividuation Part II: Environmental, Punishment, and Practical Anxiety 67
    3.4 Microindividuation Part III: Elaborations and Refinements 84
    3.5 Objection: This "Anxiety" Ain't Anxiety 92
    3.6 Taking Stock: Two Lessons for What's to Come 97

II **Anxiety's Relevance to Moral Psychology and Ethical Theory** 101

4 **Value: The Ways Anxiety Matters** 103
    4.1 Is Anxiety Ever Fitting? 105
    4.2 Is Fitting Anxiety Instrumentally Valuable? 110

- 4.3 More Than Just Instrumentally Valuable? 126
- 4.4 Two Implications 136
- 4.5 Conclusion 143

5 Virtue: Anxiety, Agency, and Good Decision Making 145
- 5.1 The Antideliberationist Challenge 147
- 5.2 Deliberation and the Skill Model of Virtuous Agency 153
- 5.3 Two Problems with the Skill Model 156
- 5.4 Vindicating Deliberation 164
- 5.5 Toward a Better Skill-Based Account of Virtuous Agency 171
- 5.6 Further Implications: Humean and Kantian Virtue 173
- 5.7 Conclusion 181

6 Progress: Anxiety and Moral Improvement 183
- 6.1 Anxiety and Moral Improvement 184
- 6.2 Anxiety and Resistance to Moral Change 187
- 6.3 Anxiety, Reformers, and Moral Improvement: A Closer Look 190
- 6.4 Lessons from the Psychology of Moral Reformers: Cultivating Practical Anxiety 197
- 6.5 Conclusion 200

III Conclusion 203

7 Conclusion: How Did We Get Here? 205
- 7.1 Chimps, Foragers, and Egyptians: Getting Here from There 206
- 7.2 Norms, Punishment, and Uncertainty 207
- 7.3 Practical Anxiety, Norm Uncertainty, and Social Regulation 211
- 7.4 Conclusion 215

Acknowledgments 217
References 219
Index 247

1 Introduction: The Philosophical Significance of Anxiety

If you ain't nervous, you're not paying attention.
—Miles Davis

This book is about the various forms of anxiety—some familiar, some not—that color and shape our lives. The objective is twofold. The first aim, developed in part I, is to deepen our understanding of what anxiety is. We talk of 'anxiety' as if the label picks out a distinctive, uniform category. But does it? There is reason for doubt. We use 'anxiety' in a variety of ways: as a label for both social worries and hardwired responses to potential threats—not to mention existential angst and clinical disorders. To make sense of this, I develop an empirically informed account of anxiety. By providing a framework that identifies different varieties of anxiety, my account brings a much needed explanation of the diversity in our talk of anxiety. Moreover, my account also demonstrates, contra skepticism from both philosophers of science and emotion theorists, that we can reconcile empirical work indicating that anxiety is an automatic, hardwired feature of our psychology with our ordinary experiences of it as a cognitive, socially driven phenomenon.

The second aim, developed in part II, is to reorient thinking about the role of emotions in moral psychology and ethical theory. Here I argue that the current focus on largely backward-looking moral emotions like guilt and shame leaves us with a picture that is badly incomplete. To get a deeper understanding of emotions' place in the moral and evaluative domains, we must also take note of the important role that more forward-looking emotions—anxiety in particular—play in moral thought and action. Building on the investigation of part I, I focus on what I call *practical anxiety*—an unappreciated variety of anxiety that not only helps individuals identify situations where they face a difficult choice, but also engages epistemic behaviors (e.g., deliberation, reflection, information gathering) that can help them determine what the correct thing to do is. By working principally to orient us toward questions about what we should do, rather than what we have done, practical anxiety can promote better moral decision making. As such, it is an emotion that plays an important role in agency, virtue, and moral progress.

Thus, my project engages with two sets of issues. First, in asking what anxiety is, I take up core questions in philosophical psychology as well as the social and cognitive sciences regarding the nature, function, and individuation of emotions. Second, by looking at the importance that anxiety has for agency, virtue, and decision making, I engage with central issues in moral psychology and ethical theory. Moreover, while these two projects are independently interesting, we will see that they are also intimately intertwined: part II's account of the importance that anxiety has for agency and ethics builds on the empirically informed account of anxiety developed in part I.

The discussion that follows further draws out the philosophical significance of anxiety. I start by highlighting some of the ways anxiety contributes positively to social and moral life (section 1.1). I then turn to methodological and terminological matters. Here I explain my naturalistic framework and say more about how I will be using 'anxiety' and other emotion labels (section 1.2). I conclude with a brief outline of the argument to come (section 1.3).

1.1 Life's Anxieties

The claim that anxiety makes an important, positive contribution to social and moral life meets an immediate hurdle. After all, folk wisdom tells us that anxiety is an inherently unpleasant, pernicious emotion.[1] Anxiety is unpleasant, no doubt. And it can clearly go awry—taking our attention away from what matters or, worse, paralyzing us when we need to act. This, of course, is obvious to anyone who has ever struggled with a bout of anxiety. A recent slew of 'anxiety memoirs' enriches the picture with tales of anxiety-wrought havoc and disaster (e.g., Berry, 2014; Stossel, 2013; Smith,

---

1. I will say more about anxiety as an emotion (rather than, say, a mood or feeling) below.

2012). But claims about the pain and trouble that anxiety can bring aren't just bits of the common lore—they also have empirical and philosophical backing. For instance, a recent review of research investigating the effects of anxiety in evaluative settings notes that it's "predominantly harmful to task performance" (Zeidner & Matthews, 2005, p. 147). And among philosophers, there is a long tradition—in both western and eastern writings—that views anxiety, and negative emotions more generally, as problematic for virtuous thought and action: the virtuous person is typically thought to display a 'tranquil mind' in the sense that there is 'harmony' or 'serenity' among her beliefs, feelings, and motives—competing impulses have been 'silenced' (e.g., Kant, 1797/1996; Annas, 1993, 2011; Hursthouse, 1999; McDowell, 1998; Confucius, 2007, p. 20; Sarkissian, 2010). In short, we seem to have a rather unflattering picture of anxiety: it is impairing, inherently unpleasant, and inconsistent with virtue.

However, while there is much that is correct in these observations about anxiety, they're not the whole story. Anxiety also has a more moderate and productive side. Here we find forms of anxiety that not only can help us see that we face a potential threat or challenge but that also bring the caution and risk-assessment efforts that better enable us work through the challenges we face. To make this more vivid, consider Henry Marsh. Marsh is one of the world's most accomplished neurosurgeons. Though he has performed over 400 brain surgeries, these procedures still make him anxious. But, importantly, he does not see his anxiety as a distraction or a curse. Rather, he sees it as the manifestation of his accumulated surgical expertise: when determining whether to remove more of a tumor—at the risk of damaging healthy brain tissue—he is guided by his anxiety. As he explains, "You stop when you start getting more anxious. That's experience" (Knausgaard, 2015; also see Marsh, 2014).

But you don't need to be a world-class brain surgeon to benefit from anxiety. The moderate twinge of helpful anxiety is a common feature of everyday life. The pinch of unease felt when talking to a new acquaintance signals that you may have said something offensive; this discomfort then brings an increased deference that can help you get your conversation back on track. Consider as well: feeling the itch of anxiety brings focus in advance of your big test; anxious about your important presentation, you decide to review it one more time and catch a subtle but significant mistake. Anxiety in situations like these—social interactions, public performances, and occasions where one may be evaluated by others—is beneficial because it functions as a regulating device: by signaling a potential danger or challenge, and by prompting caution, focusing attention, and engaging restraint, it operates as a check on overconfidence and our tendency to just go on autopilot.

Moreover, these examples are not just cherry-picked anecdotes. As David Barlow (2001)—a clinical psychologist and founder of the Center for Anxiety and Related Disorders at Boston University—explains,

> we have known for almost 100 years that our physical and intellectual performance is driven and enhanced by the experience of anxiety, at least up to a point. In 1908, Yerkes and Dodson demonstrated this in the laboratory by showing that the performance of animals on a simple task was better if they were made 'moderately anxious' than if they were experiencing no anxiety at all. Since that time, similar observations have been made concerning human performance in a wide variety of situations and contexts. Without anxiety, little would be accomplished. The performance of athletes, entertainers, executives, artisans, and students would suffer; creativity would diminish. (p. 9)

So while we tend to focus on anxiety run amok—occasions where it manifests in unfortunate, even chronic and debilitating ways—that tendency obscures the milder, and likely more common, cases of anxiety and the benefits it can bring.

Importantly, anxiety's positive contribution is not limited to facilitating social exchange or enhancing physical and intellectual performance. Contra the negative assessment suggested by the above comments from philosophers like Kant, McDowell, and Annas, anxiety can also make a positive contribution to moral thought and action. To see this, consider the remarks of the eighteenth-century abolitionist John Woolman (1952) as he recounts a particularly formative experience in his struggles with the institution of slavery:

> My employer, having a negro woman, sold her, and desired me to write a bill of sale. ... The thing was sudden; and though *I felt uneasy* at the thoughts of writing an instrument of slavery for one of my fellow-creatures, yet I remembered that I was hired by the year, that it was my master who directed me to do it, and that it was an elderly man, a member of our Society, who bought her; so through weakness I gave way, and wrote it; but at the executing of it I was *so afflicted in my mind*, that I said before my master and the Friend that I believed slave-keeping to be a practice inconsistent with the Christian religion. (pp. 26–27, emphasis added)

Here Woolman's talk of being "uneasy" and "afflicted in [his] mind" speaks to the anxiety he felt. More importantly, his anxiety appears to have been morally beneficial in two ways. First, it helped him recognize the decision he was contemplating—agreeing to write the bill of sale and thus to participate in the slave trade—might be mistaken. But his anxiety (his persistent "affliction") also prompted the reflection and reassessment that ultimately brought him to protest the sale.

In a similar vein, consider a more familiar scenario. The doctor has just told you that given the extent of your mother's Alzheimer's, it may be time to put her in a care facility. While you are inclined to follow this suggestion, the decision makes you anxious—your mother has always been terrified of nursing homes. But because of your unease about this decision you know you must make, you begin to consider whether there might be a better way to reconcile her needs and fears. As this example draws out, your anxiety about your choice prompts (potentially) valuable brainstorming. Yet it seems to do more than just get you engaged in instrumentally valuable thought. For notice: your anxiety also captures something *admirable* about you—namely, your sensitivity to the significance of the decision you must make and your awareness of the limits of your knowledge and experience with these matters. If that is right, then it suggests that anxiety in a situation like this—a situation where you face a difficult decision—has *aretaic* value. That is, your anxiety doesn't just help you make a better decision (i.e., it doesn't just have instrumental value); it's also central to your admirable character—it's the epitome of your virtuous concern. Similarly, Nelson Mandela often remarked on the *unease* that the demands of being both a father and a freedom fighter brought. In fact, these anxieties led him to reflect on "whether one was ever justified in neglecting the welfare of one's own family in order to fight for the welfare of others" (1994, p. 212). Mandela's anxiety not only reveals his sensitivity to his important—but clashing—values, it also underlies our assessment of him. Were he not anxious about how to reconcile his competing obligations to his family and the cause, our admiration of him as a moral exemplar would diminish.[2]

The emerging picture of anxiety we have here reveals it to be a complicated emotion, one that has the potential to both help and hinder our ability to negotiate the complexities of social and moral life. What are we to

---

2. See Harbin (2016) for a related, somewhat overlapping, discussion of "moral disorientations"—the situation of discomfort we experience when our moral orientation is challenged, undermined, or radically altered.

make of all this? That, in a nutshell, is the central question of this book. As a first pass at a response, we can turn to some brief claims—slogans if you will—that gesture toward my answers.

- Anxiety is a response to problematic uncertainty: it's an emotion that can help individuals recognize and respond to potential threats, dangers, and challenges.
- Not all that we call 'anxiety' is really anxiety.
- There are distinctive varieties of anxiety that we employ in the face of (evolutionarily and culturally) significant threats—not just the threat of a potential physical harm or social critique, but also, for instance, the more general practical challenges that arise when prior experience proves to be an insufficient guide about what to do.
- Though anxiety can go badly awry, it can also be very valuable.
- A particular variety of anxiety—what I call 'practical anxiety'—is central for virtuous thought and action. It represents an important form of metacognition: one that helps us identify and address conflicts in our beliefs, attitudes, and values.
- Practical anxiety's value is not merely instrumental. It can also be aretaically, perhaps even intrinsically, valuable.
- Anxiety of a moral sort plays a central role in our understanding of good moral decision making and so can shed light on larger questions about moral progress and development.
- Like other emotions, anxiety is something we can learn to regulate—even cultivate—through instruction and experience.

The remainder of this introductory chapter will give more content to these slogans by saying more about what I take anxiety to be and placing it within the context of my broader naturalistic methodology. I end with a brief summary of the arguments to come.

1.2 Anxiety as a Biocognitive Emotion

In the discussion so far, I have made use of an intuitive understanding of anxiety. But more needs to be said. For one, we use 'anxiety' to refer to a wide-ranging set of phenomena and this makes it unclear what, if anything, might unify our anxiety talk. Moreover, even if we agree that there's something that undergirds our use of 'anxiety,' there is still the challenge of explaining what sort of thing anxiety is. For starters, 'anxiety' seems to refer to a range of affective states: an emotion, a mood, and a feeling. So which is most relevant and why? Moreover, even if we focus on anxiety understood as an emotion, significant questions remain. After all, as anyone with even a passing familiarity with emotion research is aware, there's little consensus about the nature of emotions. So what does it mean to say that anxiety is an emotion? With this as backdrop, in the balance of this section, I provide an initial sketch of the account of anxiety that I will be developing in the chapters to come. In doing this, my starting place will be somewhat stipulative (as all starting places must be). The chapters that follow aim to develop and defend this initial picture, arguing that it captures the core of what we're interested in when we talk of anxiety's importance for moral and social life.

Anxiety, as I am understanding it, is a negatively valenced affective state that can be fruitfully understood on what I will call the biocognitive model of emotion (cf. Levenson, Soto, & Pole, 2007; Sripada & Stich, 2004; Levenson, 1999). As the name suggests, the biocognitive model takes emotional episodes (e.g., instances of fear, anger, disgust, joy) to be the product of two mechanisms. First, there is a biologically hardwired "core" system that consists of emotion-specific affect programs—largely encapsulated mechanisms that automatically engage stereotyped patterns of behavior to a narrow range of basic challenges and opportunities. Second, there is a more flexible, cognitive, and culturally influenced "control" system. The control system functions both to give shape to the range of stimuli that engage the core system's affect programs and to influence the patterns of behavior that result.[3]

To better draw out what understanding anxiety as a biocognitive emotion amounts to, we can start by initially characterizing anxiety as an aversive emotional response to problematic uncertainty: anxiety is typically provoked in situations where one faces a potential threat, danger, or challenge and it tends to bring behaviors aimed at helping one address the uncertainty at hand. Within the context of the biocognitive model, this characterization suggests that anxiety's biological core (the anxiety

---

3. While I take anxiety (and, as we will see, fear) to be best understood as biocognitive emotions, I remain neutral on whether all emotions should be similarly modeled.

affect program) engages a mechanism that (i) sensitizes one to situations where one faces a threat, danger, or challenge whose potential is in some way uncertain and that (ii) prompts unease and associated behaviors—risk-minimization efforts, information gathering, and so on—that are aimed at helping one address the uncertainty at hand. The control mechanism then gives (cultural and experience-based) shape to both the range of situations that are seen as problematically uncertain and the specific types of risk-minimization and information-gathering efforts that one subsequently engages in.

With this initial sketch of anxiety as a biocognitive emotion in hand, we can now turn to look at five distinctions that will help us better understand how this picture of anxiety fits within debates about the nature of emotion.

1. To get started, it will be helpful to situate our understanding anxiety as a biocognitive emotion within the context of the distinction, familiar from research in psychology, between *trait anxiety* and *state anxiety*. As commonly understood, trait anxiety refers to a stable feature of personality—namely, an individual's *tendency* to feel anxious. By contrast, state anxiety is the *immediate episode or feeling* of anxiety. Applying this, we can see trait anxiety (i.e., anxiety as a disposition or dimension of personality) as being undergirded by the core and control mechanisms of the biocognitive model. State anxiety then amounts to the felt experience of unease that one can have when those mechanisms are engaged—that is, when one sees one's situation as involving problematic uncertainty. So in thinking about anxiety as a biocognitive emotion, we have a model that incorporates *both* its state and trait dimensions. In fact, the biocognitive model's account of the relationship between state and trait—namely, that particular anxious experiences (the state) are the upshot of interactions between the underlying trait and features of one's situation—accords both with how the dominant psychological models understand this connection and with the experimental work that substantiates it (e.g., Spielberger, 1983; Endler, Edwards, & Vitelli, 1991).[4] Moreover, that we see this is significant because

---

4. In the standard experimental paradigm used to vet state/trait models of anxiety, researchers use responses to questions about trait anxiety (e.g., In social situations I tend to feel uncomfortable; I typically get nervous when I give public presentations) to predict state anxiety (e.g., self-reports of feeling anxious after having been put in a social situation or after having been made to give a public talk). Research of this

it licenses the use of research on trait anxiety in support of claims about state anxiety.[5]

2. In understanding anxiety on the biocognitive model, we get an account of it as an object-directed *emotion*—an affective state that is different in kind from moods (and feelings). This distinction and its significance merit some discussion. The difference between emotions and moods (or feelings) is, I believe, best understood in terms of the distinctive functional roles that these states play.[6] At a high level, we can see *emotions* as affective states whose core function is to monitor an individual's situation vis-à-vis their environment (what threats/opportunities are present); they do this by engaging mechanisms (the core and control systems) that forge a tight causal connection between one's appraisal of particular features of one's situation and the response behaviors that result. *Moods*, by contrast, are affective states that function to monitor an individual's internal resources (e.g., mental and physical energy levels); these assessments then act as catalysts/inhibitors to the operation of a range of mental and physical systems—particular moods work to bias an individual's subsequent beliefs, memories, feelings, and action tendencies.

Applying this to anxiety suggests the following. Instances of anxiety (the emotion) are occasions where one experiences an affective response that combines the appraisal of particular features of one's situation as potentially threatening/challenging with a range of risk-minimization and epistemic behaviors aimed at helping one address the uncertainty at hand. So understood, anxiety (the emotion) is an intentional state both in the sense

---

sort is taken to support the claim that an individual's state anxiety is the product of her trait anxiety and her situation. See Endler and Kocovski (2001) for an overview of this work.

5. As we will see (chapters 2 and 3), the legitimacy of appeals to trait anxiety research of this sort is further enhanced when the research in question also identifies self-reports of feelings of unease or anxiety-relatedphysiological changes among those with high trait anxiety scores—it bolsters the inference that the experimental findings are the result of anxiety, not something else.

6. What follows is meant as an articulation of the emotion/mood distinction as it applies to discussion of anxiety and not as a full-fledged argument for the resulting account. (For insightful defenses of the picture I am presenting, see Wong, 2016, and Sizer, 2006. For alternatives, see Prinz, 2004, pp. 182–188; Price, 2006; Goldie, 2000; and Colombetti, 2014.)

that it has content or "aboutness" and in the sense that it is directed at something in particular (e.g., a person, one's circumstances, the decision at hand). Moreover, and as with emotions in general, this content is evaluatively loaded: to feel anxious about the meeting with your boss is to see the meeting as *potentially threatening*; to be anxious when walking through the woods is to be *concerned* about the dangers that may be lurking in the trees.

By contrast, someone in an anxious mood (because, say, she's psychologically overwhelmed or fatigued) will experience a sense of unease or worry that either isn't directed at anything in particular or is only "about" very general/diffuse features of one's situation (e.g., a broad, negative assessment about what the future holds). Moreover, this general unease will not—at least not in the first place—lead to specific risk-minimization and epistemic behaviors of the sort characteristic of anxiety the emotion. Rather, someone in an anxious mood will display certain biases. For instance, she will be more likely to see features of her situation as potentially threatening and so will be more likely to feel anxious (the emotion). But she is also more likely to experience other negative emotions like sadness and fear, and will tend to think more about past situations where she has felt overwhelmed or threatened.

With this overview of the emotion/mood distinction in hand, we can now see why it matters. For starters, because our ordinary use of 'anxiety' often fails to distinguish between anxiety the emotion and anxiety the mood, it is important for me to be clear on what my focus is—anxiety the emotion.[7] Second, in focusing on anxiety the emotion, I am taking up a project that is importantly different than other philosophical investigations of 'anxiety' that have used that label to pick out a *mood*-like state (e.g., Price, 2006; Heidegger, 1962) or a more diffuse *feeling* of unease (e.g., Ratcliffe, 2008). Finally, while anxiety the emotion and anxiety the mood are functionally distinct affective states, they nonetheless interact with one another—as well as (e.g.,) other affective/mental states—in significant ways. Thus, we can explain why, for instance, people in anxious moods more readily feel anxiety the emotion. We also get the beginnings of an

---

7. 'Anxiety' is not the only label that is ambiguous in this way. My talk of my sadness or joy can be ambiguous between the emotional state (e.g., sadness that my father has passed; joy about my successful talk) and a distinct, but similar, mood (e.g., a diffuse sadness about the state of world; a generally happy outlook on my future).

explanation of the familiar correlation between anxiety the mood and things like sadness and depression.

3. Implicit in the above discussion is the idea that anxiety is, in the first place, a forward-looking emotion. Granted, we can sometimes be anxious about things in the past (e.g., when we worry about whether we said something silly at last night's party).[8] However, as a response that—like fear—concerns threats and challenges, anxiety is an emotion that, at its core, is oriented toward the future (e.g., anxiety about, say, your big talk tomorrow or whether to take the new job). In this way, anxiety contrasts with emotions like guilt, sadness, and shame. Though these emotions can be forward-looking (e.g., anticipatory guilt), they are in the first place backward-looking.[9] As we will see, anxiety's forward-looking orientation is central not just to our understanding of it as an emotion, but also to our appreciation of its relevance for social and moral life.

4. In taking anxiety to be a biocognitive emotion, we are understanding it to be more than just a clinical phenomenon. But much of the empirical work on anxiety focuses on its extreme or pathological manifestations and this can leave the impression that 'anxiety' refers only to a clinical condition—an anxiety disorder. However, while 'anxiety' can be used to exclusively refer to a clinical state, I will be using the term in a broader sense. 'Anxiety' here will refer not just to extreme and pathological instances of apprehension and worry, but also to the more common and less intense twinges of unease that we experience, for instance, in a social encounter, before giving a public talk, or when thinking about what to do. Not only do I take this broader understanding of anxiety to pick out a familiar feature of everyday life, it's also one that is generally accepted (though often only implicitly acknowledged) among anxiety researchers (e.g., Barlow, 2001; Zeidner & Matthews, 2011; LeDoux, 2015). So, as we proceed, anxiety of the *non*clinical sort will be my central focus.

---

8. Though I grant that anxiety can be backward-looking, it's worth noting that examples like the one in the text invite alternative explanations—for instance, the unease isn't anxiety, but backward-looking regret about your behavior at the party or forward-looking anxiety about whether your actions will have repercussions.

9. Here too we might raise questions: Is (e.g.,) anticipatory guilt really a feeling of the emotion guilt and not instead a general unease (or anxiety) about the prospect that one is likely to feel guilt in the future?

5. Finally, on some understandings, the term 'anxiety' refers exclusively to consciously experienced worry, nervousness, and discomfort (e.g., LeDoux, 2015; McNally, 2009; Rachman, 2004).[10] However, and as will become more apparent in chapter 2, understanding anxiety as a biocognitive emotion entails that it's not an exclusively conscious state. More specifically, anxiety can manifest below the level of conscious awareness. It can also be experienced as a mere twinge of unease or a mild feeling of unsettledness (e.g., Horwitz & Wakefield, 2012; Öhman, 2008; Corr, 2008; LeDoux, 1996; Barlow, 2001). This broader understanding of 'anxiety' raises important questions that I want to flag. For starters, there are questions about the relationship between conscious and unconscious anxiety and what, if anything, might be special about anxiety when it's consciously experienced. There's also the implication that anxiety involves "multilevel" mental processing—at a minimum, it suggests that the processing of anxiety-provoking stimuli can proceed at a "higher" level that engages conscious processing and a "lower" level that does not.[11] Having noted some of the issues that arise when we allow that anxiety is not an exclusively conscious state, I want to postpone discussion of them and their significance until chapters 2 and 3.

Shifting gears a bit, the above discussion begins to draw out some of my methodological commitments. So let's now turn to questions of methodology. As a naturalist, I am concerned to see whether and how our ordinary talk of anxiety (and emotion more generally) fits with existing work in the social and cognitive sciences. So, for instance, I take seriously the skeptical possibility that there may be no unique thing that our anxiety talk refers to. If that's right, then 'anxiety' will be much like 'jade' or 'lily'—terms

---

10. These proposals generally acknowledge that conscious anxiety is (typically) produced by unconscious threat-detection mechanisms, but they deny that these mechanisms are (part of) "anxiety." More on this in chapters 2 and 3.

11. A couple of elaborations: (1) My talk of "lower"- and "higher"-level processing is distinct from the labels "low-road" and "high-road" of LeDoux 1996. Though some have taken LeDoux's terms to pick out (respectively) unconscious and conscious emotion processing, in recent work (e.g., LeDoux, 2015, pp. 209–214) he makes clear that this is not correct—both his "low-road" and "high-road" forms of processing are unconscious. (2) While my use of "lower"- and "higher"-level processing has affinities with the type 1 / type 2 distinction of dual-process theory, one needn't endorse a dual-process account to accept the account of anxiety that I will be developing. I return to this in chapters 2 and 3.

Introduction 13

that pick out heterogeneous collections rather than distinct natural kinds. While I do not believe that such skepticism is warranted, I do believe, as we will see, that some revision of our pretheoretical understanding of anxiety is needed (i.e., not everything we call 'anxiety' is, in fact, anxiety). That said, the revisions are modest—or so I will argue.[12]

My naturalistic commitments concern more than just my approach to issues in philosophical psychology and emotion theory. They also give shape to my thinking about moral psychology and ethical theory. This means that I am interested in the role that a scientifically realistic account of anxiety might have for our understanding of *human* agency and value. Emotions, both positive and negative, are central to how beings like us perceive, learn about, and assess the world. While it may be possible for, say, a Spock-like creature to perceive, learn, and assess without emotion, that's not how we do it. Thus, my methodology investigates the normative realm as it concerns beings like us—not radically idealized beings whose psychologies and frailties are much different from ours.

1.3 Puzzles and Projects: A Preview of What's to Come

If we want to understand why anxiety matters for moral psychology and ethical theory, we need to start with an understanding of what anxiety is in the first place. Thus, the book has two parts: part I develops and defends the biocognitive account of anxiety introduced above; part II then uses this account to tackle a range of issues regarding value, virtue, and decision making. As we will see, there is some modularity to my argument (e.g., much of the account of anxiety's value in part II could be retained even if one is skeptical of the model of anxiety as a biocognitive emotion developed in part I). That said, the discussion of part I is independently significant with respect to central issues in philosophical psychology and emotion theory. Moreover, we will see that the case for anxiety's significance for practical/

---

12. Here I follow others (e.g., Railton, 1989; Cohen, 2009) in denying that there is a sharp cutoff between when skepticism about the terms/concepts of a discourse is merited or not. Rather, philosophical accounts of a discourse can be more or less revisionary with regard to our commonsense, pretheoretical understanding of it. Thus, in aiming for a nonskeptical account, I am aiming for an account that is, in Railton's words, "tolerably revisionary" with regard to our commonsense conception.

moral life is stronger when paired with the account of what anxiety is from part I.

The claim that anxiety is a biocognitive emotion presumes that 'anxiety' picks out a unique category. But is this a mistake? After all, we use 'anxiety' in a variety of ways. Yet it's far from obvious whether or how these uses might fit with one another. For instance, in attributing 'anxiety' not just to humans, but to monkeys, rodents—even crayfish[13]—we seem to be picking out some kind of primitive, hardwired defense mechanism. But when we use the term in the context of the unease we experience in the face of social interactions and public performances, we appear to have something different in mind—a more conscious, cognitive state of worried apprehension. To this we can add talk of anxiety in clinical settings as well as the existential angst familiar from the writings of Kierkegaard, Sartre, and others. To many working in areas like the philosophy of science and emotion theory, seeing such a heterogeneous lot is grounds for skepticism—it's evidence that there's no common core to our anxiety talk (e.g., Griffiths, 1997; Rorty, 1980; Russell, 2003; Barrett, 2006; Rachman, 2004). If this skepticism is well founded, then the claim that anxiety is a biocognitive emotion is in trouble. There would be no unique thing that underlies our anxiety talk.

With this mess as backdrop, two puzzles emerge. The *Puzzle of Kinds* asks what, if anything, explains the striking range of experiences that get put under the label 'anxiety.' More specifically, does 'anxiety' pick out a genuine category, or is it—as the above might suggest—nothing more than a label for a motley collection of disparate phenomena? The *Puzzle of Diversity* builds from here. If 'anxiety' does pick out a uniform category, what distinguishes it from similar phenomena like fear, shame, and cognitive dissonance? Similarly, how are we to make sense of the range of "anxieties" we just surveyed?

Chapter 2 takes on the Puzzle of Kinds. In particular, observations about the diversity in our use of 'anxiety' raise questions not just about whether there is a substantive core to our anxiety talk, but also about whether that core is best understood as a biologically hardwired affect program as the biocognitive model presumes. Drawing on a significant body of work in

---

13. We find talk of crayfish anxiety in both academic circles (e.g., Fossat, Bacqué-Cazenave, et al., 2014) and the mainstream press (e.g., Gorman, 2014). For more examples and further discussion, see LeDoux (2015, pp. 37–41).

behavioral and abnormal psychology, psychopharmacology, and neuroscience, I show that these concerns are misplaced: the claim that anxiety is a biocognitive emotion fits better with the empirical findings than do the leading alternative accounts (e.g., anxiety is just a form of fear).

In chapter 3, I show how the biocognitive model allows us to make progress on the Puzzle of Diversity. Understanding anxiety as an emotion that combines a core affect program with a culturally shaped control system both allows us to explain how there can be different varieties of anxiety and provides us with a set of individuation criteria that we can use to determine which forms of anxiety are genuine and which only count as anxiety in a more adulterated or metaphorical sense. When we then apply these insights to our use of 'anxiety,' we see that we're able to vindicate much, though not all, of our anxiety talk. Moreover, the investigation of chapter 3 has two further payoffs. In looking more closely at the ways we talk about anxiety, we will develop a better understanding of the forms of problematic uncertainty it tracks. This, in turn, will allow us to identify three broad varieties of anxiety—what I call environmental, punishment, and practical anxiety—that will take center stage in part II of the book.

With the above model of anxiety in hand, I turn in part II to show how it helps us make progress on issues in moral psychology and ethical theory. Here we find three more puzzles: the Puzzle of Value, the Puzzle of Virtue, and the Puzzle of Progress.

At its core, the *Puzzle of Value* asks about the ways anxiety is valuable—or not. The case of Henry Marsh suggests that anxiety can, at least on some occasions, be useful. Similarly for the mild anxiety that helps you get your conversation with your new acquaintance back on track. But even if we grant that anxiety can sometimes be instrumentally valuable in situations like these, we might still think that—on balance—it tends to do more harm than good. Is that correct?

Pushing further, we can ask whether anxiety has noninstrumental value: Could it be morally valuable as the Woolman and Mandela quotes seem to suggest? Similarly, we have seen that virtuous thought and action are typically taken to entail tranquility of mind or harmony among one's beliefs, feelings, and motives. But as the case of your mother's Alzheimer's suggests, anxiety in the face of a difficult choice doesn't just get you to deliberate in ways that can help you come to a better decision. It can also *reflect well on you*—it can be an expression of your awareness of both what is at stake and your own fallibility. If that's correct, then anxiety may be aretaically valuable: it can contribute to the excellence of your character. How might we reconcile these competing assessments? And what might an answer to this question imply about the plausibility of the standard "harmony" model of virtue?

Related to the Puzzle of Value is the *Puzzle of Virtue*. As we just noted, the Alzheimer's case suggests not only that anxiety matters for virtue, but that it matters, in part, because it gets you to reflect on the decision you face. But this claim—that deliberation and reflection matter—is challenged by a recent, empirically motivated line of argument. This skepticism seeks to undermine the widely held thought that deliberation is essential to virtuous agency by arguing that we rarely—if ever—engage in the kind of genuine deliberation presupposed by most standard views of agency (e.g., Haidt, 2001; Doris, 2015; Prinz, 2007). What, if anything, might our understanding of anxiety and its value add to this debate?

In chapter 4, I argue in response to the Puzzle of Value that anxiety can be valuable. A key part of defanging worries on this front lies in turning our attention away from vivid but atypical cases of extreme anxiety and the unfortunate consequences it brings (Woody Allen movies come to mind here). When we focus instead on our more common—and less intense— experiences of anxiety, we see that the above concerns fade. So while it's certainly true that intense bouts (or deficits) of anxiety can be problematic, the emotion in general tends to be a fitting and beneficial response to a wide range of uncertain threats and difficult challenges. The argument for anxiety's value gains further support from the conclusion from part I that there are different kinds of anxiety—some of which, it turns out, are more valuable than others.

Having made a case for anxiety as a fitting and instrumentally valuable emotion, I then turn to argue for a more provocative claim: anxiety— more specifically, practical anxiety—is aretaically valuable. Building from examples like the above case of your decision about what to do for your Alzheimer's-stricken mother, I argue that feeling anxiety in the face of a novel or difficult decision like this is part of what it is to be a virtuous, morally concerned individual. To not be uneasy or worried in such a situation strikes us not just as odd, but as a failing—one is disturbingly detached from the significance and uncertainty inherent in the decision at hand. If that's correct, then anxiety is aretaically valuable.

Chapter 5 argues that an appreciation of practical anxiety is crucial for making sense of the central role that deliberation plays in our understanding of virtuous human agency and so is crucial to resolving the Puzzle of Virtue. To draw this out, I argue that an understanding of anxiety's role in our psychology provides important tools for disarming Doris/Haidt-style skepticism. In particular, I develop a two-part argument. First, I explain why deliberation matters for virtuous agency: in short, it's essential to our ability to come to good decisions about what to do in hard or novel situations—situations where automatic mechanisms alone are insufficient to provide us with the guidance we need. Second, I argue that practical anxiety is uniquely well suited to engage us in this deliberation. Not only is practical anxiety central to our ability to recognize that we face a hard choice, but the manner in which it (typically) does this—an unpleasant feeling of unease—acts as an alarm that spurs the deliberation and reflection that can help us better understand what the best thing to do is.

Building on the Puzzle of Virtue, we find the final puzzle—the *Puzzle of Progress*. If there is an important role for anxiety in virtuous agency and good decision making, then anxiety is likely to be a central mechanism of moral progress. Here the Woolman example is suggestive. But one might worry that his situation isn't representative—anxiety about (social) change seems more likely to bring resistance, not improvement.

Chapter 6 argues not only that anxiety is a central mechanism of moral progress, but also that understanding why this is the case provides us with insight both into when (practical) anxiety will contribute to progressive change in moral belief and attitude, and into what we can do to harness its potential as a mechanism of moral reform. To do this, I move in two steps. First, I examine the role that moral reformers—abolitionists, suffragists, and defenders of equality more generally—play in bringing genuinely progressive change in moral beliefs and attitudes. What we find is that many of these moral reformers display a distinctive, anxiety-driven form of moral doubt and concern: they are sensitive to the possibility that the correct thing to do might not be what is prescribed by existing moral conventions, and (as a result) they are motivated to figure out what the morally correct thing to do is. In the second step, I assemble insights uncovered in part I about what anxiety is and how it functions as well as lessons from psychiatry and clinical psychology regarding how we can productively shape when and how we feel anxiety. The result is an initial account of how (practical) anxiety can be cultivated so that we experience it at the right time and in the right way.

Stepping back, the answers to the five puzzles that emerge from these chapters hang together in a mutually reinforcing way. The account of part I offers an empirically informed model of what anxiety is and how it functions. This model then provides important resources that help us understand, in part II, the value of a forward-looking emotion like anxiety. With these preliminary matters dispatched, we are now ready to start our investigation. I begin with the Puzzle of Kinds.

I Unity, Diversity, and the Science of Anxiety

2 Kinds: Anxiety, Affect Programs, and the Biocognitive Model of Emotion

Anxiety is not a simple thing to grasp.
—Sigmund Freud

If we are to understand anxiety's relevance for moral psychology and ethical theory, we need to begin with an understanding of what anxiety is in the first place. But questions about the nature of anxiety are also independently interesting. Our move to understand anxiety, at least provisionally, as a biocognitive emotion allows us to draw this out—for the model makes claims about what anxiety is that do not obviously fit with how we talk and think about anxiety. For starters, if anxiety is a biocognitive emotion, then our talk of anxiety (or at least a substantive portion of it) refers to a unique and unified category. But does it? Given the tremendous diversity in our use of 'anxiety,' why isn't it more plausible to think our anxiety talk is not unified, but fractured—like our talk about lilies and jade? Moreover, even if we think 'anxiety' refers to a unified category, we still might deny it's a unique one: anxiety isn't its own thing, but rather just (say) a cultural elaboration of our fear response. Finally, even if we agree that 'anxiety' picks out a unified category and that anxiety itself is distinct from fear, there is still the challenge of showing that it should be understood as a biocognitive emotion—specifically, that there is an anxiety affect program that gets shaped by a set of control systems. Addressing these issues is the core project of this chapter.

To do this, I begin by saying more about both the biocognitive model of emotion in general and its application to anxiety in particular. With this in hand, I turn to explain why understanding anxiety in this way invites the first two challenges from above—whether 'anxiety' picks out a genuine category and whether it is distinct from fear (section 2.1). I then propose a general strategy for tackling this pair of worries and draw on a range of empirical findings to show that, unlike 'lily' and 'phlogiston,' there is a substantive and distinct foundation underlying our anxiety talk (sections 2.2 and 2.3). With the first two challenges addressed, I turn to the third project—explaining what kind of thing anxiety is. Here I draw on additional empirical work to argue that there is an anxiety affect program and an associated set of control systems (section 2.4).

The result of all this will be a better understanding of what it means to say that anxiety is a biocognitive emotion and a richer appreciation for why it makes sense to understand anxiety in this way. This, in turn, will provide us with a substantive, empirically informed model of anxiety that will play an important role in the investigation of chapter 3, where we will use it both to show that much of our anxiety talk can be vindicated and to identify three important subtypes or varieties of anxiety. Our model will also provide a foundation for the discussion of anxiety's value in part II.

2.1 The Biocognitive Model and Two Causes for Concern

2.1.1 The Biocognitive Model

The starting place for the biocognitive model of emotion is the idea that (many) emotions are evolutionarily and culturally shaped responses to perceived threats and opportunities.[1] So, to experience a given emotion (anger, joy, fear, anxiety, etc.) is to respond to a particular threat/opportunity with a distinctive suite of attentional, physiological, expressive, motor, and cognitive behavioral routines. Though this much is shared by most accounts of what emotions are, the distinctive feature of the biocognitive model is the claim that both the perception of threats/opportunities and the subsequent responses are the upshot of two distinctive systems: a biologically hardwired "core" system and a more flexible, cognitive, and culturally shaped "control" system. Consider, for instance, the following comments from the psychologist Robert Levenson (1999; also see figure 2.1):

At the core of the emotion system is a remarkably durable, simple, and efficient "processor," designed early in evolution to cope effectively with a few very basic, ubiquitous problems (e.g. Ekman, 1992; Lazarus, 1991; Levenson, 1994; Tooby &

---

1. Recall from section 1.2 that I take it to be an open question as to whether all or most emotion phenomena should be understood on the biocognitive model.

Kinds

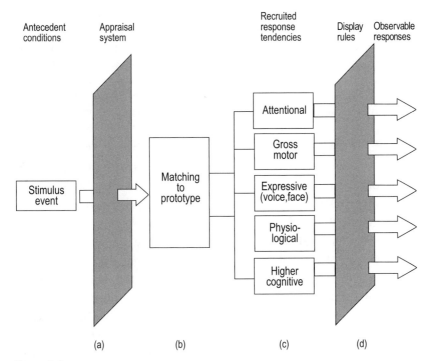

Figure 2.1
The biocognitive model of emotional episodes. The operation of the core system is depicted by elements (b) and (c); the control system's functions are represented as structures (a) and (d). More specifically, on the biocognitive model, we have in the move from (a) to (b) the appraisal system scanning information to identify stimuli representing threats and opportunities. What counts as a threat/opportunity is a function of the hardwired content of a particular affect program (e.g., contamination for disgust, challenge for anger) as enriched and modified by culture and individual experience (e.g., an experience with spoiled milk). In the transition from (b) to (c), a screened stimulus has been identified as a match for the prototype of a particular affect program. Given the match, the associated suite of (e.g.,) attentional, motor, expressive, physiological, and higher cognitive response systems is then recruited. In the move from (c) to (d), these recruited responses can then be modified by particular display rules. The resulting output is a distinctive, emotion-specific pattern of observable behavior. (For the sake of simplicity, I have omitted potential feedback loops; they will be discussed in section 2.5. Figure adapted from Levenson, 1999, p. 490.)

Cosmides, 1990) in time-tested, highly predictable, and quite automatic (e.g. Zajonc, 1984) ways. Surrounding this core system is a more recently evolved, highly flexible, and much less predictable set of control mechanisms that are designed to influence the actions of the core system. Whereas the core system is largely hard-wired and not capable of major modification in response to experience, the control mechanisms are exquisitely sensitive to learning, fine-tuning their operating parameters across the course of life. ... The control system acts on the "input" to the core system by altering the conditions that set the core system into action (e.g. Lazarus, 1991; Scherer, 1984; Smith & Ellsworth, 1985), and it acts on the "output" of the core system by intercepting tendencies to respond to prototypic situations in characteristic, stereotypical ways and modulating the translation between response tendencies and resultant behaviours (e.g. Ekman & Friesen, 1969; Hochschild, 1979). (pp. 483–484)[2]

Fleshing out the Levenson quote, we can see the core system (consisting of a set of affect programs, one per emotion type) as a mechanism that serves two functions. First, it continually scans incoming (sensory) information, screening it against a small number of hardwired prototypical threats and opportunities. Second, having detected a match, the core system automatically recruits systems that engage a coordinated suite of behaviors—behaviors that have been evolutionarily shaped to help the individual address the threat or opportunity at hand. So, for instance, in the part of the core system associated with anger (the anger affect program), we have a mechanism that integrates a capacity for detecting a particular kind of threat—for example, conspecific aggression or encroachment—with systems that bring the coordinated combination of behaviors characteristic of a "fight" response. Which specific systems are recruited, and which behaviors they prompt, will be a function of the particular affect program that has been engaged. Generally speaking, the affect programs of the core system will tend to engage mechanisms and processes responsible for (i) shifts in attention, (ii) physiological changes, (iii) the activation of particular motor programs, (iv) the engagement of distinctive vocalization routines and facial expressions, and (v) the gating of additional, higher-level cognitive processing (Levenson, 1999; Sripada & Stich, 2004; Griffiths, 1997, pp. 81, 97–99).

While the affect programs of the core system bring hardwired content and automatic processing, the control system makes use of content acquired via culture and individual experience as well as processing that is more

---

2. Also see, for example, Levenson (1999); Levenson, Soto, and Pole (2007); Sripada and Stich (2004); Lazarus (1999); Fiske (2000); Izard (2007); Hofmann, Ellard, and Siegle (2012); Cisler, Olatunji, Feldner, and Forsyth (2010); Zeidner and Matthews (2011); Öhman (2008); Corr (2008); Baumeister, Vohs, DeWall, and Zhang (2007); and de Sousa (1987, pp. 181–184).

strategic and controlled. These content and processing resources allow the control system to, in a sense, act as a filter on the inputs to, and outputs of, the core system. These filters function to affect both how one appraises emotion-eliciting stimuli and how one subsequently responds. To better see this, consider some examples. After an unfortunate experience with spoiled milk, you come to be disgusted by the smell of bad dairy products, perhaps even ripe cheeses. On the biocognitive account, this change in your disgust sensitivity is the upshot of the input side of your control system acquiring new content about what should be appraised as a contaminant and so trigger the disgust affect program (Sripada & Stich, 2004, p. 150; Kelly, 2011). We find something similar with regard to the control system's effects on the outputs of the core system's affect programs. For instance, experiments by the psychologist Paul Ekman and his colleagues provide evidence of culture affecting the behavioral tendencies of particular emotions. One well-known example involved both American and Japanese subjects. These individuals watched a stressful movie either by themselves or in the presence of an observer. The results revealed that cultural influences affected the subjects' emotional outputs. In particular, while American subjects displayed the same negative expression in both situations, the Japanese subjects masked the negative expression with a smile—but only when watching the film in the presence of the observer (Ekman, 1971; Griffiths, 1997, pp. 50–55). On the biocognitive model, these results are the upshot of cultural variations in the content of the control systems of the American and Japanese subjects—it's an example of how differences in the content of the control system's output filter can shape the behavioral responses that would otherwise have been provoked by the core system's affect programs.[3] Moreover, the control system tends to modify the inputs to, and outputs of, the core system in ways that are *functionally integrated* in the sense that what one sees as emotionally salient gives shape to the behaviors that result (Lazarus, 1999; Fiske, 2000; Öhman, 2008). For instance, Daniel Fessler's anthropological studies of Californians and Sumatrans illustrate how social

---

3. As we will see in the discussion of the repressors' coping strategy (sections 2.4.2 and 2.4.3), culture and individual learning can give shape to more than just the "display rules" that govern the (facial) expressions associated with particular emotions; they can also affect, for instance, attentional tendencies and forms of higher cognitive processing.

influences can produce culturally distinctive shame sensitivity-response combinations (Fessler, 2007).[4]

Before turning to raise worries about whether anxiety is plausibly understood as a biocognitive emotion, it is worth pausing to highlight two general virtues of the biocognitive model. First, the model helps reconcile the observation that many emotional episodes—not just instances of anxiety—appear to engage two distinct sets of capacities: (i) a set of hardwired capacities that we (and other primates) engage in the face of basic, recurrent threats and opportunities, and (ii) a more complex set of capacities that bring a broader, more refined set of culturally and environmentally tuned sensitivities and responses. Second, the model secures this reconciliation while also allowing us a degree of neutrality on some of the more contentious issues regarding the nature of emotions (cf. chapter 1). For instance, we can accept the biocognitive model without taking a stand on, say, whether the content of emotions is essentially propositional or conceptual in nature or whether emotions are best understood as (akin to) perceptual states. Given the deep disagreement we find about the nature of emotion, the biocognitive model's ability to remain neutral on questions like these is a significant advantage.

2.1.2 Challenge 1: Does 'Anxiety' Pick Out a Unified Category?

As we noted above, understanding anxiety as a biocognitive emotion presumes that 'anxiety' refers to a unified category—that the term picks out a psychological phenomenon with a common core. But establishing this is not a trivial task. After all, even a little reflection on 'anxiety' suggests it refers to a motley crew. Consider, for instance, the following (quasi-)synonyms that are employed in both everyday and professional contexts: worry, panic, fear, stress, apprehension, angst, unease, and preoccupation. Add to this the collection of clinical categories that we find in psychiatric tomes like the *Diagnostic and Statistical Manual of Mental Disorders* (the

---

4. It is worth noting that though culturally driven shaping of affect programs will tend to bring functionally integrated combinations of sensitivity and response, this does not guarantee that the resulting package will be "rational." Ripe cheese may seem ripe, but it's not going to kill you—in fact, it's likely to have nutritional and gustatory value (Sripada & Stich, 2004). I will say more about the "rationality" of emotion (especially anxiety) in chapter 4.

DSM)—things like Social Anxiety Disorder, General Anxiety Disorder, Agoraphobia, and Scrupulosity.[5] In addition to these "official" anxiety disorders, we also have a looser collection of clinical labels: test anxiety, dating anxiety, public speaking anxiety, and the like. Going in a different direction, we find things like existential anxiety—roughly, uncertainty about one's being and place in the world—that are familiar features of ordinary experience and philosophical work in the continental tradition (e.g., Kierkegaard, 1844/2006; Sartre, 1943).

Given the striking diversity we seem to have in the labels and phenomena associated with 'anxiety,' one might reasonably doubt that the term picks out a unified category. Why not think instead that like 'lily,' it picks out a heterogeneous lot or, like 'phlogiston,' it fails to refer to anything at all? This is not an idle worry. As the psychologist Paul Hoch (1949) explains, "Although it is widely recognized that anxiety is the most pervasive psychological phenomenon of our time ... there has been little or no agreement on its definition" (p. v). Though we have made significant progress in understanding anxiety since Hoch made his assessment, the general worry—is there anything that underlies and unifies our anxiety talk?—persists. Some of these lingering concerns result from general worries about the tenability of purported psychological and emotion categories. After all, if the categories of the physical and biological sciences are susceptible to this skepticism (as the above examples of phlogiston and lilies suggest), then the categories of the psychological sciences are presumably just as vulnerable—if not more so (Griffiths, 1997; Russell, 2003; Barrett, 2006; Kendler, Zachar, & Craver, 2011).[6] But there are also anxiety-specific sources

---

5. Compounding the challenge is the fact that which clinical categories go on this list depends on which version of the *DSM* one consults (for discussion see LeDoux, 2015, pp. 11–14, as well as Horwitz & Wakefield, 2012, chap. 5).

6. On this front, consider talk of 'aggression'. Though often taken as a label for a unified type of behavior—a set of action tendencies with a common psychobiological core—empirical work now suggests it is more like 'jade': an outward appearance that belies significant differences below the surface. For instance, Moyer (1976) documents how the seemingly similar "aggressive" behaviors found both on occasions when one is attacked by a predator and when one is competing for a mate are driven by very different underlying psychobiological mechanisms. For another example, see the discussion of fear in Griffiths (1997) (also see Scarantino & Griffiths, 2011; Russell 2003).

of skepticism—many of which build on observations about the diversity of our anxiety talk and the fact that, even 60 years after Hoch's remarks, there is still no universally accepted definition of 'anxiety' (Rachman, 2004, p. 7; Barlow, 2001, pp. 6–8; Baumeister & Tice, 1990). In light of all this, there's reason to worry whether our anxiety talk (or a substantive portion of it) picks out a unified category.

2.1.3 Challenge 2: Uniqueness—Is Anxiety Just a Kind of Fear?

A related worry grants that 'anxiety' refers to a unified category, but denies that it's best understood as the distinct emotion anxiety. Rather, this objection maintains that the range of phenomena we call anxiety are better understood as a (culturally modified) form of fear (e.g., Tappolet, 2016, pp. 50–51; Price, 2006). This line of thought gains support from two sources. First, there is our lived experience of fear and anxiety as responses whose phenomenology and elicitors (various types of threats and dangers) overlap in significant ways. Second, there is the precedent that we find in early research on this pair of emotions. Fear and anxiety, at least initially, were not thought to be distinct emotions in any substantive sense. Rather, they were thought to be the upshot of a *single* defense mechanism (e.g., Miller, 1959). Moreover, while more recent research functionally differentiated the two responses, this work left open whether the posited functional differences were just at the surface or whether they reflected deeper differences in the underlying mechanisms—differences of the sort we would want to see if we were to understand anxiety and fear as distinct psychological phenomena (e.g., Rachman, 2004, p. 5; Epstein, 1972). In light of this, the second challenge to the claim that anxiety is a biocognitive emotion is the demand to show that the category 'anxiety' picks out is not a form of fear, but rather a distinct emotion: anxiety.[7]

---

7. Making the case for anxiety as a genuine emotion requires distinguishing it not just from fear, but from other seemingly similar emotions and affective states (e.g., shame, embarrassment, cognitive dissonance). Given the prominence of the fear/anxiety distinction among emotion researchers, I see this as the most pressing rival hypothesis to my account of anxiety. That said, I will have more to say about how anxiety differs from other rivals in chapter 3.

2.1.4 Summing Up

Before moving to address these two challenges, it will be useful to emphasize why it's important to address them. To the extent that these skeptical challenges are well founded, it means there is no (single) thing—no distinctive mechanism or psychological process—that underlies and unifies our use of 'anxiety.' This would suggest that (much of) our anxiety talk was systematically in error. It would also mean that philosophical and scientific inquiry—our investigation of what anxiety is, what it does, and why it is valuable—is in need of significant revision and reorientation. Granted, if 'anxiety' proved not to be a unique or unified category, we might still be able to use the label to categorize and make sense of a narrower range of human interests and culturally bounded phenomena (Goldie, 2004, chap. 4). But within the context of part II of this book, that would come at a significant cost.

To see this, suppose 'anxiety' was like 'jade' in the sense of picking out a collection of distinct things (jadeite and nephrite).[8] On such a scenario, we could still use the label to categorize and make sense of a range of behaviors and experiences in much the way that 'jade' is still useful for (novice) gem collectors and buyers of green-stoned baubles. But there would be real limitations on what we could do along these lines.[9] For instance, it would be false (or at least badly misleading) to say that anxiety is a valuable part of one's character or that it plays a role in progressive moral inquiry. It would be false (or misleading) in much the same way that saying jade is more valuable than gold is. After all, while these claims purport to be general or categorical evaluations about anxiety and jade, they are, in actuality, just loose ways of speaking: the claims are true (if they are true) only with respect to certain specifications of what 'anxiety' and 'jade' refer to. We find similar limitations when we turn to matters of explanation and justification for evaluative claims about anxiety. In answering a question like "Why is anxiety a valuable part of a person's character?" we often appeal to claims about anxiety's nature and function (e.g., it is a sensitivity

---

8. Though I won't pursue the point here, I believe a similar set of concerns follows if anxiety is not jade-like, but rather a weakly genetically constrained amalgam of cultural influences and individual experiences (e.g., Goldie, 2000, pp. 98–99).

9. How significant these limitations are would turn on what alternative account of anxiety we endorse.

to uncertainty that brings reflection and reassessment). And so for these explanations/justifications to have force, those claims need to be true. But if anxiety is jade-like, then these claims about its nature/function will only be true in an attenuated sense (for a similar point, see Griffiths, 2004b, pp. 908–909). Thus, if skepticism about anxiety is well founded, it will come at a real cost.

2.2 A Way Forward: Predictive and Explanatory Power

Addressing the above pair of challenges requires showing that a substantive portion of our anxiety talk picks out a unique and unified category. As a first step toward understanding what this would involve, notice that in focusing on anxiety, we are focusing on a phenomenon that is, broadly speaking, of a psychological or biological nature. Recognizing this brings some initial answers to questions about what type of category anxiety might refer to. In particular, if 'anxiety' picks out a genuine category (i.e., one that's unique and unified), then it—like the basic categories of the biological and social sciences more generally (e.g., 'species,' 'psychopath,' 'capitalism')—is unlikely to refer to something that has a distinct, underlying essence. Rather, the categories of the biological and social sciences are generally thought to be better understood on an *antiessentialist* model of kinds. As Paul Griffiths and Andrea Scarantino explain, an

> essentialist notion of natural kinds [i.e., a notion that specifies a set of necessary and sufficient conditions] applies to categories like gold, but it is unsuitable for natural kinds in the biological and social sciences. ... In those disciplines, variability among kind members is the norm, borderline cases often emerge, and generalizations tend to be exception-ridden and only locally valid. (Scarantino and Griffiths, 2011, p. 2; also see Scarantino, 2009, pp. 949–951)

Fleshing this out, the basic antiessentialist picture—for example, the homeostatic property cluster account of Boyd (1991, 1999) or the stable property cluster model of Slater (2015)—maintains that a purported category is genuine to the extent that it picks out a collection of properties that are projectable: the category has predictive and explanatory power that can contribute to scientific understanding. Importantly, no single property in such a collection is necessary; rather, what is required is that these properties tend to regularly and stably clump together in ways that support meaningful generalizations and predictions.

Since we are interested in categories that deliver reliable predictions and informative explanations over a wide range of phenomena, we can follow Boyd, Slater, and others in setting the following as a minimal threshold that must be met for a category to count as projectable:

Minimal Projectability. We have evidence of a minimally projectable category to the extent that we can (i) identify a set of generally co-occurring features that are involved in a network of causal relations with each other and with other kind-like things, (ii) develop theories couched in terms of these categories that make successful predictions over a wide range of phenomena, and (iii) intervene in the co-occurring features to produce novel effects.

Moreover, since the defense of the robustness of a given category will be stronger to the extent that we can explain why the properties in question tend to reliably and stably clump together, we can propose a stronger test for being a genuine category:

Robust Projectability. We have evidence of a robustly projectable category to the extent that we have evidence not just for (i)–(iii) above, but also evidence that (iv) there is a (homeostatic) mechanism that undergirds the interactions of the relevant co-occurring features.

Given the distinction between minimal and robust projectability, we can see that we are better able to substantiate a positive answer to the first challenge—Does "anxiety" pick out a unified category?—to extent that we can show it to be *robustly projectable*. After all, meeting condition (iv) provides additional evidence that the predictive and explanatory power delivered by a stably co-occurring set of features is not some fluke, and so provides support that the category in question picks out something with a unified core—a genuine kind-like thing (e.g., Peacocke, 2004; Kornblith, 1993).[10] Moreover, we also have a test that helps with the second challenge: showing that the unified category that 'anxiety' picks out is not a

---

10. Two points of elaboration. First, it is worth flagging that condition (iii)—the ability to intervene to produce novel effects—also provides evidence that the predictive and explanatory power of a category is not an accident. What condition (iv) demands is, for instance, that the interventions of (iii) be such that they support the claim that the category in question is regulated by an underlying mechanism. Second, the reference to 'mechanism' in (iv) is meant to be neutral with regard to the kind of mechanism needed (e.g., neural, chemical, psychological).

form of fear, but rather anxiety. In particular, to the extent that we have evidence that the robustly projectable thing undergirding our anxiety talk is different from the robustly projectable thing that underwrites our talk of fear, we have evidence that anxiety and fear are unique kinds. In short, we now have a general and stringent test for whether a purported category like 'anxiety' is genuine in the sense of being unique and unified: Is it a robustly projectable category in the sense that it meets conditions (i)–(iv)?[11]

2.3 The Case for Anxiety as a Genuine Category

With an account of robust projectability and its significance in hand, we can now turn to empirical research that purports to be investigating anxiety to see if there is anything in this work that supports understanding 'anxiety' as a unified and unique category. As a first step, it will be helpful to say a little more about how anxiety and fear are generally understood among emotion researchers. This will allow us to formulate a set of predictions that we can use to assess whether anxiety passes our robust projectability test.

2.3.1 Background and Predictions

Work on evolutionary origins anxiety and fear suggests that these emotions originated as defensive mechanisms: they are tools that make individuals more sensitive to threats and dangers—be it predators, cliff edges, or conspecific aggression.[12] That said, while these two emotional responses share a common defensive function, they are generally thought to differ in two respects. First, the elicitation conditions for fear and anxiety differ with regard to the (un)certainty of the threat in question. Fear is a response to clear and present dangers in one's environment. Anxiety, by contrast, is a

---

11. It is worth noting that our robust projectability test is one prominent and particularly demanding way of demonstrating the scientific robustness of a purported category. However, it is not the only way one might attempt to do this. Thus, in using robust projectability to make my case for anxiety as a unique and unified category, I take myself to be setting a high bar. If one is inclined toward something less demanding as the standard (e.g., Prinz, 2004; Tooby & Cosmides, 1990), all the better for me.
12. For investigations of anxiety and fear in evolutionary terms, see, for example, Kurth (2016); Avery, Clauss, and Blackford (2016); Öhman (2008, 1986); Gilbert (2001); Marks and Nesse (1994); and Baumeister and Tice (1990). I will return to questions about anxiety and fear's evolutionary origins in chapter 7.

response to situations where the nature of the threat is uncertain in the sense of involving a danger whose potential is unpredictable, uncontrollable, or otherwise open to question. Second, there are significant differences in the behavioral tendencies associated with fear and anxiety. Because fear concerns *clear* threats, it typically engages specific, situation-appropriate responses (e.g., particular fight/flight/freeze behaviors; tonic immobility). Anxiety, by contrast, concerns situations involving *unclear* threats. So it typically leads to more general risk-minimization efforts (e.g., avoidance behaviors) as well as epistemic behaviors that are aimed at helping one address the uncertainty about the presumed threat (e.g., information gathering). While I will have more to say about the kind of uncertainty associated with anxiety (section 3.3), the key point for present purposes is that assessments of (un)certainty and their ties to particular behavioral tendencies are the core of the (conceptual and functional) distinction between fear and anxiety: there is a threshold regarding how certain one is about the nature of a perceived threat that, when crossed, allows for the engagement of the specific behavior characteristic of fear (fight/flight/freeze and the like); threat assessments that remain below this threshold prompt the risk-minimization and epistemic behaviors distinctive of anxiety (Davis, Walker, et al., 2010; Öhman, 2008; Corr, 2008; Gray & McNaughton, 2000).

Bringing these observations about research on the evolutionary origins of fear and anxiety together, we can extract basic functional characterizations of these emotions that, in line with our antiessentialist methodology (section 2.2), locate them within the larger causal processes distinctive of threat detection and response:

Core fear. A defensive response that is triggered by clear and present dangers in one's surroundings, and that engages specific, situation-appropriate behaviors (e.g., fight/flight/freeze).

Core anxiety. A defensive response that is triggered by threats and challenges that are unpredictable, uncontrollable, or otherwise uncertain in nature, and that prompts general patterns of risk-assessment and risk-minimization behavior.

Not only do these characterizations resonate with our own experiences of these emotions, but they provide us with the material we need to formulate predictions we can use to determine whether anxiety and fear are robustly projectable in a way that will allow us to assess the two challenges from section 2.1.[13] Turning to details, we can identify four broad sets of predictions about anxiety and fear:

P1: Similar threat detection. As defensive responses, we should expect both fear and anxiety to be triggered by stimuli that are threat-relevant from an evolutionary point of view. We should also expect them to enhance an individual's awareness of and sensitivity to threats and dangers.

P2: Similar defense mobilization. As defense mechanisms, we should expect that instances of anxiety and fear should tend to engage similar, threat-relevant physiological changes—things like heightened levels of arousal and increases in heart rate.

P3: Distinct defensive responses. Fear and anxiety should display different action tendencies—differences that correspond to (e.g.,) the proximity and certainty of the danger at hand. In particular, since fear is a response to imminent threats, we should see a tendency toward patterns of fight/flight/freeze behavior in the face of (physically, temporally) near or certain threats. By contrast, we should find a tendency toward more general risk-assessment and risk-avoidance behaviors when a potential threat is more distant and uncertain.

P4: Distinct underlying mechanisms. Our functional characterizations predict that we should be able to intervene in ways that not only disrupt the patterns of behavior characteristic of anxiety and fear, but do so in ways that allow for dissociations of these two responses. More specifically, if anxiety and fear are distinct psychological responses, then there should be evidence that they engage (e.g.,) different chemical pathways and neural structures. For instance, a wealth of neuroscientific research implicates the extended amygdala complex (EAC) as undergirding threat-detection and threat-response capabilities.[14] Thus, if anxiety and fear are genuine but distinct defensive responses, we should expect not only that they will engage the

---

13. Recall the methodological point from section 1.2: this starting place, while intuitive and grounded in empirical work on anxiety, is (by necessity) somewhat stipulative. The discussion that follows aims to remove this stipulative air by showing that much of our anxiety talk fits within the account we will be developing.

14. The extended amygdala complex consists of both the central and medial nuclei of the amygdala as well as the bed nucleus of the stria terminalis. (For details, see, e.g., Alheid & Heimer, 1988, and LeDoux, 2000.)

EAC, but that there will be differences in the specific structures within the complex that are engaged by episodes of anxiety and fear.

In what follows, I will show that these predictions are borne out by three broad lines of research: (i) behavioral and physiological investigation of responses to threat cues, (ii) psychopharmacological work concerning the chemical pathways underlying fear and anxiety, and (iii) neuroanatomical research from lesion studies and brain imaging work. Moreover, because the research we will be reviewing provides the foundation for our current understanding of the cognitive architecture that undergirds fear and anxiety (for recent overviews, see Avery, Clauss, & Blackford, 2016; LeDoux, 2015; Davis, Walker, et al., 2010; Öhman, 2008), they allow us to make a strong case for the distinct and robust projectability of anxiety. This will not only allow us to address our first two challenges, but will also allow us to draw out important findings for our subsequent discussion and defense of the anxiety affect program and the biocognitive model.

2.3.2 Behavioral and Physiological Evidence

If anxiety and fear are mechanisms that facilitate one's ability to recognize and respond to threats, then we should expect them to bring attentional biases toward threatening stimuli as well as physiological changes associated with the presence of a threat (e.g., arousal, increased cortisol levels). We should also expect to see differences in the larger action tendencies that conform with our theoretical characterizations of these emotions: imminent threats should be associated with the fight/flight/freeze response of fear, while for more distant and uncertain threats we should see the risk-assessment and risk-minimization behaviors of anxiety.

To begin to assess these predictions, we can start with P1—the predictions concerning threat detection and attentional biases. If anxiety and fear are threat-detection mechanisms, then they should affect attentional systems in ways that make threats more salient; they should make threats appear to "pop out" from their surroundings. And they do. To see this, consider results from visual search experiments. In this work, participants are tasked with picking out target images among a set of distractors. Here we find that threatening target images (e.g., spiders, snakes) are located more quickly than nonthreatening ones (e.g., mushrooms, flowers)—a result that supports the claim that we have a general attentional bias toward stimuli that are threat-relevant (e.g., Brosch & Sharma, 2005; Öhman, Lundqvist,

& Esteves, 2001). More importantly, we also find that the anxious and phobic individuals (as determined by self-report measures) are faster than nonanxious/nonphobic control subjects to pick out threatening target images, but that there is no difference in the response times of these two groups with regard to locating unthreatening target images. That is, anxiety and fear seem to accentuate the "pop-out" effect for threats. More specifically, because anxious/phobic individuals are faster only with respect to identifying threatening images, these results are generally taken to demonstrate that anxiety and fear function as a threat-detection mechanism (rather than reflecting, say, a general skittishness) (Öhman, Flykt, & Esteves, 2001).

Not only have these results been widely replicated (e.g., Shasteen, Sasson, & Pinkham, 2014; Rinck, Reinecke, et al., 2005; Miltner, Kriechel, et al., 2004), but related work has extended the basic findings. Two features of this subsequent work are of particular note for the discussion to come. First, we have results showing that there are anxiety- and fear-driven attentional biases not just to *environmental* dangers like snakes and spiders, but also to *social* threats like angry and fearful faces. For instance, anxious/phobic individuals are quicker to focus their attention on threatening faces than on happy or neutral ones (Bradley, Mogg, Falla, & Hamilton, 1998; Derryberry & Reed, 2002). They are also quicker to follow the gaze of fearful faces than neutral ones (e.g., Mathews, Fox, Yiend, & Calder, 2003). Second, anxious/phobic subjects report higher levels of state anxiety and fear after completing the pop-out task than do controls—a result that provides further evidence implicating anxiety and fear as responsible for the threat detection rather than some more general mechanism (e.g., Rinck, Reinecke, et al., 2005).

Let's now turn to evidence showing that anxiety and fear display the physiological changes characteristic of looming dangers (i.e., P2). On this front, a standard experimental paradigm measures skin-conductance responses in both anxious/phobic individuals and normal controls as they are presented with a range of threatening and unthreatening images (e.g., snakes and spiders versus flowers and mushrooms). Since increased skin conductance is a standard measure of arousal, we should expect to find more pronounced responses in anxious/phobic individuals when viewing threatening images. And we do. While the skin-conductance responses of anxious/phobic subjects were no different from controls with regard to the neutral stimuli, they showed significantly elevated responses (compared to controls) to the threatening images (Öhman & Soares, 1993). Thus, we get support for the claim that anxiety and fear are defense mechanisms—they prompt the kinds of physiological changes (e.g., increased arousal) we would expect to see in an individual facing a threat. As with the visual search experiments, these results have been widely replicated (e.g., Wangelin, Bradley, et al., 2014; Öhman & Soares, 1998, 1994; Soares & Öhman, 1993a, 1993b). And similar results have also been found for social threats: we see more pronounced skin-conductance responses to angry faces in comparison to neutral ones (e.g., Wangelin, Bradley, et al., 2014; Parra, Esteves, Flykt, & Öhman, 1997; Esteves, Dimberg, & Öhman, 1994). Moreover, anxious/phobic subjects report feeling more avoidant, more aroused, and less in control when viewing the masked threat stimuli (Öhman & Soares, 1994). So here too we get evidence that anxiety and fear are responsible for these physiological changes.[15]

Finally, consider the prediction from above concerning differences in the response tendencies—namely, that reducing the proximity or certainty of a threat should bring a shift from fear-related behaviors to anxiety-related responses (i.e., P3). On this front, we get confirmation from research on animal models (mostly rats and mice) as well as work that extends these findings to humans. The basic setup for the rodent-based research is simple: observe what happens when a mouse is presented with (un)certain threats. In the classic version of this work, a cat is put into a mouse's enclosure (i.e., the introduction of an imminent threat). Unsurprisingly, we find that introducing the cat brings a characteristic fear response in the mouse: flight (burrowing), freezing, and defensive vocalizations. By contrast, exposure to cat odor (i.e., introducing a less certain threat) brings the more general patterns of risk assessment associated with (rodent) anxiety: "head out" peaking from a burrow, cautious exploration of the surroundings, and increased vigilance (Blanchard, Yudko, Rodgers, & Blanchard, 1993; Blanchard, Griebel, Henrie, & Blanchard, 1997; Blanchard & Blanchard, 2008; Gray & McNaughton, 2000).

Similar findings—that is, more (less) imminent threats bring fear-related (anxiety-related) behavior—have been found in humans. However, since IRB panels frown on experiments that expose humans to the equivalent

---

15. As we will see (section 2.4), while these results provide support for P2, the larger picture of anxiety's (and fear's) physiological effects is more complicated.

of the above cat-threat condition, most of this research uses responses to questionnaires or computer simulations. For instance, using vignettes that describe a range of threat scenarios (e.g., imminent attack in a dark parking lot, hearing strange noises at night), we find subjects reporting that they would respond with fight/flight-like responses (e.g., look for weapon, run away) when presented with scenarios describing certain threats. By contrast, when the vignettes describe situations where the nature of the threat is less certain, subjects indicate they would respond with more risk-assessment behaviors (e.g., investigate, cautious approach) (Blanchard, Hynd, et al., 2001; Perkins & Corr, 2006). We get similar results from an experimental setup using computer-simulated threat scenarios to assess flight/approach tendencies in response to imminent and distant threats. Here again we see that the more imminent the threat, the more likely the individual is to flee rather than approach (Perkins, Ettinger, et al., 2009; Alvarez, Chen, et al., 2011; Phelps, O'Connor, et al., 2001).

Taken together, these behavioral findings provide support for three of the above predictions. We get evidence that both anxiety and fear enhance threat sensitivity (P1), that they both bring physiological changes associated with preparation for danger (P2), and that they engage distinctive patterns of behavior that are sensitive to the (un)certainty of the threat at hand (P3). As we will see, work in psychopharmacology and neuroscience not only bolsters these findings but also provides significant support for P4: anxiety and fear are undergirded by distinct causal mechanisms.

2.3.3 Psychopharmacological Evidence

Given the above account of the functional differences between anxiety and fear (section 2.3.1), we should expect that antianxiety drugs (i.e., anxiolytics like lorazepam and diazepam) should both reduce sensitivity to ambiguous threats and attenuate the associated risk-minimization and epistemic behaviors. Similarly, we should see corresponding effects for drugs used to treat fear and panic disorders (i.e., panicolytics like citalopram)—namely, reduced sensitivity to imminent threats and less pronounced fear-related behaviors.

Work on rodents suggests that anxiety and fear are doubly dissociable in a manner that indicates they are regulated by different chemical pathways. Recall, for instance, the behavioral findings discussed above. That work shows that an imminent danger (e.g., presence of a cat) brings the fight/flight/freeze response of fear, while an uncertain threat (e.g., cat odor) prompts efforts toward risk assessment and minimization. Building on this basic finding, we see that when rats and mice are given panicolytics, the fear-related responses are blocked, though the anxiety-related behavior remains unaffected. We also see the converse when anxiolytics are administered: anxiety-related behavior is blocked but there is no similar change in fear-related behavior (Blanchard, Yudko, Rodgers, & Blanchard, 1993; Blanchard, Griebel, Henrie, & Blanchard, 1997; Gray & McNaughton, 2000).[16]

Variations of this psychopharmacological research operationalize fear and anxiety in terms of distinctive startle responses (startle reactions, in general, are defensive reactions elicited by sudden, unexpected stimuli). This startle-based research is significant not only because it builds from and further affirms the above findings regarding anxiolytics, but also because, as we will see, it provides an experimental design that can be extended to humans. On the rodent version of this work, fear is operationally defined in terms of an enhanced short-duration startle response to a *predictable* threat. For instance, rats are conditioned to associate a certain tone with electric shocks: the conditioning makes the tone a reliable signal for the threat (the shock). Fear is then defined as an enhanced startle response when the shock is paired with the tone in comparison to the shock alone (this is called 'fear-potentiated startle')—a proposal that fits well with our understanding of fear as a response to immanent dangers (here, predictable shock). Anxiety, by contrast, is operationally defined in terms of an enhanced startle response to an *unpredictable* threat. For instance, rats—as nocturnal critters—respond with cautious risk-assessment behavior when transitioned from a dark enclosure to a brightly lit one. This allows us to define anxiety as an enhanced, long-duration startle response in rats when moved from dark to light as compared to the startle response when they remain in the dark (this is "light-enhanced startle"); here too we have something that accords with our picture of anxiety as a sustained state of apprehension to an uncertain threat. In line with the earlier findings, this startle-based

---

16. We find a similar double dissociation in rodent experiments using elevated T-mazes. In this work, anxiety is operationalized as apprehension to entering the (potentially dangerous) maze and fear is defined as fleeing the maze when dropped into it. Anxiolytics block apprehension to entering, but not fleeing; panicolytics block fleeing, but not apprehension to entering (Pultronier, Zangrossi, & de Barros Viana, 2003; Teixeira, Zangrossi, & Graeff, 2000).

research affirms the ability of anxiolytics to reduce anxiety—but not fear-related behaviors (e.g., de Jongh, Groenink, Van der Gugten, and Olivier, 2002; Walker & Davis, 1997, 2002a).

In experiments on humans, the setup is slightly different. Fear is still operationalized as fear-potentiated startle. But because, in contrast to rodents, we are diurnal and not nocturnal, a revised definition of anxiety is used—'dark-enhanced startle': the enhanced long-duration startle reaction that is seen when a human participant is moved from light to dark (in comparison to their startle responses when they remain in the light). The results from startle research of this sort, while not as robust or well understood as the work on rodents, nonetheless suggest that findings from the rodent studies carry over: anxiolytics block anxiety-related behavior (i.e., dark-enhanced startle) but have no effect on fear-related responses (i.e., fear-potentiated startle) (Baas, Grillon, et al., 2002).[17]

Taken together, this psychopharmacological research provides further support for the predictions about behavioral differences between anxiety and fear in the face of (un)certain threats (P3). We also get evidence that these responses engage distinct—and dissociable—chemical pathways (P4), though we saw there were limitations in our ability to extend the results from the rodent studies to humans. So while we have some confirmation that the disassociations of the rodent research also occur in humans, we should not put too much weight on these findings. Fortunately, we get additional—independent—evidence from lesion and imaging studies.

2.3.4 Neuroanatomical Evidence

Some of the most provocative research validating the robust projectability of anxiety comes from lesion and imaging studies indicating that anxiety and fear engage distinct neuroanatomical structures within the extended amygdala complex (EAC). As such, it significantly bolsters the psychopharmacological evidence supporting the prediction that patterns of behavior characteristic of these emotions are underwritten by different homeostatic mechanisms (i.e., P4).

---

17. More specifically, whether we see anxiolytic effects like this in humans appears to depend on (inter alia) which anxiolytic drug is used, though how exactly these drugs have their effects is not well understood (see Davis, Walker, et al., 2010, for discussion).

On this front, first consider the lesion studies. Here we find a wealth of research implicating the central nucleus of the amygdala (CeA) as a neural structure that plays a distinctive role in underwriting fear and the bed nucleus of the stria terminalis (BNST) as a neural structure that plays a distinctive role in underwriting anxiety.[18] The basic setup of this research builds from the startle-based paradigms of the behavioral and psychopharmacological work we looked at above. More specifically, the lesion studies retain fear-potentiated startle as the behavioral measure for fear, though they operationalize anxiety in a slightly different way—in terms of what is called CRH-enhanced startle.[19] Using these measures for fear and anxiety, researchers have again found a double dissociation. Lesions to the CeA completely block fear-potentiated startle (Hitchcock & Davis, 1987; Campeau & Davis, 1995), but lesions to the BNST have no effect on fear-potentiated startle (Hitchcock & Davis, 1991; Gewirtz, McNish, & Davis, 1998).[20] By contrast, lesions to the BNST completely block CRH-enhanced startle, while lesions to the CeA have no effect (Lee & Davis, 1997a, 1997b). Again, dissociations of this sort are exactly what we would expect to find if fear and anxiety are underwritten by distinct neural mechanisms.[21]

---

18. To be clear, the claim here is not that the CeA and BNST are (uniquely) responsible for, respectively, fear and anxiety. Rather, the claim is that these structures (or portions of them) are implicated in the larger mechanisms that underwrite fear and anxiety. For instance, research suggests that the anterior cingulate cortex (ACC) also plays an important role in encoding information about the (un)certainty of punishments and rewards (Monosov, 2017).
19. More specifically, CRH-enhanced startle is an anxiety measure that takes advantage of the role that CRH—that is, corticotropin-releasing hormone—plays in generating prolonged anxiety-related responses. In particular, when rats are infused with CRH, we find a dose-dependent increase in long-lasting startle sensitivity. Moreover, this enhancement of startle sensitivity can be reduced by anxiolytics but not panicolytics (Swerdlow, Geyer, Vale, & Koob, 1986; Liang, Melia, et al., 1992). Results like these implicate CRH startle responses as indicative of anxiety. This is turn allows for an anxiety measure—CFH-enhanced startle—that can be used in lesion studies. On this definition, anxiety is understood as an increase in post-CFH infusion startle-response amplitude in comparison to preinfusion levels.
20. Similar results have been found using a different paradigm—one that operationalized fear in terms of conditioned freezing behaviors and blood pressure responses. (For details, see Iwata, LeDoux, et al., 1986, and LeDoux, Iwata, Cicchetti, & Reis, 1988.)
21. In this general vein, Walker and Davis (2002b) bring further support by showing that engaging distinct startle elicitors through *both* the CeA and BNST produces an

Though one might be wary of taking the results of rodent lesion studies as evidence for the scientific robustness of anxiety and fear in humans, the force of such concerns is undercut by two recent lines of brain imaging research. Before turning to discuss these results, however, a little background on this imaging research will be helpful.

Interpreting imaging results is a complex matter, because of technical limitations (e.g., image resolution) as well as methodological issues (e.g., how to extract claims about the role of a given brain region from a particular set of imaging results) (Klein, 2010; Raichle & Mintun, 2006). Moreover, these challenges are more pronounced when the brain structure being studied is small and when there is evidence that a given structure is implicated in a range of roles—both of which are the case for the BNST. However, recent advances in neuroscientific research on anxiety and fear have done much to address these issues. For instance, new ultra-high-resolution imaging technology better enables researchers to target small structures (Avery, Clauss, & Blackford, 2016, p. 133). And an increasing body of results from different labs and across a range of experimental designs (see below) warrant increased confidence in our understanding of what the BNST and CeA do. In fact, we find a growing consensus that the structural and functional findings from recent rodent research carry over to humans. Consider, for instance, the assessment of the neuroscientist Joseph LeDoux (2015): "Studies in healthy humans have confirmed the role of the BNST in processing uncertainty. The BNST thus seems to do for uncertainty what the amygdala [the CeA, in particular] does when there is a specific and certain threat stimulus" (pp. 105–106; also see Avery, Clauss, & Blackford, 2016; Davis, Walker, et al., 2010). With this background in hand, we can now turn to the details of this imaging work.

The first line of research uses fMRI scans of human subjects to understand which brain structures are activated in response to fear- and anxiety-eliciting threats. In the basic experimental setup, participants undergo fMRI brain imaging as they are presented with a range of threatening and nonthreatening stimuli. Moreover, the threat stimuli used are designed to

---

additive result in subsequent startle responses, while engaging the distinct startle elicitors though *just one* of these structures fails to be additive. Put another way, that the dual startle elicitors bring a magnified result only when engaged through different structures suggests that these structures engage distinct threat-processing pathways.

be either fear-eliciting (e.g., a predicable shock) or anxiety-eliciting (e.g., an unpredictable shock) in a manner that accords with the basic picture we have been working with: fear is a response to certain threats, while anxiety concerns situations where the nature of the threat is uncontrollable, unpredictable, or otherwise uncertain. As such, the setup allows researchers to test whether the above findings from rodent lesion studies can be extended to humans. For instance, Alvarez, Chen, et al. (2011) used virtual reality scenarios to investigate brain regions associated with fear- and anxiety-provoking situations. In this experiment, participants were told that they would hear a tone at regular intervals as they viewed three computer-generated scenes: walking through a bank, a casino, and a restaurant. They were also told that when viewing the bank scene, they would be subjected to shocks shortly after the tones (the "predictable-threat" scenario), when in the casino, they would be subjected to random shocks unrelated to the tone (the "unpredictable-threat" scenario), and when in the restaurant, they would not be subjected to any shocks (the "safe" scenario). Consistent with results from rodent models implicating the BNST as part of the neural mechanism that underwrites responses to uncertain dangers, only the unpredictable-threat scenario produced sustained activity in the BNST.[22] Following a similar paradigm, Phelps, O'Connor, et al. (2001) investigated brain activity associated with imminent threats. Using fMRI imaging, they found that there was rapid but brief amygdala activation to predictable verbal threat cues in comparison to safe cues (e.g., "If you see a red patch, you will receive a shock" versus "If you see a green patch, there will be no shock"). Taken together, these human imaging results provide further evidence that the central findings of the rodent research carry over to human neural architecture: the CeA and BNST are structures that play distinctive roles in underwriting (respectively) fear and anxiety.[23]

---

22. Alvarez and colleagues also found that skin-conductance responses showed linear progression from safe, to predicable, to unpredictable threat scenarios indicating a *ramping up* of *felt apprehension* in the subject across the three conditions. Thus we get further support both for the above predictions (in P2 and P3) regarding fear and anxiety as engaging distinct but overlapping defense-oriented physiological changes and for the claim that fear and anxiety (not, say, some more general mechanism) are doing the work.
23. We get additional support from research by Leah Somerville and her colleagues. For instance, Somerville, Wagner, et al. (2013) showed both that (i) brain structures

The second line of research uses ultra-high-resolution imaging technologies to extend findings from optogenetic research on rodent fear and anxiety neurocircuity. Optogenetic studies are of particular significance for our purposes because they allow researchers to develop fine-grained mappings of the neural circuits that underlie specific brain structures.[24] In this regard, recent optogenetic work on rodents provides a rich picture of the structural and functional connections of the extended amygdala complex—one that provides robust support for the existence of a "fear circuit" and an "anxiety circuit." More specifically, we see that there is a fear circuit that runs through the central amygdala and engages fight/flight/freeze behaviors in a response to imminent/predictable threats. We also find that there is an anxiety circuit that runs through the BNST and brings risk-assessment and risk-minimization behaviors in response to distant/unpredictable threats (Kim, Adhikari, et al., 2013; Jennings, Sparta, et al., 2011). In fact, optogenetic work on mice suggests that different regions within the BNST play different roles in processing uncertain threats: some regions of the BNST appear to prompt anxiety-related behaviors (anxiogenic effects), while others curb them (anxiolytic effects). It is thought that this architecture allows for the fine-tuning of the anxiety response to particular features of the situation at hand (Kim, Adhikari, et al., 2013; Jennings, Sparta, et al., 2011).

While these findings regarding the neural circuitry of rodents are important, the real significance for our purposes comes from recent ultra-high-resolution imaging work that suggests these results can be extended to humans (see figure 2.2). In contrast to the imaging work discussed above (which looked to see which brain regions were activated by fear- and

---

theorized to underlie fear (e.g., the CeA) were activated by predictably appearing threats, but not unpredictably appearing ones, and (ii) structures involved in anxiety (e.g., the BNST) showed greater activation for unpredictably appearing threats than for predictably appearing ones. Also see Somerville, Whalen, and Kelley (2010) for similar confirmation of the roles of the CeA and BNST in fear- and anxiety-related behaviors in response to temporally distant threats.

24. In brief, optogenetic experiments involve surgically injecting a virus into a rat's brain. The virus contains a light-sensitive protein, and it is inserted into the brain region to be studied. After allowing the protein to work its way through the neural structure to be studied, researchers then shine light on the protein (via fiber-optic cables) to map the neural circuitry of the targeted brain region. (See LeDoux, 2015, pp. 98–100.)

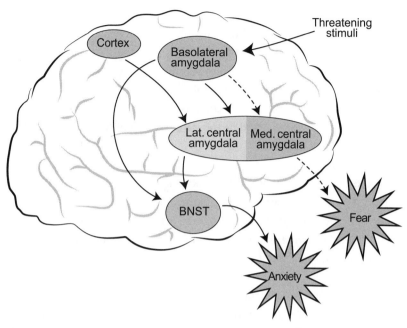

Figure 2.2
Anxiety and fear circuits. Solid lines represent the core of the BNST-centric anxiety circuit; dashed lines represent the core of the CeA-centric fear circuit. (Adapted from Davis, Walker, et al., 2010.)

anxiety-eliciting stimuli), the work of interest to us here investigates structural and functional connections both within the extended amygdala complex and between the EAC and other brain regions. What we find provides initial confirmation that the structural connections within the human EAC are very similar to those found in the optogenetic research on rodents (Avery, Clauss, et al., 2014; Oler, Birn, et al., 2012).[25]

More provocatively for the discussion to come, this imaging work also identified distinct connections in humans that have not been found in

---

25. Additional evidence supporting the extension of the rodent findings to primates comes from imaging work on monkeys and humans. For instance, PET scans of rhesus monkeys have shown that activation of BNST was correlated with anxious behavior in threatening (versus secure) situations (Fox, Shelton, et al., 2008; Kalin, Shelton, et al., 2005). The investigation of Oler, Birn, et al. (2012) nicely enriches these findings through a comparative analysis of imaging results from rhesus monkeys and humans. For similar findings in macaques see Hoffman, Gothard, et al. (2007).

either rodent or nonhuman primates. In particular, humans exhibit functional connections between the BNST and the paracingulate gyrus (i.e., the medial portion of the prefrontal cortex—a structure that has been implicated in, among other things, executive function, attention, and memory). That we see evidence of this connection is significant because it helps make sense both of anxiety's cognitive dimension (e.g., its tendency to produce ruminations and worries) and of imaging work implicating the prefrontal cortex in anxiety disorders (Avery, Clauss, et al., 2014; McMenamin, Langeslag, et al., 2014).

Taken as a whole, these lesion and imaging results complement and extend the behavioral and psychopharmacological results we have already looked at. They provide further support for the prediction of P4 that anxiety and fear are underwritten by distinct causal mechanisms—namely, a BNST-centric neural circuit for anxiety and a CeA-centric circuit for fear.

2.3.5 Summing Up: Silencing the Skeptic

The research we have reviewed delivers a widely replicated and diverse set of findings in support of our four predictions and so provides important initial support for our account of anxiety as a biocognitive emotion. Though these findings operationalize anxiety and fear in different ways (e.g., startle responses to conditioned shocks, threats of (un)predictable shocks, depictions of threatening images), there are common themes that unify this work. We start with the familiar observation that imminent dangers bring more pronounced defensive responses than do less certain threats. If you are a mouse, this means flight and burrowing when you see a cat, but cautious exploration if you just catch a whiff. For humans, the basic pattern is the same: when we see the snake or the mugger approaching, we try to escape, but the proverbial "bump in the night" is more likely to just bring increased vigilance and attention to our surroundings. Moreover, in transitioning these observations to the lab, we take advantage of the fact that there is a basic startle response that is common to both of these defensive responses, but that manifests in different ways in the face of (un)certainty: a short-duration response to imminent or predictable threats, but a longer-lasting response when the threat is less certain—differences that map to the broader patterns of behavior characteristic of fear and anxiety.

So while one might challenge particular pieces of the above argument, the combined results provide diverse and converging lines of support for the claim that 'anxiety' picks out a unique and unified category. Contra the two skeptical challenges from section 2.1, we can now see both that the characteristic behaviors of fear and anxiety are underwritten by distinct and dissociable causal mechanisms, and that we can intervene on these mechanisms (via lesioning and drugs) to produce novel effects. But to say that just is to say that 'fear' and 'anxiety' pick out distinct psychological phenomena. Moreover, the case for this will be further solidified when we turn (in sections 2.4 and 3.1) to make a case for the claim that the psychological categories 'fear' and 'anxiety' pick out are undergirded by distinct affect programs.

2.4 What Kind of Thing Might Anxiety Be?

Having made a case both for the conclusion that 'anxiety' picks out a unified category and for the claim that anxiety is distinct from fear, there is still the challenge of showing that it should be understood as a biocognitive emotion—an affective state that combines a hardwired affect program and a culturally shaped control system. So, in what follows, I begin by formulating a set of predictions about what we should expect to see in research on anxiety if anxiety is underwritten by an affect program. I then show that the research bears these predictions out. This investigation will, in turn, point us to evidence that the inputs to, and outputs of, this affect program are shaped by cultural influences / individual experiences of the sort we would expect to see if anxiety were a biocognitive emotion. I then conclude by showing why these empirical findings are not well explained by leading alternative accounts of what anxiety is.

2.4.1 Predictions

As standardly understood, affect programs are hardwired systems or modules that provide rapid, automatically engaged stereotyped responses to evolutionarily salient dangers and opportunities (Griffiths, 1997; Ekman, 1971, 1992, 1999). Applying this to the case of anxiety produces four predictions (following the above convention, I will label these P5–P8).[26] Given

---

26. As we will see below, I do not take these four predictions to be exhaustive, though (following Griffiths, 1997) I take them to be among the most important (cf. Ekman, 1992, 1999).

that affect programs are *hardwired, evolutionarily honed mechanisms*, we can make two predictions:

P5: Presence in primates. We should expect to see evidence of anxiety, or proto-versions of it, in nonhuman primates and other mammals.

P6: Distinct physiology and neural activity. We should also find that anxiety is tied to distinct neural mechanism and that it prompts distinctive physiological responses.

Moreover, given that affect programs bring *fast-acting, encapsulated responses* (contrast: more strategic and controlled processing), we can make two further predictions:

P7: Rapid onset. Anxiety should be engaged quickly—typically prior to conscious awareness.

P8: Automatic appraisal. Anxiety should involve an appraisal of potential threats that is automatic in the sense that it is resistant to voluntary control and involves minimal engagement of strategic cognitive processing.

In theory, with P5–P8 in hand, determining whether there is an anxiety affect program should be straightforward: we just look to research of the sort discussed in section 2.3 and see whether it confirms our predictions. In practice, however, things get messy. As suggested by our discussion of both the quasi-synonyms for anxiety (section 2.1.2) and emotional episodes more generally, emotions—and so affect programs—are embedded within larger social-psychological systems. Moreover, these larger systems bring in processes that are more flexible, controllable, and culturally shaped than are the hardwired, automatic processes characteristic of affect programs. This means that as we look for evidence relevant to assessing our predictions about an anxiety affect program, we will also find that there's more to our experiences of anxiety than what comes from the anxiety affect program alone—a finding that, as we will see, is best accounted for by understanding anxiety as a biocognitive emotion.

2.4.2 The Case for an Anxiety Affect Program

The investigation of whether 'anxiety' picks out a genuine category (section 2.3) provides us with significant resources with regard to assessing the first pair of predictions from above: anxiety's presence in nonhumans (P5) and its distinctive physiology and neural profile (P6). Taking these in turn, much of the research on anxiety reviewed above builds from animal models—mice, rats, macaques, and rhesus monkeys. Thus it affirms that there is (proto)anxiety in nonhuman primates and other mammals. Moreover, much of this work (especially the lesion studies and imaging research) also supports the claim that anxiety is associated with distinctive patterns of neural activity. In particular, we saw evidence that anxiety is undergirded by distinct neural circuitry—a BNST-centric circuit within the extended amygdala complex. In the present context, these neuroscientific findings have further significance: because they implicate *subcortical* neural structures as the drivers of anxious episodes, they also provide (defeasible) evidence for P8—namely, that anxiety employs automatic appraisal mechanisms that minimally engage strategic cognitive processing.[27]

However, evidence of distinctive neural activity is not the whole of P6—though it is comparatively weighty (more on why below). There is also the expectation that anxiety brings distinctive physiological activity. But here the research is more difficult to interpret. We have already reviewed evidence (e.g., in the context of the behavioral research on anxiety in section 2.3.2) that anxiety brings increases in arousal—just the sort of result we would expect to find from a threat-detection mechanism. However, other research investigating whether anxiety has a characteristic physiological profile challenges those findings. For instance, in a review of this work, the psychologist Jochen Fahrenberg (1992) concluded that "over many decades research has failed to substantiate the physiological correlates that are assumed for emotionality and trait anxiety. There is virtually no distinct finding that has been reliably replicated" (pp. 212–213). In light of this, one might reasonably worry whether we have evidence affirming the "distinctive physiology" portion of P6.

However, more recent research suggests that the earlier failures to find a connection between anxiety and particular physiological responses fade once the data from subjects classified as "repressors" are omitted from the analyses (e.g., Brown, Tomarken, et al., 1996; Philips & Steel, 2002; Blackhart, Eckel, & Tice, 2007; Derakshan, Eysenck, & Myers, 2007). Repressors are individuals who display the physiological and behavioral responses associated with anxiety (e.g., increases in arousal, threat-oriented

---

27. This evidence is defeasible since some subcortical structures may be capable of producing conscious processing (Merker, 2007).

attentional biases) but who deny feeling anxious. According to the standard interpretation of the repressor phenomenon, these individuals have developed a coping strategy that involves distracting themselves from the anxiety-provoking stimuli. So understood, repressors appear to be processing threats via two independent channels (Derakshan, Eysenck, & Myers, 2007, and, more generally, LeDoux, 2015, 2008). First, there is the low-level processing that quickly identifies potential threats and automatically engages both threat-relevant physiological changes and efforts at *distraction*. Second, there is the higher-level processing that brings a slower, more strategic appraisal of the situation. But because of the distraction behaviors that were (quickly) initiated by the low-level processing, the subsequent—and independent—higher-level processing deems there to be nothing to be anxious about. So we have a situation where the subjects' self-reports belie the anxiety their physiological changes suggest they are experiencing. Thus, if this picture of repressors is correct (see Dickson, Moberly, et al., 2009, for concerns), it appears that the difficulty finding correlations between self-reports and physiological changes noted by Fahrenberg may result from a failure to countenance the possibility of disassociations between these two processing channels. In light of this, it appears we do have evidence that anxiety is associated with a distinctive physiological response, it just tends to be masked by the distraction efforts of repressors.

Stepping back, we can draw two conclusions from our investigation of P6. First, the evidence we have just looked at suggests that anxiety has a distinctive neural profile and prompts (threat-relevant) physiological changes—though these changes can be masked by (e.g.,) the distraction efforts that we find in the coping strategy of repressors. Second, we get evidence of the complexity of anxious episodes. In particular, we see that the processing of anxiety-provoking stimuli can proceed via (at least) two independent routes: the quick, automatic low-level pathway that is characteristic of an anxiety affect program, and the slower, more strategic higher-level processing channel that drives (e.g.,) repressive coping (Hofmann, Ellard, & Siegle, 2012).

Setting aside these observations about multilevel anxious processing for the moment (we will come back to them in section 2.4.3), let's return to the case for an anxiety affect program. In particular, let's turn to P7—that is, the prediction that anxiety will display a quick, preconscious onset. We get support for this from three sources, physiological, neural-anatomical, and behavioral. First, and as we have seen (section 2.3), skin-conductance responses reveal that anxious individuals demonstrate a greater sensitivity to threatening stimuli (e.g., photos of snakes and angry faces) than we find in nonanxious individuals. Yet we do not see a similar difference with regard to nonthreatening stimuli (e.g., flowers, neutral faces).[28] Because this research uses masked stimuli—that is, photos that are presented too quickly for subjects to be consciously aware of them—the results indicate that the greater sensitivity found in anxious individuals is the upshot of *preconscious* detection. And because we see the difference only with regard to danger-related stimuli, we have evidence for anxiety bringing a specific form of threat sensitivity, rather than (say) a general skittishness (Öhman & Soares, 1999; Parra, Esteves, et al., 1997). Second, at the neural level, fMRI studies indicate that anxious individuals show greater activation in the extended amygdala complex (EAC) in the presence of unattended threat-relevant stimuli (Bishop, Duncan, & Lawrence, 2004). Since, as we have seen, the EAC is a *subcortical* structure associated with responses to threats, and since these are responses to *unattended* threat stimuli, these results provide further support for anxiety displaying the quick, preconscious onset predicted by P7. Finally, response times on various threat-detection tasks indicate that anxious individuals display rapid, automatic attentional biases toward threatening stimuli. For instance, in comparison to nonanxious individuals, anxious subjects are quicker both to focus their attention on threatening faces (Bradley, Mogg, et al., 1998; Derryberry & Reed, 2002) and to follow the gaze of fearful faces (Mathews, Fox, et al., 2003). But we do not find similar differences between anxious and nonanxious individuals with regard to happy faces. Thus, these results provide more evidence of anxiety as a rapid response to threats (as opposed to emotional expression in general). Taken together, this trio of findings provides a diverse range of support for the prediction that anxiety involves the kind of preconscious, threat-oriented detection capacity we would expect to find if there was an anxiety affect program.

---

28. In the discussion that follows, I use 'anxious individuals' to refer not to individuals with clinical levels of anxiety, but rather to subjects with high trait anxiety scores as measured by (e.g.,) Spielberger's (1983) State-Trait Anxiety Inventory (STAI). Recall the discussion in section 1.2.

Finally, consider P8: the prediction that anxiety will involve an automatic appraisal of stimuli that minimally engages higher, strategic cognitive processes. From the above discussion, we can see that anxiety brings attentional biases toward threating stimuli that, given their speed, provide evidence that anxiety engages automatic, minimally strategic processing. This picture is bolstered by research using behavioral measures (e.g., attentional blink) that shows that anxious individuals employ less strategic attentional control than do nonanxious individuals when assessing threat-relevant stimuli (Fox, Russo, & Georgiou, 2005). Similarly, fMRI studies show that, in comparison with low-anxious individuals, high-anxious individuals display less activity in the rostral anterior cingulate cortex (ACC) when presented with images of fearful faces (as opposed to images of neutral ones). This is significant because the rostral ACC is considered a key structure involved in "top-down" attentional control (Bishop, Duncan, Brett, & Lawrence, 2004). So less rostral ACC activity is evidence of less strategic and more automatic processing, and so provides further support for our prediction.

However, other work indicates that anxiety also engages higher, controlled and strategic processing. For instance, anxious individuals display a threat-sensitivity bias when making predictive inferences: they are more likely to provide threat-relevant terms (as opposed to neutral terms) as answers to ambiguous prompts (e.g., completing 'the plane ___' with 'crashed' rather than 'swerved' in response to 'In low visibility, the plane approached the mountain and the passengers began to shout'). Because this bias occurs only when the anxious individuals are afforded a substantial time delay between the ambiguous prompt and their response, the threat bias is thought to be the result of strategic—not automatic—processing (Calvo & Castillo, 2001).[29]

While this might seem to undermine the case for anxiety engaging the automatic appraisal characteristic of an affect program, it is actually just the kind of result we should expect if anxiety is (as the above discussion suggests) an emotion that involves multilevel processing. While the bigger picture of anxious episodes will become clearer below (section 2.4.3), recognizing that anxiety engages multilevel processing suggests the following

---

29. For similar results using a different experimental paradigm (a word-pairing task) see Derryberry and Reed (1997).

interpretation of these experimental results. The initial (lower-level) automatic processing of the anxiety affect program identifies something in the ambiguous prompts as potentially threatening. But because of uncertainty about the particular nature of this threat, additional, higher-level processing resources are recruited to help the individual better assess the uncertainty they face (Hofmann, Ellard, & Siegle, 2012). Put another way, anxiety itself principally involves automatic processing—though part of what that automatic processing functions to do is gate (as needed) additional, higher/strategic processing resources. So understood, the experimental results regarding predictive inference do not undermine the support we have gathered for our prediction about anxiety and automatic processing.[30]

The above investigation of our predictions brings together four independent lines of support for an anxiety affect program. But one might resist nonetheless on the grounds that we have no evidence for two particularly important features of affect programs: there is little evidence that anxiety has a *characteristic facial expression* or that it is a *pancultural* response. Since these features are often taken as the sine qua non of an affect program (e.g., Ekman, 1971), not finding evidence of them for anxiety would seem devastating. However, I believe this concern is overblown.

First, while the importance of a facial expression was emphasized by Ekman, its status as the most important marker has faded as emotion theorists increasingly look for a broader range of features—and place increasing weight on neuroscientific evidence—in support of claims about affect programs (e.g., Griffiths, 1997; Scarantino & Griffiths, 2011; Panksepp & Panksepp, 2000; LeDoux, 2008, 2015). In fact, Ekman himself now hedges on whether we must have evidence of a distinctive facial expression to be warranted in making claims about affect programs; he is now inclined to draw on a more diverse range of features—features of the sort that we have been focusing on (e.g., Ekman, 1992, 1999). The reason for the change of heart seems to be that while the presence of a distinctive facial expression serves

---

30. Additional empirical support for anxiety functioning to gate higher, strategic processing comes from work on animal models and pharmacological studies. This work indicates that persistent uncertainty about a threat brings the recruitment of additional processing resources that help assess the nature of the threat at hand. (See, e.g., Gray & McNaughton, 2000; Griffiths & Scarantino, 2005; and Corr, 2008.) More on this when we turn to discuss the biocognitive model below.

as a good proxy for an underlying affect program, it is merely that: a proxy. Moreover, advances in neuroscience made over the last 40+ years now allow us to better (and more directly) assess whether a particular pattern of behavior is the upshot of a distinct, hardwired mechanism. Hence, the shift away from facial expressions as the sine qua non of an affect program.[31]

Let's turn now to the charge that anxiety is not a pancultural phenomenon. Here I protest. The prima facie plausibility of this charge is, I believe, grounded in two observations: the absence of a distinctive facial expression for anxiety and the difficulties that early emotion researchers had in distinguishing anxiety from fear (e.g., Izard, 1972). Not only does the discussion to this point undermine both of these grounds for doubt, but there is also positive evidence of anxiety's panculturality—namely, the neuroscientific results that we have discussed indicating that there is a hardwired anxiety circuit in humans, monkeys, and rodents (section 2.3).[32]

---

31. Cashing in my earlier promissory note, notice that a similar line of thought helps substantiate the earlier observation that neural evidence should be given greater weight than evidence regarding physiological change when assessing P6.

32. While I do not know of any research that directly investigates whether anxiety, in general, is a pancultural emotion, there is a range of work that tackles the issue indirectly. For instance, a World Health Organization study investigated the prevalence of psychiatric disorders in 18 nations across Africa, the Americas, Asia and the Pacific, Europe, and the Middle East. Anxiety disorders like General Anxiety Disorder and Social Anxiety Disorder were found in all countries (Kessler, Angermeyer, et al., 2007). While, as we will see (section 4.2.2), there is reason to be concerned about the methodology of these studies, those concerns focus on the measures when used to identify anxiety *disorders*, not the more general issue we are interested in here—namely, whether anxiety (pathological or not) is a pancultural phenomenon. On this matter, the measures used do provide evidence of anxiety symptoms in all 18 nations and so provide indirect evidence for anxiety as a pancultural phenomenon. In a different vein, anthropological investigations of alcohol use in traditional, small-scale societies reveal excessive drinking is used primarily as an *antidote for anxiety* about (e.g.,) economic and social stability—thus providing further evidence of anxiety across a range of groups and cultures (Horton, 1943; Schaffer, 1976). This finding fits well with recent work showing both that anxiety disorders and addiction are highly comorbid and that the underlying neural mechanisms may interact in ways that facilitate the perpetuation of addiction as a response to anxiety (Grant, Stinson, et al., 2004).

Bringing this discussion to a close, we can turn to Paul Griffiths's work to assess the force of the case we have made for an anxiety affect program. While Griffiths is skeptical about whether our emotion talk displays the unity of a genuine category, he argues that there are *subsets* of our talk of specific emotions that pick out affect programs. To make this argument, he shows—much as we have just done—that (substantive) portions of our talk of fear, disgust, surprise, and joy display features that tell for the presence of an underlying affect program: there are (proto)versions of the responses in primates, they are associated with distinct neural and physiological activity, they display rapid onset, and they engage automatic appraisal mechanisms (1997, pp. 77–84). Moreover, Griffiths is sensitive to criticisms of Ekman's emphasis on facial expressions and, as a result, suggests (as I have) that distinctive neural activity might provide better evidence for an affect program than facial expressions do (pp. 85–87). Recognizing these parallels is significant given Griffiths's general skepticism about emotions; it means that the case we have made for an anxiety affect program is *just as compelling* as the case he makes for responses like fear, surprise, disgust, and joy.

However, we have seen that there is more to anxious episodes than just the anxiety affect program. In particular, we have seen evidence that anxiety involves not just the low-level automatic processing characteristic of affect programs, but also more strategic and controlled forms of cognition. For some, findings like these—especially when combined with observations about the wide range of states we call "anxiety"—argue against the claim that anxiety is, or engages, an affect program. This approach has two sides: one critical, one constructive. On the critical side, the objection holds that if anxiety is, or engages, an affect program, the resulting account will be excessively revisionary—it won't do justice to how we talk about or experience anxiety (Goldie, 2000, pp. 99–101; Roberts, 2003, pp. 24–36; Prinz, 2004, pp. 81–86). However, while this worry may have force against some accounts of emotions as affect programs (e.g., Griffiths's 1997 account of fear), we will see (chapter 3) that it is misplaced when leveled against our biocognitive account of anxiety. On the constructive side, we get an alternative account of the nature of emotions like anxiety, one that downplays hardwired biological elements and emphasizes cultural influences (e.g., Goldie, 2000, chap. 4). On this alternative proposal, anxiety is best understood as a form of higher cognition—an affective state that is underwritten by a culturally shaped set of controlled and strategic processes. However, though this "cultural-cognitive" model may be a good fit for some emotions (e.g., love, grief), as we will see below, it is poorly equipped to make sense of what we have learned about anxiety.[33]

2.4.3 From an Anxiety Affect Program to the Biocognitive Model

To make a case for anxiety as a biocognitive emotion, I will begin by focusing on two pairs of features of the model that draw out the plausibility of understanding anxiety in this way rather than on the alternative cultural-cognitive model discussed above. I will then tie the discussion of these features in with some of the neuroimaging results we noted earlier.

To get started, first notice that on the biocognitive model, culture and experience can shape the operation of the core system, but these shaping effects are anchored in, and constrained by, the hardwired features of the core system. This predicts that we have a combined system that is *biased* in the sense that certain emotional sensitivities and response patterns should be easier to acquire than others. Second, as we have seen (section 2.1.1), the biocognitive model views the control system as tending to modify the inputs to, and outputs of, the core system in ways that are *functionally integrated* in the sense that what you see as emotionally salient (and how you see it as such) gives shape—via the associated affect program—to the behaviors that result.

These first two features of the biocognitive model—bias and functional integration—fit well with what we know about anxiety. For instance, Arne Öhman and his colleagues have shown that it's easier to acquire anxieties (and fears) to stimuli that are threat-relevant from an evolutionary point of view (e.g., snakes and angry faces) than to those that are not (e.g., flowers or happy faces). In one version of this research, the Öhman team showed that while individuals can learn (via conditioning) to respond with a startle reaction to both threatening and benign images, the conditioning to the threatening stimuli is more robust in the sense that only these images continue to elicit a startle response in masked presentations (i.e., when the threatening images are hidden within a series of quickly appearing neutral images) (Öhman & Soares, 1993; Esteves, Dimberg, & Öhman, 1994; Parra,

---

33. Though I will not pursue it here, I believe a similar line of argument can be made against the psychological constructivism of LeDoux (2015), Barrett (2012), and Russell (2003).

Esteves, et al., 1997). In a second version of this work, Öhman and colleagues showed that conditioned startle responses could even be acquired to masked images—but *only when* the masked images involved threat-relevant stimuli (Esteves, Dimberg, et al., 1994; Öhman & Soares, 1999). Taken together, experimental results like these indicate that anxiety displays the kinds of biases we would expect to see if it were, as we are hypothesizing, a biocognitive emotion. Moreover, we have also reviewed (section 2.3) a wealth of work indicating both that anxiety combines a sensitivity to uncertain threats with risk-assessment and risk-minimization efforts, and that this combination contrasts with the fight/flight/freeze response prompted by more certain threats.[34]

Moreover, while these data about bias and functional integration are easily accommodated by the biocognitive model, this is not the case for the cultural-cognitive alternative. In particular, because the cultural-cognitive model takes anxiety to be underwritten by a set of flexible, strategic planning mechanisms, it's hard to see how it could explain why anxiety displays the biases toward evolutionarily salient threats that it does (cf. Goldie, 2000, pp. 110–111).

The second pair of features provide more direct support for a biocognitive account of anxiety. Here the first thing to notice is that the model allows emotional processing to be engaged on at least two "levels." (1) Within the core system, we find low-level processing that, as we have seen (e.g., section 2.1.1; also figure 2.1), screens incoming information against a set of prototypical threats/opportunities and recruits the associated combination of response tendencies (e.g., particular motor programs, vocalization routines). This processing is "low-level" in the sense that it's quick, coarse-grained, automatic, and operates below the level of conscious awareness. (2) In addition to engaging things like motor programs and vocalization routines, the core system can also prompt the recruitment of further, higher-level and potentially conscious processing. This additional processing is "higher-level" both in the sense that it involves more strategic and controlled cognition, and in the sense that the particular form of the processing can be shaped by cultural influences and individual experiences. Moreover, the response tendencies initiated by the core system—for example, motor programs, vocalization routines, higher-level processing—are

---

34. Section 3.3 will bring more evidence of functional integration in anxiety.

coordinated but independent behaviors. They are *coordinated* in the sense that they represent evolutionarily shaped responses to particular threats and opportunities (e.g., the distinctive motor, expressive, and physiological changes of the fight response that are recruited in the face of aggression from a conspecific). They are *independent* in the sense that they engage distinct systems—for instance, motor systems, systems responsible for vocalizations, as well as higher-level processing systems.

That the biocognitive model accommodates distinct forms of emotion processing complements the above explanation of the experimental results regarding things like predictive inferences (section 2.4.2). Recall that the work on predictive inferences indicates that anxiety can engage strategic processing. This raised a question: If anxious episodes are just the upshot of the lower-level, automatic processing of the anxiety affect program, then what are we to make of this higher-level, strategic processing? In response, I argued that the results could be explained on the assumption that the anxiety experienced in these predictive inferences begins as a (lower-level) automatic assessment of a potential threat, but given the ambiguity of the prompt, this initial automatic response ends up recruiting additional (higher-level) controlled processing. The biocognitive model complements this explanation by locating anxiety's automatic gating of higher-level processing within a more general and widely accepted framework.

Moreover, this second pair of features—that is, multilevel processing and coordinated but independent systems—also provide us with a richer theoretical understanding of the "repressor" phenomenon discussed above. If emotions engage initial lower-level processing, which can, in turn, recruit additional higher-level resources, and if those higher-level processing resources are coordinated with—but independent of—the engagement of other response behaviors (e.g., motor, expressive), then disassociations of these systems should be possible. In particular, it should be possible for the outputs of systems that engage (e.g.,) physiological changes and attentional narrowing to come apart from those resulting from higher cognitive processing. But notice: this is the very kind of separation that we find in repressors. Fleshing this out, in repressors, the lower-level processing of the core system identifies a threat and automatically prompts a distinctive set of behaviors—not just threat-relevant physiological changes and higher-level processing, but also the repressor's distinctive distraction efforts. But because the distraction efforts take hold before the (slower) higher-level processing runs its course, and because these systems function independently of one another, we get the disassociation characteristic of the repressor phenomenon—a physiological response associated with being anxious, but a self-report that denies this.

Again, these explanatory payoffs provide support for understanding anxiety as a biocognitive emotion. Because the biocognitive model makes room for multilevel processing, it is well equipped to accommodate the data about (e.g.,) predictive inferences and repressors. By contrast, the cultural-cognitive proposal—with its emphasis on higher cognitive processing—seems less able to explain these phenomena.

A final piece of support for understanding anxiety on the biocognitive model comes from some of the neuroimaging results we discussed earlier (section 2.3.4). In particular, if anxiety is a biocognitive emotion, then anxious episodes should engage elements of both the core and control systems. While we get some confirmation of this from the above discussion of predictive inferences and repressors, we find further support in imaging work on the neural connections of the human BNST. In particular, ultra-high-resolution fMRI work has shown not only that the human BNST is structurally connected to other parts of the "anxiety circuit" associated with the anxiety affect program (i.e., the core system), but also that there are functional connections between the BNST and the prefrontal cortex—a "higher cognitive" structure thought to be responsible for things like attention, memory, and executive function (Avery, Clauss, et al., 2014; McMenamin, Langeslag, et al., 2014). In short, we have neuroimaging evidence that anxiety—as predicted—engages both the core and control systems.

2.5 Conclusion

Before moving to the Puzzle of Diversity and questions of individuation, we should take stock of what we have accomplished so far. In short, we have made a strong case for understanding anxiety on the biocognitive model. Drawing on work from Griffiths and others, we developed a framework for determining whether 'anxiety' is a unique and unified category. Then, drawing on a range of empirical research, we used this framework to show that 'anxiety' picks out a unified category, one that is distinct from fear (a conclusion that will be further bolstered in chapter 3). But this empirical work had further significance: it helped draw out that anxiety is best understood as an affective state that combines a biologically hardwired core and a culturally influenced set of control mechanisms—that is, a biocognitive emotion. As we will see, this result provides us with a start toward a more comprehensive, empirically informed account of anxiety and so a foundation for our investigation of anxiety's importance for social and moral life.

3 Diversity: Varieties of Anxiety and Vindication

I've heard there are troubles of more than one kind; some come from ahead, and some come from behind.
—Dr. Seuss

We have made significant progress in our understanding of anxiety as a biocognitive emotion. But we still need to assess which portions of our wide-ranging use of 'anxiety' are captured by the biocognitive account we have developed. As we have seen (e.g., sections 2.1, 2.4.2), if the result is a highly revisionary picture—if little in our anxiety talk is about anxiety the (biocognitive) emotion—then that would tell against our proposal. It would suggest something like the cultural-cognitive model might be a better fit. We also need to determine what structure might undergird the discussion of different varieties of anxiety that we find among folk and theorist alike. Progress on these fronts will not only position us to address the Puzzle of Diversity, it will allow us to better understand both how anxiety differs from similar emotions (macroindividuation) and what subtypes of anxiety there are (microindividuation).

As we will see, the two elements of the biocognitive model—the core and control systems—provide us with important resources. More specifically, we can take the presence of the anxiety affect program as our criterion for macroindividuation (section 3.1). We can also use the presence of the anxiety affect program, in combination with observations about the predictive and explanatory power of content within the control system, as our criterion for microindividuation (sections 3.2–3.4). Moreover, these macro- and microindividuation criteria provide the foundation we need to assess which portions of our anxiety talk are legitimate (section 3.5).

The payoff of this chapter is threefold. First, we will see that our biocognitive account of anxiety allows us to vindicate much, though not all, of our anxiety talk—thus providing further support for the argument of chapter 2. Second, by looking more closely at questions of microindividuation, we will gain further support for the earlier conclusion that anxiety and fear are distinct emotions. Third, in looking more closely at the ways we talk about anxiety, we will develop a better understanding of the forms of problematic uncertainty it tracks. This, in turn will set up the final payoff: we will identify (in section 3.3) three broad varieties of anxiety—what I call environmental, punishment, and practical anxiety—that will take center stage in part II of the book, where we will investigate the importance of (particular varieties of) anxiety for social and moral life.

3.1 Macroindividuation and the Anxiety Affect Program

A central lesson of the discussion so far is that we have good reason to think there is an anxiety affect program in much the sense that Griffiths and Ekman take there to be affect programs for other emotions like fear, anger, sadness, and joy. In light of this, we can follow them (and others) in using this as a criterion for macroindividuation—a way of demarcating general emotion categories. More specifically, the proposal is this: we have reason to endorse a general emotion category (e.g., fear, anxiety, anger, joy) to the extent that we have evidence of a hardwired system—an affect program—that brings rapid, automatically engaged stereotyped patterns of response behaviors to particular evolutionarily salient dangers or opportunities.

If this is our macroindividuation criterion, then by building on the discussion of the differences between anxiety and fear from chapter 2, we can extract a set of features that tell for the presence of such a mechanism. Call these the Affect Program Features—the APFs for short:

(APF 1) Stereotyped patterns of stimulus-response behavior that map to (evolutionarily salient) threats and opportunities

(APF 2) Presence in primates

(APF 3) Distinctive neural and physiological activity

(APF 4) Rapid onset

(APF 5) Automatic appraisal

Together, the five APFs provide us with a set of independent tests for whether a purported emotion phenomenon is underwritten by an affect program and so for whether we have a distinct emotion category. Moreover, by looking for differences in how a purported category exhibits these features (especially APF 1 and APF 3), we get a principled way of distinguishing emotion types. In particular, to the extent that we see evidence of distinct patterns of stereotyped stimulus-response behavior (APF 1) that correspond with (or, better, are underwritten by) distinct neural activity and physiological changes (APF 3), we have evidence of distinct affect programs and so distinct emotions.

Applying this test provides further support for the conclusion from chapter 2 that anxiety is not a form of fear, but rather its own emotion. More specifically, the evidence we reviewed indicates not only that anxiety and fear exhibit distinct patterns of stimulus-response behavior (APF 1), but also that these stimulus-response differences are underwritten by distinct neural structures—the BNST-centric circuit for anxiety and the CeA-centric circuit for fear (APF 3). We can also use the affect program criterion to distinguish anxiety from other seemingly similar emotions. Consider shame, an emotion that strikes some as either a variant of anxiety or a part of a "family" of emotions that includes anxiety (e.g., Baumeister & Tice, 1990; Gilbert, 2001). If shame really is a kind of anxiety (or vice versa), then we should see significant overlap between the two responses with regard to the APFs. But we don't. For one, they appear to have different functional roles: unlike anxiety, shame is not a (forward-looking) response to problematic uncertainty, but rather a (backward-looking) response to situations where one believes one has violated a norm in a way that reflects poorly on oneself as a person (Bastin, Harrison, et al., 2016; Roberts, 2003; Tangney, Miller, Flicker, & Barrow, 1996; cf. section 1.2). So we see little overlap with regard to APF 1. More significantly, the two responses also appear to involve very different patterns of neural activity (i.e., no overlap with regard to APF 3). As we have seen, anxiety is underwritten by the BNST and the extended amygdala complex (EAC) more generally. By contrast, feelings of shame show little association with the amygdala, but significant engagement of the insula, the anterior cingulate cortex, and the prefrontal cortex (Bastin, Harrison, et al., 2016; Michl, Meindl, et al., 2014).[1]

---

1. We see similar differences in the neural and physiological activity associated with anxiety and embarrassment (e.g., Bastin, Harrison, et al., 2016; Cutlip & Leary, 1993;

Taken together, these results provide good evidence that anxiety and shame should be understood as distinct emotions.[2]

In addition to distinguishing anxiety from other emotions, our macro-individuation criterion also allows us to explain how it differs from more general affect-based phenomena like cognitive dissonance. There are clearly affinities between anxiety and cognitive dissonance. Both are aversive responses that, at least at a high level, appear to share a similar functional profile: responses to threats and challenges that bring a range of defensive behaviors. But these broad similarities hide important differences. To draw this out, some background will be helpful. Cognitive dissonance was initially understood as an aversive state that occurs when an individual simultaneously holds two cognitions (e.g., beliefs, attitudes, opinions) that are psychologically inconsistent. Given the aversive nature of this conflict, one tries to reduce it by rejecting or revising one of the dissonance-producing cognitions (Festinger, 1957). But this initial formulation of cognitive dissonance was considered too vague to be capable of generating testable predictions—for example, what is a "psychologically inconsistent" set of cognitions and why do they motivate revision?[3] As standardly elaborated, cognitive dissonance and the revisions it brings are thought to be undergirded by one's *sense of self*. As the psychologist Eliot Aronson (2008) explains, "Dissonance-reducing behavior is ego-defensive behavior; by reducing dissonance, we maintain a positive image of ourselves—an image that depicts us as good, or smart, or worthwhile" (p. 192).

If this is the correct way to understand cognitive dissonance, then it appears to be something that is, functionally speaking, both narrower and broader than what we find in the anxiety affect program. It is *narrower* in the sense that (i) it is elicited, not by a general, problematic uncertainty,

---

Harris, 1990). This is significant since embarrassment is also thought by some to be part of the anxiety "family" (e.g., Leary & Kowalski, 1995, pp. 82ff.; Roberts, 2003, p. 233).

2. I suspect the reason the two are thought to be part of the same family lies in the fact that both tend to be elicited in social situations and both can prompt withdrawal and appeasement behaviors. But given the significant differences noted in the text, these affinities seem better explained by the tendency for social anxiety to, in certain situations, provoke shame (and vice versa). We will return to this in chapter 7.

3. See Aronson (1968) for discussion of the development and refinement of dissonance theory.

Diversity

but rather by situations where one has cognitions that pose a specific threat to one's sense of self (cf. Gilbert, 2001), as well as in the sense that (ii) it prompts largely ego-defensive behaviors (rather than the more general tendencies toward risk minimization and information gathering that we find for anxiety). Cognitive dissonance is *broader* than anxiety in the sense that, while it is concerned with threats to one's sense of self, it is not restricted to occasions where those threats are uncertain (as we would expect to find were it related to anxiety). In fact, the engagement of cognitive dissonance arguably requires that the threat be sufficiently certain—otherwise it would be hard to understand why one would be motivated to revise or reject one of the conflicting cognitions.

These asymmetries reveal important functional differences between anxiety and cognitive dissonance that suggest the two should not be assimilated (i.e., insufficient overlap with respect to APF 1). More importantly, to my knowledge, there is no work suggesting nonhuman primates might experience (proto)cognitive dissonance (i.e., unlike anxiety, cognitive dissonance fails to secure APF 2). Nor is there evidence that cognitive dissonance displays the distinctive neural activity (e.g., activity in subcortical structures) that we would expect to see if it were undergirded by an affect program—much less the BNST activity we would want to see if we classify it as a kind of anxiety (so no support for APF 3 either). In light of these differences, it seems cognitive dissonance is most plausibly understood as a psychological construct that cuts across the phenomena that the anxiety affect program—and the biocognitive model more generally—seek to explain.[4]

---

4. The functional gloss on anxiety as sensitivity and responsiveness to problematic uncertainty raises questions about how anxiety differs from the mere recognition of uncertainty. What to say here turns on what, exactly, this 'recognition of uncertainty' amounts to. On one interpretation, the mere recognition of uncertainty amounts to a situation where one sees one's situation as presenting a potential threat/challenge, but where one doesn't engage in the risk-minimization and risk-assessment behaviors associated with anxiety. Such a case is best understood as a case where one's appraisal of the uncertain threat falls below the threshold for being problematic. Thus, the anxiety affect program is not engaged and we do not have an instance of anxiety (the biocognitive emotion). Understood in another way, the mere recognition of uncertainty amounts to a state where one sees one's situation as uncertain—one lacks relevant information—but where one does not also see one's situation as threatening. On this reading, one may well engage in the epistemic behaviors associated with anxiety. But because one's situation does not involve a threat, this

3.2 Microindividuation Part I: Specifying a Standard

While identifying a criterion of macroindividuation is progress, we still have a further, more difficult set of microindividuation questions to answer. Our earlier discussion of the biocognitive model (and the antiessentialist methodology more generally) suggests a way forward. More specifically, we need a way of specifying both what purported varieties of anxiety *share* such that they count as genuine subtypes of anxiety, and how they *differ* such that there is also a distinction to be made between them with regard to their scientific credentials (i.e., do they have robust predictive and explanatory power?).

My basic proposal is twofold. First, we can say that a purported subtype of anxiety A counts as a genuine variety of anxiety to the extent that we have evidence that the anxiety affect program is a *component* or *constitutive* element of A. So understood, A's relation to the anxiety affect program is akin to the way that many understand the relationship between anger and indignation: to feel indignation is to feel a distinctive kind of anger or to feel anger in combination with certain other (cognitive or affective) elements (e.g., Roberts, 2003, pp. 215–216). The key here is that a given manifestation of indignation will include the engagement of the anger affect program.[5]

Second, we can distinguish A and B as genuine varieties of anxiety to the extent that each has substantive predictive and explanatory power. Importantly, the predictive and explanatory power we need here will not be as substantive as what we find with respect to the anxiety affect program. After

---

seems best described as a case of curiosity, not anxiety. I say more about this in Kurth (forthcoming b), section 4.

5. It is worth noting that not all emotions associated with 'anger' will meet the component test articulated in the text. For instance, some emotion researchers maintain that anger is a component of vengefulness (e.g., Frank, 1988; French, 2001, pp. 94ff.). However, while there certainly is an important connection between the two, it appears possible for there to be vengeance that does not engage the anger affect program. More specifically, the engagement of the anger affect program is generally thought to involve things like the making of a threat expression, the rapid engagement of motor programs associated with violent action, and quick increases in heart rate and blood pressure (Griffiths, 2004a, p. 909). But if that is correct, then it is hard to locate something with those features in the feelings of vengeance one might experience toward an intellectual rival or that sustain one's efforts to get even for an offense suffered years ago.

all, the claim is not that practical anxiety, say, is itself a distinct *emotion*, but rather the weaker claim that it is a distinct *variety* of anxiety. Recognizing this reveals that what we need is evidence that *A* and *B* display the kind of predictive and explanatory power we would expect to see given our theoretical account of their function (more on what this amounts to below).

To flesh out this account of microindividuation, I will work through some examples. In doing this, I am not trying to give a complete taxonomy of all the subtypes of anxiety that exist. Rather, my aim is to identify—and substantiate—the three varieties of anxiety introduced above: environmental, punishment, and practical anxiety. As we will see, not only does this trio capture much of the structure that underlies our anxiety talk, but these three forms of anxiety also play an important role in our understanding of anxiety's value (chapters 4–6).

3.3 Microindividuation Part II: Environmental, Punishment, and Practical Anxiety

Recall some of the examples of anxiety discussed in chapter 1. First, there were the cases of the unease that we experience when walking in woods or through the streets of a strange city late at night—anxiety that brings increased attentiveness and caution with regard to our surroundings. There was also the anxiety of social interaction: what we feel when we are worried that we might say something silly or on occasions where the eyes of our social peers/superiors are on us. In these cases, we are concerned about how we might be judged and so tend to be more deferential toward those whose good opinions we seek. Finally, there were the examples of Nelson Mandela, the abolitionist John Woolman, and the neurosurgeon Henry Marsh, whose anxiety about what they ought to do regarding a novel or difficult choice prompted a range of epistemic behaviors—reflection, deliberation, reassessment, and the like.

Not only are bouts of anxiety like these familiar, they also suggest that anxious episodes clump in interesting ways. More specifically, they suggest both (i) that uncertain threats and challenges of particular sorts—Will I be injured? Am I being negatively evaluated by others? What is the right thing to do?—might trigger distinctive patterns of anxious behavior, and (ii) that the behaviors triggered are geared toward helping one address the particular kind of uncertainty one faces.

This idea gets further support from an independently theorized set of distinctions in research on how uncertainty shapes decision making. The work in question aims to identify the various places where uncertainty can complicate the decision-making process (see Bach & Dolan, 2012, for a review). Here we find three types of uncertainty that are of particular interest for our purposes: state uncertainty, rule uncertainty, and outcome uncertainty. (1) State uncertainty is *uncertainty about the current state of one's environment* (e.g., what dangers or opportunities are present). Uncertainty of this sort creates problems for decision making insofar as it undermines one's ability to understand and assess one's options. (2) Rule uncertainty involves making decisions in the face of *uncertainty about which rule to apply* to a given choice. It enters the decision-making process either when one faces vague or conflicting rules, or when one doesn't have enough experience to know which rule to apply. (3) Outcome uncertainty is *uncertainty about what will happen* given that one acts (or has acted) according to a particular rule. In these cases, though the rule that one is following is clear, it is only probabilistically associated with a particular result—hence, one's uncertainty about the outcome.

The emerging picture, then, is one on which we have (at least) three general varieties of anxiety that correspond to the above examples and that get independent backing from work examining how uncertainty can enter into decision making. In what follows, I characterize these three varieties of anxiety—what I call environmental, punishment, and practical anxiety—arguing not only that we should understand them as genuine subtypes of anxiety but also that they capture much of the structure of anxious experience (Kurth, 2015, 2016; cf. Endler, Parker, Bagby, & Cox, 1991).

3.3.1 Characterizing Environmental, Punishment, and Practical Anxiety

To make a case for environmental, punishment, and practical anxiety as genuine varieties of anxiety, we need to start with a general picture of their characteristic concerns—an initial account of their distinctive elicitors and subsequent response tendencies that fits with our general understanding of anxiety as a response to problematic uncertainty (i.e., a response to situations where one faces a threat or challenge whose nature is unpredictable, uncontrollable, or otherwise open to question). With this in hand, we will be positioned to formulate a set of predictions that we can use to assess whether environmental, punishment, and practical anxiety satisfy

Diversity 69

our two-part microindividuation test. So consider the following, first-pass accounts of these three types of anxiety:

Environmental anxiety. Environmental anxiety is anxiety about potential physical dangers. In the paradigmatic case, it is triggered by the possibility of something in one's environment that could bring physical harm (e.g., predators, cliff edges, conspecific aggression). It typically brings response behaviors that emphasize caution in one's movements (e.g., withdrawal, avoidance) and increased vigilance toward one's surroundings.

Punishment anxiety. Punishment anxiety is anxiety about the possibility of receiving negative evaluations or sanctions from others. The paradigmatic source of this type of anxiety is uncertainty about the outcome of a (public) performance, action, or social encounter—will one be viewed negatively and what consequences will occur if one is? As such, it tends to prompt socially oriented risk-minimization efforts (e.g., deference; efforts to ingratiate, flatter, or even appease).

Practical anxiety. Practical anxiety is anxiety about what the correct or appropriate thing to do is. Its paradigmatic elicitors are situations where one is uncertain about what the (social, moral) norms prescribe or prohibit (call this 'norm uncertainty'). It can also be prompted by uncertainty about how one might influence future, potentially threatening events (call this 'novelty'). Anxiety of this sort tends to result in epistemic behaviors (e.g., inquiry, deliberation, reflection, (re)assessment) aimed at helping one better understand and so respond to the situation at hand.

With these initial (rough) characterizations in hand, we can make four general observations. First, I do not take this trio to be exhaustive of the subtypes of anxiety—that might be the case, but determining whether it is would require (as we will see in section 3.4) a much richer empirical picture of anxious episodes than we currently have. Second, the boundaries between these three varieties of anxiety are blurry. This is to be expected. For starters, we are dealing with biological/social kinds for which this fuzziness is the norm (recall the discussion from section 2.2). But notice as well that experiences of these forms of anxiety are likely to transition from one form to another fairly fluidly. Walking back to your hotel after dinner, you start to feel uneasy about the dark street you find yourself on and so start paying closer attention to what's around you (environmental anxiety). Now at an unfamiliar intersection, you start to worry—"Should I turn left, or retrace my steps?" (practical anxiety). Safely back at the hotel, you stop at the bar for a drink. You see your colleague there and she looks at you with a puzzled face. You start to feel uncomfortable: Is she thinking that you have (again) gotten yourself lost (punishment anxiety)? Third, it's possible to experience more than one of these anxiety subtypes at once: I can feel uncertain about both what the correct thing to do is (practical anxiety) and whether I'll be reprimanded if I make the wrong choice (punishment anxiety).[6]

Finally, and most significantly, the characteristic concerns and action tendencies we see in these three forms of anxiety suggest that each is bound up with (or unified by) a distinctive kind of motivation.[7] Environmental anxiety, as a concern about physical harm that brings avoidance and withdrawal tendencies, carries a *self-defense motivation*. We find something similar—though importantly different—in punishment anxiety. As a response to potential negative evaluation that prompts deference and appeasement behaviors, it also engages a kind of defensive motivation. But here it is a motivation to defend one's "social self," not one's "physical self"; it is an *ego-defensive motivation* in the face of a potentially threatening social encounter, not the self-preservation response to a possible physical danger. In contrast to both of these defensive motivations, practical anxiety brings what we might call an *accuracy motivation*: it is a form of anxiety triggered by uncertainty about what to do that brings a range of epistemic behaviors. Moreover, in engaging in these epistemic efforts, one is trying to get it right—trying to determine what the correct or optimal thing to do is. The picture of environmental, punishment, and practical anxiety that emerges from these observations is one that meshes with our understanding of anxiety as a biocognitive emotion: these varieties of anxiety engage distinct, functionally integrated processes within the biocognitive model's control system—processes that underwrite the characteristic combinations of situational sensitivities, motivations, and behaviors we've noted.

---

6. The idea that we can feel more than one emotion at a time is not unique to (subtypes of) anxiety. As Heidi Maibom (2014) notes, "Emotions are seldom felt in isolation, particularly in isolation from related emotions" (p. 7). Also see (e.g.,) work investigating the co-occurrence of guilt and shame (e.g., Deonna, Rodogno, & Teroni, 2011; Tangney & Dearing, 2002).

7. We will return to the motivational dimension of these varieties of anxiety in chapters 4 and 5.

With these initial characterizations of environmental, punishment, and practical anxiety in hand, we can turn to the project of validating their credentials as genuine varieties of anxiety. As a first step, notice the significant parallels between the above discussion of how researchers exploring the significance of uncertainty in decision making have carved up conceptual space and our three forms of anxiety. In particular, the characteristic concerns we have identified for environmental, punishment, and practical anxiety significantly overlap with (respectively) the sources of state, outcome, and rule uncertainty. This overlap shouldn't be surprising. After all, that we find these parallels between varieties of anxiety and forms of decision-making uncertainty makes perfect sense given the account of anxiety we have been developing. For on that account, anxiety is a tool that helps individuals recognize and respond to problematic *uncertainty* in its various manifestations.

While we have characterized three varieties of anxiety that both resonate with familiar instances of ordinary anxious episodes and map onto a parallel set of distinctions made about uncertainty in decision making, we need more. In particular, to see if environmental, punishment, and practical anxiety count as genuine varieties of anxiety, we need a set of predictions we can use to determine if they pass the two-part test from above. So consider the following:

P9: Engages the anxiety affect program. We should see evidence that the anxiety affect program is engaged (e.g., BNST activity) when individuals are in situations that involve the forms of uncertainty characteristic of environmental, punishment, and practical anxiety.

P10: Distinctive patterns of stimulus-response behavior. We should find evidence of the patterns of stimulus-response behavior characteristic of environmental, punishment, and practical anxiety; we should also see evidence that this behavior is underwritten by anxiety.

P11: Engagement of distinctive cognitive processes. We should find evidence that the stimulus-response behaviors characteristic of environmental, punishment, and practical anxiety are underwritten by distinctive cognitive processes or mechanisms. More specifically, we are looking for evidence of distinct subtypes of anxiety (not distinct general emotion types). So there should be evidence that the mechanisms responsible for the subtype-specific stimulus-response behaviors are mechanisms of the biocognitive model's control system (e.g., strategic and controlled processing, not the operation of an affect program).

With these predictions in hand, we can turn to empirical work to determine if they are met. As we will see, we find support from three sources: behavioral research, abnormal psychology, and neuroscience.

3.3.2 Evidence from Behavioral Research

So far, we just have anecdotal evidence for the systematic and robust regularities in the eliciting conditions and behavioral tendencies that are part of our characterizations of environmental, punishment, and practical anxiety. If these are genuine subtypes of anxiety, we should be able to find more systematic support for these patterns of behavior—patterns that would support the predictions of P10. On this front, we get confirmation from a range of work investigating how anxiety manifests itself in various situations.

For instance, work by the psychologist Norman Endler regarding individual personality differences indicates that tendencies to become anxious cluster into (at least) three kinds of situations (Endler, Hunt, & Rosenstein, 1962; Endler & Kocovski, 2001; Endler, Parker, et al., 1991):

Physical dangers: A tendency to become anxious when there is a possibility of bodily harm

Social threats: A tendency to become anxious in situations where there is a possibility of being evaluated or observed by others

Ambiguous threats: A tendency to become anxious in situations whose novelty or difficulty makes one uncertain about what to do or what will happen

Not only have Endler's results been widely replicated (e.g., Endler, 1997; Endler, Crooks, & Parker, 1997; Flett, Endler, & Fairlie, 1999; Trotter & Endler, 1999), there is also a tight fit between his groupings and our account of the dangers that characteristically elicit environmental, punishment, and practical anxiety. Moreover, Endler's work on the types of situations that provoke anxiety comports with other research on the distinctive behavioral tendencies that result from feeling anxious in these different kinds of situations. To see this, and so get more support for P10, we can look more closely at the evidence supporting these three elicitor-behavior links.

Environmental anxiety: Linking physical harm and avoidance behavior. We have already seen evidence that anxiety about the possibility of physical harm tends to bring avoidance and escape behaviors (section 2.3.2). Recall, for instance, the results from questionnaire-based studies indicating that tendencies toward avoidance and escape increase as the chance of physical harm becomes more likely (Blanchard, Hynd, et al., 2001; Perkins & Corr, 2006). There was also the research using computer-simulated threat scenarios indicating not only that there is a transition from approach to avoidance behavior as a threat become more imminent, but also that this tendency toward greater avoidance is reduced when individuals are given antianxiety drugs like lorazepam (Perkins, Ettinger, et al., 2009). Together, these results provide some initial affirmation that environmental anxiety meets P10: they both support the prediction of a link between the recognition of a potential physical harm and subsequent avoidance efforts, and implicate anxiety as having a role in driving this pattern of recognition-and-response behavior.

Punishment anxiety: Linking social evaluation/sanction and deference. As predicted by our account of the stimulus-response behavior characteristic of punishment anxiety, individuals anxious about how they are being evaluated tend to show greater deference toward others and to be more cautious in what they say and do (see Leary & Kowalski, 1995, chap. 8, for an overview). For instance, in comparison to the non–socially anxious, socially anxious individuals display more conversational deference: they interrupt others less often (Natale, Entin, & Jaffe, 1979), smile more frequently (Pilkonis, 1977), and offer more confirmations of what others have said (Leary, Knight, & Johnson, 1987).[8] We find similar results with regard to increased caution. For example, anxious individuals who are concerned about how a social interaction is going tend to have shorter conversations, speak more quietly, and make less eye contact than do nonanxious individuals in similar situations (Ammerman & Hersan, 1986; Burgio, Merluzzi, & Pryor, 1986). And anxious individuals concerned about whether they are making a good impression on others in conversations tend to express less information about themselves (Leary, Knight, & Johnson, 1987; Snell, 1989), and when they do share information, they are less revealing in the stories

---

8. In what follows, and in line with the discussion of section 1.2, I use 'socially anxious individuals' to refer, not to those with social anxiety disorder or some other form of clinical anxiety, but rather to individuals with high scores on measures of trait anxiety (e.g., STAI).

they tell (DePaulo, Kenny, et al., 1990; Greenberg, Pyszczynski, & Stine, 1985). Taken together, these findings provide evidence that punishment anxiety meets P10: not only do we see the sorts of deference and appeasement behaviors predicted by our characterization of punishment anxiety, we also find support for an underlying role for anxiety in linking the two.[9]

Practical anxiety: Linking norm uncertainty and information gathering. Finally, in line with our account of practical anxiety, we find that individuals anxious about what to do or what will happen tend to engage in information gathering and other epistemic behaviors aimed at helping them work though the uncertainty they face. On this front, much of the empirical work comes from political scientists investigating how emotions affect political participation and decision making. Since practical anxiety will play an important role in part II, it will be helpful to have a more detailed discussion of the associated behavioral evidence.

Here we can begin with work by Michael MacKuen and his colleagues. They investigated how feelings of anger and anxiety in response to a challenge to one's political policy preferences affected one's subsequent actions and attitudes (MacKuen, Wolak, et al., 2010). To explore this question, the MacKuen team developed a web-based environment that presented subjects with an informative (but fake) news story about a school's decision to change its affirmative action policy. The story was designed to either affirm or challenge the policy preferences that the subjects had reported on a pretest questionnaire. The web-based environment also provided subjects with the opportunity to explore, if they wished, additional information that would affirm, challenge, or be neutral with regard to the news story they had read.[10]

---

9. Related work points to differences in behavioral responses that map to (and so provide additional support for) our distinction between environmental anxiety and punishment anxiety. For instance, individuals anxious about *physical harms* (e.g., possible shocks) prefer to be with others (Schachter, 1959)—presumably because they see being with others as a source of protection and support. By contrast, for those who are anxious about *social evaluation*, being with others is the very source of their problem, so unsurprisingly, they tend to avoid and withdraw from others (Himadi, Arkowitz, et al., 1980; Weeks, Rodebagh, et al., 2008).
10. MacKuen and colleagues talk generally about 'anxiety,' not 'practical anxiety' (that's a term I've coined). But as the discussion in the text indicates, and as is readily apparent in their own presentation, they are picking out a particular variety of

In the present context, MacKuen's experimental design is significant for two reasons. First, the strategy of challenging subjects' stances on affirmative action policy fits nicely with our focus on uncertainty about what to do in the face of vague or conflicting norms. After all, affirmative action is a policy that is supported—and challenged—by independently plausible norms: equity norms say one should support affirmative action efforts, while meritocratic norms tell one not to. Thus, situations that raise questions about whether one should continue to support (oppose) affirmative action are situations that are likely to introduce the type of norm uncertainty that prompts practical anxiety. Second, by creating an environment that can induce distinct emotions (anger or anxiety) and that provides subjects with the opportunity to explore additional information sources, the experimental design provides a rather direct test of the claim that practical anxiety engages epistemic behaviors that help one work through uncertainty about what to do. The results indicate that it does. Subjects for whom the fake news story provoked anxiety sought out *more* information about affirmative action policy, were more interested in learning more about *both* sides of the issue, and—perhaps most interestingly—were more willing to *explore new solutions*. By contrast, those who experienced anger were less interested in informing themselves, and when they did seek out more information, they tended to just look for things that were in line with their initial views about affirmative action policy. In short, these emotions "have a direct influence over both attention and open-mindedness"—anxiety brings increases, anger does not (p. 455; also see Tiedens & Linton, 2001).[11]

---

anxiety—one concerned with uncertainty about what to do rather than, say, uncertainty about how one might be evaluated. For instance, there was little in the experimental design to make subjects think they were being observed or evaluated, and so little that might prompt social or punishment anxiety (rather than practical anxiety). In particular, subjects were not required to do anything once they had read the news story: they could engage—or not—with the web platform, nor were there any observers present.

11. We get additional confirmation of our predictions about practical anxiety through a different paradigm. In earlier work, the MacKuen team found similar results via correlation analyses (e.g., Marcus, Neuman, & MacKuen, 2000). This research examined data from U.S. presidential elections from 1980 to 1996 and found that voters' self-reported anxiety about a political candidate was correlated with their interest in the upcoming election, their intention to seek out more information about the candidates, and their knowledge about where the candidates stood

Additional research along these lines deepens and extends the MacKuen findings that implicate anxiety about what to do or what will happen as a driver of epistemic behaviors (e.g., information gathering and reassessment). For instance, Nicholas Valentino and his colleagues used an experimental setup much like MacKuen's (Valentino, Hutchings, Banks, & Davis, 2008). Participants were presented with a (fake) news story about the economic policies of the candidates in the 2004 presidential election. The story was designed to prompt uncertainty by challenging the participants' preexisting economic policy preferences. After reading the story, participants were asked to indicate the extent to which what they read made them feel angry, anxious, disgusted, or enthusiastic. As with MacKuen's setup, the participants were then presented with a web portal that allowed them to explore (or not) additional news items about the candidates and the issues.

The Valentino group found that, in comparison with the other participants, individuals made anxious by the initial news story *explored a greater range* of subsequent articles. Moreover, only the anxious individuals showed *improvement in their knowledge* about the issues (as measured by scores on true/false questions about the content of the stories available through the portal). Not only do these results confirm the MacKuen results, they also extend them by identifying a tie between being anxious and becoming more informed (rather than merely being more interested in reviewing a range of information sources). Moreover, and more importantly, because the Valentino experimental setup assessed the emotion-inducing effects of the initial story before subjects were given access to the web portal (the MacKuen setup had put the manipulation check at the end), we have a paradigm that allows us to better gauge the extent to which the postmanipulation behavior was driven by the induced emotions. The Valentino group's resulting regression analyses show that anxiety had a causal role in bringing about the increases in information seeking and retention seen in

---

on various issues. Moreover, the correlations they found remained significant even after controlling for the most plausible alternative drivers of this voter interest and knowledge of this sort—for example, education level, general political attentiveness, and strength of partisanship. These basic findings have been further confirmed using data from the 2000 and 2004 election cycles (Marcus, MacKuen, & Neuman, 2011; cf. Ladd & Lenz, 2008).

the anxious subjects. Feelings of anger, disgust, and enthusiasm, by contrast, had no causal impact.[12]

Looking at these results regarding the role of emotion in political decision making as a whole, a clear pattern emerges: uncertainty about what to do or what will happen prompts epistemic behaviors that are geared toward helping one address the uncertainty at hand. Put another way, when anxiety "signals novelty or danger ... people will engage to find out what is going on" (Marcus, Neuman, & MacKuen, 2000, p. 82). As such, we see that practical anxiety meets the predictions of P10: we not only have evidence of a robust connection between uncertainty about what to do and epistemic behaviors, but also evidence that anxiety undergirds this connection.

Speaking more generally, the cumulative result of the behavioral experiments we have reviewed confirms that the functional accounts we are taking to be characteristic of environmental, punishment, and practical anxiety are not just one-off results based on anecdotes. Rather, they suggest we have a collection of stably recurring causal chains whereby uncertainty of a particular sort (regarding, e.g., physical harm, social evaluation, or norm conflict) brings distinctive response behaviors (e.g., avoidance, deference, information gathering). Thus we have solid support for P10 and so for the claim that these are genuine varieties of anxiety.

3.3.3 Evidence from Abnormal Psychology

A second line of research not only bolsters the case for P10, but also provides support for P11. In particular, research in psychiatry and clinical psychology points to anxiety disorders that (i) appear to correspond to the types of threats associated with environmental, punishment, and practical anxiety, and so (ii) suggests the associated behaviors are underwritten by the kinds of strategic and controlled processing we would expect to see if they were subtypes of anxiety.

---

12. Ted Brader (2005, 2006) affirms a distinctive causal role for anxiety in promoting open-minded information gathering and processing using a different experimental paradigm—one that compared the effects that anxiety- and enthusiasm-inducing political campaign advertisements had on political interest, engagement, and candidate preferences. Also see Huddy, Feldman, and Cassese (2007), which used self-reported survey results to investigate the impact of anxiety and anger on information gathering and processing about political policy matters regarding the Iraq War.

For instance, animal phobias and agoraphobia are generally seen as clinical manifestations of what we are calling environmental anxiety (e.g., Marks & Nesse, 1994; Öhman, 2008). Similarly, an anxiety disorder called scrupulosity provides support for punishment and practical anxiety. Scrupulosity is a form of obsessive-compulsive anxiety disorder that concerns moral and religious wrongdoing. More specifically, individuals suffering from scrupulosity exhibit patterns of obsessive behaviors that fall along two dimensions: (a) fears about sinning or doing wrong, and (b) fears about punishment for having sinned or done wrong (Abramowitz, 2008, pp. 156–158). Moreover, each type of obsession tends to provoke its own distinctive sets of compulsions: type (a) obsessions tend to provoke efforts to seek information and reassurance about the correct way to act, while type (b) obsessions typically bring efforts to avoid situations where one might do wrong, and prayer and other efforts to repent when one finds oneself having done wrong (pp. 163–168). The following excerpts from clinical case reports nicely illustrate these two forms of scrupulosity:

[*Type (a)*.] [Ken] viewed himself as a representative of the Catholic Church, yet often doubted whether he had taken "the moral high ground" and adhered to "the requirements of Catholic law," especially in situations that presented moral ambiguity. To resolve uncertainty regarding his behavior, Ken engaged in excessive reassurance seeking by mentally reviewing his behavior, referring to the Bible, and asking others (e.g., priests, relatives) for assurances. (p. 165)

[*Type (b)*.] Paul's obsessions included persistent unwanted sexual thoughts that occurred whenever he saw any sort of religious icon. For example, if he saw a cross, he would think, "Could I insert this in my rectum?" ... Paul worked hard to avoid all of the external cues. He could not attend church, see the priest or certain members of the congregation, or confront any religious icons. If these stimuli were encountered, Paul engaged in prayer rituals to atone for his sinful and blasphemous thoughts. (p. 159)

While there is much to say about these excerpts and the phenomenon of scrupulosity in general,[13] the key point for present purposes is that these two types of scrupulosity fit nicely with our two forms of anxiety. Type (a) scrupulosity gives us an example of the behavior distinctive of practical anxiety: Ken's anxiety results from concerns about what to do given a *normatively ambiguous* situation and brings *epistemic behaviors*—efforts to seek

---

13. See Summers and Sinnott-Armstrong (2015) and Shoemaker (2015, chap. 5) for a general discussion of the (moral) significance of scrupulosity.

assurance from experts (e.g., priests)—aimed at addressing this normative uncertainty. Type (b) scrupulosity gives us an example of the behavior distinctive of punishment anxiety: Paul's anxiety results from the belief that he may face *punishment* for having done wrong (e.g., having blasphemous thoughts) and brings actions (e.g., prayer) aimed at *lessening the chance or severity of punishment*.[14]

While these clinical findings provide additional support for P10, they are also evidence that these varieties of anxiety engage distinctive cognitive processes (P11). As we have seen (section 3.3.1), the biocognitive model suggests environmental, punishment, and practical anxiety represent distinct, functionally integrated systems within the control mechanism. If so, then it should possible for there to be distinctive breakdowns in those systems— breakdowns that manifest as extreme versions of the basic response tendencies of these forms of anxiety. Thus, it's significant that the breakdowns we see in these clinical conditions appear to involve the strategic processing of the control system's appraisal- and output-regulating mechanisms: these phobic and scrupulous individuals exaggerate their assessments of (condition-specific) potential physical and social threats; they also respond to these threats in similarly exaggerated ways. In short, finding evidence of these disorders provides support for P11: the stimulus-response behaviors distinctive of environmental, punishment, and practical anxiety are underwritten by mechanisms of the control system.[15]

---

14. While individuals suffering from scrupulosity will often exhibit both type (a) and type (b) behaviors, these two dimensions are doubly dissociable (as indicated by the above case reports).

15. Here I follow others in appealing to clinical research as a guide to the functioning of (normal) psychological processes (e.g., Doris, 2015; Maibom, 2005; Nichols, 2004; Roskies, 2003). Though one might object to appeals of this sort, there's reason to think such worries are misguided in the present context. As the clinical psychologist Bunmi Olatunji explains, looking to disorders can illuminate our understanding of the nature of well-functioning cognitive systems: "A substantial body of empirical research supports theoretical propositions that clinical obsessive-compulsive symptoms [including those associated with scrupulosity] have their origins in *normally occurring phenomena* (e.g., Salkovskis, 1999) and that such symptoms occur on a continuum, with many individuals in the general population reporting subclinical obsessions and compulsions (e.g., Gibbs, 1996)" (Olatunji, Abramowitz, et al., 2007, p. 774, emphasis added). For a more general discussion of the relevance of pathologi-

3.3.4 Evidence from Neuroscience

The above findings from behavioral research and abnormal psychology provide two independent lines of support for P10 and P11. This leaves P9: the prediction that environmental, punishment, and practical anxiety engage the anxiety affect program. On this front, we find support from research in neuroscience. In particular, recent imaging work implicates the BNST in human responses to threat scenarios that correspond to our characterizations of the elicitors distinctive of environmental, punishment, and practical anxiety. And given the BNST's prominence as a neural structure underlying the anxiety affect program (section 2.3.4), this research works to affirm P9.[16]

If environmental anxiety engages the anxiety affect program in the way that I have been suggesting, then we should see BNST activity when individuals are subjected to the possibility of physical harm—be it from predators, cliff edges, or other humans. This is what we find. For instance, in Straube, Mentzel, and Miltner, 2007, subjects with self-reported spider fears and non-spider-fearing control subjects were scanned as they were presented with a series of images of spiders or mushrooms. The subjects were told that these images would appear between 10 and 18 seconds after the presentation of an anticipatory symbol (e.g., "%" cued spiders, while "#" cued mushrooms). So while subjects would know a spider image was coming when they saw the "%," they would not know when. Thus, we get a setup that brings the kind of unpredictable threat associated with anxiety. As such, we should see increased BNST activity in the spider-fearful subjects both in comparison to their responses to mushrooms and in comparison to the responses of the control participants. And we do. Moreover, similar imaging results implicating the BNST have been found in a more complicated experimental setup that used live tarantulas, rather than spider images (Mobbs, Yu, et al., 2010).

In another experiment, Coaster, Rogers, et al. (2011) monitored BNST activity as participants read scenarios describing the possibility of them suffering either serious physical harms (e.g., an X% chance of broken bones,

---

cal conditions for our understanding of normal cognitive processing, see Bach and Dolan (2012); Ellis and Young (1988); and Shallice (1988).

16. To date, there has been fairly little imaging work on the BNST (see Avery, Clauss, & Blackford, 2016, for an overview). This is, in part, because we have only recently developed the ultra-fine-grained imaging technology needed to study a structure as small as the BNST (cf. section 2.3). So while the results are provocative, we should be cautious in the inferences we draw from them.

paralysis, death) or only minor injuries (e.g., an X% chance of skin scrapes, toe stubbings). Here they found more BNST activity with regard to the serious physical threats than for the minor ones—which is what we would expect to find given these were stories about more/less severe *potential* injuries. Together, this work supports our account of environmental anxiety as a genuine variety of anxiety: we see increased BNST activation in the face of a range of situations involving the possibility of serious physical harm.

In a similar vein, given our characterizations of punishment and practical anxiety, we should expect to find increased BNST activity in situations involving both potential social evaluation/sanction and norm uncertainty. Though less imaging work has been done along these lines, we have some interesting results nonetheless.

First consider findings supporting our account of punishment anxiety. On this front, Leah Somerville and colleagues put subjects in a scanner as they were shown a video of a line that purported to represent their own real-time physiological state. The participants were also told that they would accumulate electric shocks (to be administered at the end of the session) every time the line passed through a preestablished threshold. In reality, however, the line was not a measure of the subject's physiology, but rather a computer-generated image of a line slowly fluctuating above and below the threshold bar. The imaging results showed that BNST activity increased as the line approached the threshold bar (Somerville, Whalen, & Kelley, 2010). Importantly for our purposes, since the instructions given to subjects both indicated that they had some control over the line's movement and that they should try to "avoid accumulating shocks," the experimental design represents a type of *performance situation*. As such, the BNST activity we see in these subjects suggests activation of the anxiety circuit in the face of possible negative evaluations of their performance—their efforts to the contrary, they were unable to exert enough control to keep the line below the threshold. This is just what our account of punishment anxiety predicts.[17]

Turning to practical anxiety, we find support from work in neuroeconomics. We have seen that practical anxiety is anxiety that concerns uncertainty

---

17. Using a different paradigm, Schlund, Hudgins, et al. (2013) found increased BNST activity in response to potential monetary losses for poor performance on a cued button-pushing task—another type of situation where subjects seem to be experiencing anxiety about potential evaluation and punishment.

about what the correct thing to do is. Moreover, we also noted that paradigmatic elicitors of practical anxiety are cases of norm uncertainty—cases where the norms and expectations governing the situation are vague, conflicting, or otherwise difficult to make sense of. In neuroeconomics, decision-making uncertainty of this sort is often operationalized through card tasks: decks of cards of varying colors provide information about potential monetary payoffs and subjects are tasked with developing a strategy that will allow them to maximize their payout.

In the version of the card task relevant here, there were two decks. While the cards in the "low-uncertainty" deck provided payoff information that made it easy for participants to develop a winning strategy, the cards in the "high-uncertainty" deck provided little information and thus developing a winning strategy was very difficult (in fact, most participants ended up losing money). As such, the experimental setup allows us to compare decision-making situations where it's clear what rule/strategy to follow against situations where it's very unclear what rule/strategy one should employ. Our account of practical anxiety predicts that we should see increased BNST activity when subjects played from the high-uncertainty deck. That is what we find. More specifically, compared with controls, subjects with generalized anxiety disorder (GAD) showed increased BNST activity when playing from the high-uncertainty deck. But there were no differences between controls and GAD subjects when playing from the low-uncertainty deck (Yassa, Hazlett, et al., 2012).[18]

---

18. As suggested by the discussion in the text, there were no differences in BNST activity in the control participants (i.e., healthy individuals without GAD) between the high- and low-uncertainty games. This might suggest that the results are disorder-specific, and so have no implications for our general understanding of (practical) anxiety. Here I make two observations. First, as we noted in section 3.3.3, clinical levels of anxiety are generally thought to provide insight into the operation of normally functioning anxiety; this is especially true with regard to matters of threat detection. Second, notice that in comparison to the other research reviewed in this section, the gambling task used here involved a decidedly low-stakes threat—small monetary losses (not tarantulas or shocks!). Thus, the fact that we only see BNST activity in the GAD participants might well reflect their more pronounced sensitivity to small threats of this sort and so tell for a comparable (though less pronounced) sensitivity in normals. For further discussion, see Avery, Clauss, and Blackford (2016, p. 137).

Thus, we have evidence of BNST activity in the very kinds of situations that are characteristic of our three varieties of anxiety. This work is significant in two ways. First, by providing evidence of BNST activity, it supports the claim that environmental, punishment, and practical anxiety engage the anxiety affect program (by way of APF 3) and so count as genuine varieties of anxiety (P9). Second, it provides further evidence of the distinctive patterns of situational sensitivity and response characteristic of these three varieties of anxiety (P10).

3.3.5 Where Things Stand

Our two-part microindividuation test holds that if environmental, punishment, and practical anxiety are to count as genuine subtypes of anxiety, we need evidence that they (i) engage the anxiety affect program and (ii) pick out minimally or robustly projectable categories. The three lines of research that we have just reviewed support our trio of predictions (P9–P11) and so suggest these tests have been met. Not only do all three of these responses appear to engage neural structures central to the anxiety affect program (e.g., the BNST), they also display patterns of situational sensitivity and behavioral responses that appear to be underwritten by distinctive elements of the biocognitive model's control system.

Moreover, in our discussion both of the research on where uncertainty can enter decision making (section 3.3.1) and of the empirical findings more generally (sections 3.3.2–3.3.4), we saw that these three forms of anxiety are responses to prominent and recurring forms of uncertainty—Will I be hurt? Am I being negatively evaluated? What is the correct thing to do? This is significant for two reasons. First, it provides evidence that cultural forces have shaped the evolution of anxiety (the biocognitive emotion) in ways that suggest environmental, punishment, and practical anxiety represent refinements of a basic anxiety response.[19] Second, the breadth in the range of situations that provoke these subtypes of anxiety suggests that they capture much of the structure of ordinary anxious episodes and so provides initial assurance that much of our anxiety talk is—contra the skeptic (section 2.4.2)—well founded. In our biocognitive account of anxiety, we have a proposal that not only picks out a *genuine category* but also one

---

19. We will return to this possibility in chapter 7; I have taken up in detail elsewhere (Kurth, 2016).

that has *broad application*. In the next section, I will work through some more examples of our everyday anxiety talk. Doing this will reveal how the discussion so far allows us to make principled microindividuation claims—distinctions about what does, and does not, count as a variety of anxiety. The result will be further evidence that our biocognitive model captures a significant portion of our anxiety talk.[20]

3.4 Microindividuation Part III: Elaborations and Refinements

Recalling some of the examples of our anxiety talk from chapter 2, the discussion that follows takes a closer look at 'anxiety' as it is used with regard to existential matters, social/evaluative situations, and moral contexts. As with the above, the task is to determine whether these uses meet our two-part microindividuation criterion. That said, since the forms of anxiety we will be surveying have received less systematic attention, the discussion that follows will be more schematic.

3.4.1 Existential Anxiety

Assessing talk of existential anxiety is difficult given that the term has different connotations depending on which existentialist author one considers (e.g., Kierkegaard or Sartre). If we focus on Kierkegaard's version (1844/2006), we get a rendering of existential anxiety that is perhaps best glossed as a feeling of uncertainty about one's purpose brought on by the recognition of one's freedom to make life-shaping choices. Kierkegaard introduces this idea through the analogy of an individual standing on a cliff edge:

Anxiety may be compared with dizziness. He whose eye happens to look down into the yawning abyss becomes dizzy. But what is the reason for this? It is just as much in his own eye as in the abyss, for suppose he had not looked down. Hence, anxiety is the dizziness of freedom, which emerges when the spirit wants to posit the synthesis and freedom looks down into its own possibility, laying hold of finiteness to

---

20. A qualification: given how unsettled our understanding of psychological disorders is, in what follows, I will set aside questions about how anxiety disorders fit within the framework I am developing. (For thoughtful, general discussions of the nature and classification of psychological disorders, see Griffiths, 2004a; Horwitz & Wakefield, 2012; Kendler, Zachar, & Craver, 2011; Murphy, 2005; and Murphy & Stich, 2000.)

support itself. Freedom succumbs to dizziness. (1844/2006, p. 61; cf. LeDoux, 2015, pp. 253–254)

Recalling our two-part individuation criterion, how should we understand the connection between Kierkegaard's account of existential anxiety and the anxiety affect program we have been looking at? In particular, is the anxiety affect program a component or constitutive element of Kierkegaard's existential anxiety?

Given the above discussion, I do not believe a plausible case can be made for this. The first reason for doubt concerns the intentionality (or aboutness) associated with existential anxiety. As Kierkegaard describes it, existential anxiety conveys a very general negative assessment—roughly, an amorphous unease about one's future or freedom. If this is correct, then, given the discussion of section 1.2, existential anxiety is likely better understood as a mood or feeling than an emotion. This assessment gets further support from the emphasis Kierkegaard puts on the analogy between anxiety and dizziness—for dizziness seems more a feeling than an emotion.[21] Second, even if we grant existential anxiety is an emotion, there's reason to doubt whether it engages the anxiety affect program. Notice, for instance, that on Kierkegaard's account existential anxiety seems to lack the automatic appraisal characteristic of an affect program (i.e., no APF 4). As I understand his explanation, anxiety is the result of someone surveying, or "look[ing] down on," her freedom and "synthesizing" its infinite and finite dimensions. Such surveying and synthesizing sound less like the operation of a fast-acting, automatic assessment mechanism and more like high-level, controlled processing. Together these differences provide good reason for doubting that existential anxiety meets the tests for being a form of anxiety (the biocognitive emotion).

The more plausible possibility, I suspect, is that existential anxiety is an emotion that bears some interesting *ontogenetic* relationship to the anxiety affect program (or, given Kierkegaard's analogy, an ontogenetic tie to the processes that underlie *dizziness*). So understood, existential anxiety and the anxiety affect program have no (substantive) shared mechanisms—the

---

21. See Ratcliffe (2008, chaps. 1–2) for discussion of 'anxiety' as used by philosophers working in the phenomenological tradition. There he argues that anxiety is best understood as a feeling or mood, not an emotion.

connection between them is merely a historical or developmental one.[22] If that is right, then existential anxiety is not a genuine kind of anxiety; instances of it do not engage the anxiety affect program in the above component sense—its role is (at best) ontogenetic.

3.4.2 Social, Test, and Cocktail Party Anxiety

As we noted at the beginning of the chapter, we find talk of a wide range of broadly "social" anxieties among both ordinary people and psychologists. These include both anxieties that arise with regard to social interactions in general and anxieties that manifest themselves in particular social situations—public speaking, test taking, dating, and the like. What does our microindividuation criterion, and biocognitive account of anxiety more generally, tell us about these social anxieties? Which, if any, might suitably engage the anxiety affect program and have the predictive and explanatory power to count as genuine varieties of anxiety?

For the beginnings of an answer, we can start by noting two points of broad agreement among social and clinical psychologists. The first concerns the basic characterization of 'social anxiety.' As standardly understood, social anxiety is (i) an aversive emotional response provoked by the possibility of observation or evaluation by others that (ii) brings associated worries, increased arousal, and distinctive patterns of risk-minimization behavior (e.g., deference, excuse making, apology, withdrawal, avoidance) (Barlow, 2001, pp. 455–456; Gilbert, 2001; Leary & Kowalski, 1995; Marks & Gelder, 1966). The second point of agreement is that labels for anxieties associated with particular kinds of performances—speaking in public, taking a test, playing a sport, using computers, and so on—should be understood as *subtypes* of social anxiety as characterized above. The underlying thought here is that performances of these sorts are occasions where observation and evaluation by others are possible (Barlow, 2001, pp. 455–456; Leary & Kowalski, 1995; Zeidner & Matthews, 2005).[23]

---

22. Griffiths (1997) speculates that this might be the best way to understand the relationship between guilt and fear. As he sees it, guilt might be the result of an experience of fear in a social exchange early in infancy that leads to the existence of the pattern of thoughts, behaviors, and so on that is distinctive of guilt (p. 122).

23. This second claim regarding things like public speaking and test anxiety being subkinds of social anxiety is potentially more controversial. I say potentially because we lack much of the comparative data we would need for a full assessment of the

With these two points of consensus in hand, we can explore the relationship between these assorted social anxieties and our biocognitive model. Do they count as genuine varieties of anxiety on a par with environmental or practical anxiety? Or are they better understood as akin to existential anxiety—phenomena for which there is only a loose (metaphorical or ontogenetic) connection to the anxiety affect program? Since my primary goal here is not to develop a comprehensive taxonomy, but rather to merely illustrate how our biocognitive framework allows us to identify varieties of anxiety that count as genuine categories in virtue of their predictive and explanatory power, I will limit myself to two observations on this front.

First, the above characterization of social anxiety's behavioral and physiological profile suggests there are strong affinities between it and punishment anxiety. Punishment anxiety, recall, is a form of anxiety that helps one see that one might be subject to evaluation and punishment and that prompts things like deference and appeasement efforts aimed at helping one minimize (or avoid) punishment. In the context of the biocognitive model, social anxiety, then, might plausibly be seen as a cultural elaboration of punishment anxiety: it is punishment anxiety where cultural influences (acting through the anxiety control system) have brought a further expansion in both the range of situations that elicit the response, and the ways one subsequently responds.[24]

If that is correct, then we should expect the first part of our microindividuation test to be met—social and performance anxiety should engage the anxiety affect program. While more research is needed on this front, we have some evidence that this is the case. For instance, based on observations of wild and captive nonhuman primates, we find evidence of what appears to be (proto)anxiety on occasions where there is social instability (Cheney & Sayfarth, 2007) or when subordinates interact with dominants (Dutton, Clark, & Dickins, 1997). More importantly, the behaviors taken to be indicative of primate (social) anxiety (e.g., scratching) are blocked by anxiolytics like lorazepam (Schino, Troisi, et al., 1991). Thus, in support of social

---

relationship between these various phenomena. See Zeidner and Matthews (2005) for further discussion.

24. As we will see below (section 3.5), there are a variety of different ways these expansions might come about.

anxiety engaging the anxiety affect program, we have evidence for both APF 2 (presence in primates) and APF 3 (distinct neural/physiological activity).

Second, to the extent that we have evidence that a particular subtype of social anxiety has a collection of features (e.g., elicitation conditions, behavior tendencies, perhaps even first-person phenomenology) that display substantive predictive and explanatory power, we have reason to take it to have met our second microindividuation test. Here work by psychologists on particular social anxiety measures suggests that things like test anxiety (Zeidner, 1998), sports anxiety (Woodman & Hardy, 2001), public speaking anxiety (McCroskey & Beatty, 1984), and even computer anxiety (Thorpe & Brosnan, 2007) may make the cut.[25] By contrast, more fine-grained phenomena—say, how-to-act-at-cocktail-party anxiety—are likely to fall short. This is not because there is no anxiety among cocktail party attendees. Rather, it's that for a phenomenon like this, there is unlikely to be a collection of features with predictive and explanatory power across an interesting range of individuals and situations (Griffiths, 1997).

Taken together, these findings provide initial support that many—but not all—of the 'anxieties' of social and performance situations meet our two-part microindividuation test.

3.4.3 Moral Anxiety

Elsewhere I have discussed a form of anxiety that I call moral anxiety (Kurth, 2015). Moral anxiety, as a gloss, is an aversive emotional response to uncertainty about the correctness of a moral decision one is contemplating (or has made). When one feels morally anxious, one tends to do things that are aimed at both resolving one's underlying uncertainty (e.g., information gathering, reflection, deliberation), and minimizing the risks that come with having to act in the face of such uncertainty (e.g., deferring to "moral authorities"). What does our biocognitive model suggest about how we should understand moral anxiety? Is it a distinct variety of anxiety, a subtype of practical anxiety, or something else altogether?[26]

---

25. The case for treating a particular subtype of social anxiety as genuine is stronger to the extent that the personality measures associated with it build on more than just the self-reports (e.g., supplementation by peer reports or physiological responses).

26. Freud (1926/1959) also uses the label 'moral anxiety.' For him, the term picks out anxiety that results from conflict between the biological drivers of the id and the

Four pieces of evidence suggest moral anxiety might be a distinct variety of anxiety—something on a par with punishment or practical anxiety. First, misattribution research implicates feelings of anxiety as central to doing the right thing in the face of temptation or uncertainty. More specifically, individuals who were led to believe their feelings of unease were the result of a pill, not their anxiety, were more likely to cheat if given the opportunity than were controls who had not been led to misattribute their unease (e.g., Dienstbier & Hunter, 1971; Schachter & Latané, 1964). Similar results have been found with regard to fairness: individuals led to misattribute their anxiety are more likely than controls to divide resources in a manner they themselves deem unfair (Jackson, Gaertner, & Batson, 2016). Second, experimental work by Adam Perkins and colleagues (Perkins, Leonard, et al., 2013) indicates that taking antianxiety medications makes individuals more "ruthless." In particular, Perkins's team found that there was a dose-dependent increase in individuals' willingness to endorse courses of action in moral dilemmas that involved directly harming others. For instance, in contrast with controls, individuals who had taken the antianxiety pills were more willing to endorse pushing a large man off a bridge to save five others from being killed by a runaway trolley. Given that the willingness to inflict such harms increased as individuals were given stronger doses of the drug (i.e., there is dose dependence), these results suggest a causal relationship between anxiety and harm sensitivity (and so evidence that the anxiety affect program is engaged).[27] Third, the psychologist Karl Aquino's work on moral identity suggests that we have a capacity for anxiety that is attuned to moral violations. In particular, Aquino's work suggests that recognizing that one's decision to act in a particular way will conflict with one's conception of oneself as a moral person is associated with the unease

---

moral/social ideals of the superego: one experiences Freudian moral anxiety when one has violated (or believes one is likely to violate) a moral/social norm. As such, the phenomenon Freud identifies is more akin to what we have labeled 'punishment anxiety.' For further discussion, see Zeidner and Matthews (2011, pp. 80–85); cf. Velleman (2003).

27. There is some reason to question the Perkins "ruthlessness" results: the moral vignettes they used were drawn from Greene, Sommerville, et al. (2001)—a study whose methodology has been called into question (e.g., Berker, 2009; McGuire, Langdon, et al., 2009). Whether these concerns carry over to the Perkins results is an open question.

and stress characteristic of anxiety (Aquino, Freeman, et al., 2009). Finally, recall the investigation by Michael MacKuen et al. (2010) of the effect of anxiety on moral/political issues like the appropriateness of one's views on affirmative action. As we have seen, this work indicates that anxiety brings a greater willingness to compromise and explore alternative solutions.

Taken together, these results are provocative. They suggest there may be a distinctly moral variety of anxiety—something that is on a par with punishment, practical, or environmental anxiety with regard to its ability to meet our two-part microindividuation test. However, more cautiously—and I suspect more plausibly—we might see these results, not as evidence of a distinctly moral form of anxiety, but rather as evidence of moral content being acquired (in the anxiety control system) as the result of enculturation and individual learning. If this alternative picture is correct, then moral anxiety is likely to be better understood, not as a distinct variety of anxiety, but rather as a subtype of practical anxiety. This proposal gets further support from its fit with a common theoretical picture on which the moral domain is a subset of the practical domain.[28]

3.4.4 Mapping Varieties of Anxiety

Bringing this discussion of some of the phenomena that we call 'anxiety' to a close, figure 3.1 summarizes the various types of anxiety we have identified and the relations between them.

3.4.5 Vindicating Talk of Anxiety

Summing up this discussion of individuation, we can make a few general observations. First, we have seen that our biocognitive account of anxiety provides us with macro- and microindividuation criteria that allow us to make principled and plausible decisions about what does, and does not, count as a genuine variety of anxiety. We have also seen how these tools can be used to taxonomize various varieties of anxiety. On this front, we have made some initial progress. While the results are far from complete, they nonetheless provide us with a picture that captures much of the structure of anxious episodes. Further developing this picture will require, among other

---

28. I say more about moral anxiety in chapters 5 and 6.

Diversity

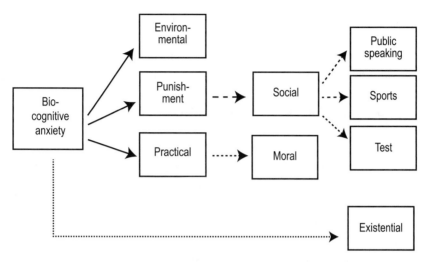

Figure 3.1
Varieties of anxiety. Smaller dashes indicate we have less evidence that the category is plausibly seen as a genuine subtype of anxiety.

things, more empirical data and a better understanding of how culture and individual experience give shape to anxious episodes.[29]

An additional consequence of our progress here is that we secure further support for the claim that much, though not all, of our anxiety talk is legitimate. Not only does the account of environmental, punishment, and practical anxiety capture a substantive core of anxious episodes, but—as our discussion of various "social" anxieties reveals—it also accommodates much of our everyday and academic anxiety talk. 'Anxiety,' as we typically use the term, refers to a phenomenon that, as the biocognitive model details, has the anxiety affect program at is core. But the operation of this basic, hardwired threat-detection and threat-response system is also

---

29. It is worth noting that the basic strategy for (macro- and microindividuation) that we have been employing has broader application. Anxiety, after all, is not the only emotion for which we find talk of distinct varieties or subtypes. There is, for instance, fear and its various (clinical and nonclinical) phobias. There is also an "anger family" that is thought to include things like outrage, indignation, contempt, and (perhaps) vengeance. So here too we can ask questions about microindividuation. And we can answer these questions by making use of the pair of microindividuation criteria we developed in section 3.2.

influenced by a set of control filters—higher cognitive structures that give shape both to the types of threats that trigger anxiety and to the behaviors that result. Thus, the concern that our biocognitive account of anxiety would prove excessively revisionary can be set aside.

3.5   Objection: This "Anxiety" Ain't Anxiety

The discussion to this point might raise worries about how to reconcile the largely biological picture of anxiety that we have been looking at with the anxiety of our ordinary experience. After all, implicit in the gloss we just gave is the suggestion that—according to the biocognitive account—anxiety is both typically an automatic response to a particular set of external stimuli (angry faces, snakes), and something that often operates below the level of conscious awareness: though later higher-level, strategic processing can be engaged, this only occurs downstream from the initial, automatic appraisal. Such a picture is, as I have discovered, likely to strike some as odd, if not just downright confused. After all, anxiety as we often experience it seems to be internally driven—it is the upshot of our conscious ruminations and worries about all sorts of things (LeDoux, 2015; Rachman, 2004; Zeidner & Matthews, 2011, chap. 7). To better see this, consider the following:

Gala. After being introduced to a new acquaintance at a fancy gala, you start worrying about whether you're making a good impression—or whether you will (again) say something silly or stupid. Now you're anxious. Worse, you notice that you have started to sweat and fidget—so now you're even more anxious. You quickly apologize for being clumsy and, looking toward the door, start trying to figure out a way to extricate yourself from the conversation.

Not only is this a familiar sort of experience, but recognizing it as such helps draw out two worries about the biocognitive account of anxiety. First, in the example, we seem to have anxiety manifesting itself via an alternative, largely cognitive route. More specifically, the anxiety you experience at the party is not the upshot of the kind of causal sequence we have been focusing on—one whereby an automatic low-level appraisal generates physiological changes, risk-minimization behavior, and higher-level (potentially conscious) processing (recall figure 2.1 from chapter 2). Rather, in this case, your anxiety appears to be driven by (largely) conscious, higher-level appraisals that then bring physiological changes, risk-minimization behavior, and further higher-level processing. As such, anxiety seems better understood not as a biocognitive emotion, but on the cultural-cognitive model discussed in section 2.4.2. Second, thinking of anxiety on the biocognitive model suggests it's unable to explain the (potentially debilitating) cycles of worry and rumination that we see in the example (e.g., situations where recognizing one is anxious makes one more so). Since worry and rumination are prominent features of ordinary anxious experience, the biocognitive model seems to have again gotten something wrong.

To address these worries, we need to say more about two aspects of the model that we have only noted in passing: the existence of significant feedback loops and the control system's tendency to acquire new content via culture and individual experience.

Taking these in turn, recall figure 2.1. One important way in which this schematic gives an oversimplified picture of anxious episodes is by omitting feedback loops (cf. Levenson, 1999, pp. 490–491). Of particular note for present purposes are the loops that begin from the outputted behaviors on the right side of the figure (e.g., attentional, gross motor, physiological, and higher cognitive behavior) and that feed back as inputted stimuli on the left side. Drawing out the feedback loops implicit in the biocognitive model is important because it allows us to capture both the dynamic, self-regulating nature of anxious episodes and their potential to bring debilitating cycles of worry.[30]

To flesh this out, first consider a toy instance of this dynamic self-regulation. The automatic appraisal of a possible threat brings (via the core system) both a narrowing of focus in one's attentional systems and increases in physiological arousal. These response behaviors then become feedback: they themselves are taken as stimuli to be appraised (e.g., when one feels

---

30. Research in neuroscience supports the presence of feedback loops of this sort. For instance, as we have seen, fear and anxiety are grounded in distinct neural circuits (the central nucleus of the amygdala for fear, and the bed nucleus of the stria terminalis for anxiety). While both structures have been shown to get significant inputs from specific sensory systems (e.g., visual, auditory), the anxiety circuit is distinct in that it is also (more) extensively connected to cortical areas involved in higher cognitive processing (e.g., prefrontal cortex, hippocampus). This additional set of inputs is generally thought to help explain why (in comparison with fear) anxiety has a more significant cognitive dimension. For further discussion, see LeDoux (2015, chap. 4) and the citations there. Also see Colombetti (2014).

the spike in arousal, one appraises one's situation as more threatening). This, in turn, prompts additional anxious behavior (e.g., information gathering, higher cognitive processing). These anxious behaviors, however, fail to locate any actual dangers, which then reduces one's appraisal of the situation as threatening and so brings a reversal in the earlier changes in attention and arousal (Corr, 2008; Lewis, 2005; Mathews, 1990).

While this toy example illustrates how feedback loops allow anxiety to operate as a dynamic, self-regulating system, it also reveals how anxiety can generate the kinds of debilitating cycles of worry that we saw in the gala example. For instance, socially anxious individuals are more likely to approach social exchanges with increased self-focus: they are more sensitive to clues about the impression they are making on others and more attuned to their own behavior (e.g., fidgeting, increased arousal) (Clark & Wells, 1995; Heerey & Kring, 2007; Leary, Kowalski, & Campbell, 1988). As such, when they come to appraise their situation as socially threatening (e.g., they appraise an ambiguous facial expression as conveying a possible negative evaluation—as a possible social threat), they tend to respond by turning greater attention on themselves and engaging in conscious cognitive assessments of their own actions. This self-focused attention and rumination can be fed back into the appraisal system: feelings of unease can act as catalysts to thoughts that one may have (again) made a bad impression and so increase one's tendency to appraise subsequent ambiguous information as threatening. If this happens, a vicious cycle of worry can ensue.[31] With this in hand, we can see—contra the initial worry—that the biocognitive model explains how anxiety can generate vicious spirals of worry and rumination.

While this is progress, there is still the challenge of showing that the biocognitive model can explain how anxiety can be initiated and sustained by conscious, higher-level cognitive processing. To address this worry, we need to say more about the control system's tendency to accumulate content. Initially, we glossed the control system as a kind of filter that both scans/selects for potential threats and opportunities, thereby affecting the inputs

---

31. Empirical work suggests that the tendency for self-focus/rumination to lead to vicious cycles is determined in part by one's belief that one cannot control one's anxiety once one recognizes that one is anxious (e.g., Barlow, 2001; Rapee, Craske, et al., 1996).

to the core system, and gives shape to the (motor, higher cognitive, express) behaviors activated by a given affect program (anger, fear, joy, etc.) in the core system. Pressing beyond this metaphor, we can understand these "filters" as cognitive structures that consist of mental representations of particular beliefs and values—representations that supply the content that drives the control system's effects on what one sees as emotionally significant and how one subsequently responds (Sripada & Stich, 2004; cf. Prinz, 2004, pp. 100–102).[32] Moreover, as we noted above (section 3.3), individual experiences and cultural influences provide these structures with content that can affect the genetically hardwired tendencies of particular affect programs. For instance, an individual's interaction with her environment can modify and add to her innate beliefs and values by, (e.g.,) making her sensitive to the specific threats and opportunities of her locale. Culture and social learning can provide an additional source of content: internalizing cultural mores and practices can accentuate (or silence) existing aspects of an individual's value structures; they can also add new elements. The result will be an augmented representation of what counts as, say, danger (fear), contamination (disgust), or success (joy) (Izard, 2007; Levenson, 1999; Prinz, 2004; Sripada & Stich, 2004).[33]

---

32. I follow Sripada and Stich in understanding these beliefs and values broadly. Thus, 'beliefs' includes inter alia content (purporting to be) about oneself, the world, and past events; 'values' includes inter alia content concerning norms, goals, drives, and ideals.

33. I want to remain neutral on the details regarding how culture and experience combine with, and give shape to, the gene-based content of the control system. The important thing for present purposes is that this likely happens in a variety of ways. One possibility is that these influences on gene-based content are the result of *culturally driven co-option* or *modification*. Dan Kelly (2011, chaps. 4–5) has developed a proposal of this sort with regard to the disgust response that underlies violations of social and moral norms (e.g., food taboos, incest prohibitions). Alternatively, culture and experience could influence the gene-based content of value structures through *learned associations*. Jesse Prinz (2004) develops a proposal of this sort (pp. 100–102). As he sees it, an emotion like fear is linked to collections of mental representations that provide hardwired content about what is to be feared and how one is to respond. This hardwired content can be added to and altered through learned associations—that is, through individual experiences, one can come to fear a wider range of things (e.g., one's boss, handguns, tornadoes). Carroll Izard (2007) provides a more general model on which the operation of basic emotions / affect programs

Applying this basic picture to the case of anxiety helps us explain how instances of anxiety can be initiated and sustained by conscious, higher-level processing. As we have seen, the control system's content is a collection of beliefs and values. But notice: when threat- (and so anxiety-)relevant beliefs are combined with particular values and situation-specific events, the result can be anxiety-provoking ruminations and worries of the sort we found in the gala example. Fleshing this out, if past experiences leave you believing that you typically make bad first impressions, then finding yourself being introduced to a new acquaintance can bring conscious worries about whether you are going to again embarrass yourself—worries that, given your concern to avoid embarrassing yourself—make you more likely to appraise ambiguous information as threatening and so more likely to feel anxious. So we have an explanation for how anxiety can be engaged by conscious, cognitive processing.

Stepping back, we can now have a richer understanding of the biocognitive model—one that helps us explain the pair of observations about the cognitive dimensions of anxiety. The values and beliefs of the anxiety control system bring content grounded in culture and experience that colors both what makes one anxious and how one subsequently responds. Recognizing this explains how anxiety can be evoked by such a wide range of things—be it snakes, angry faces, tests, or cocktail parties. Moreover, because past experience can dispose us to see particular situations as threatening, we get an understanding of both how thinking about such a situation can make someone anxious, and how recognizing that one is anxious can make one even more so. Thus, we see how anxiety can be internally driven—prompted by conscious ruminations and worries—and how this can lead to potentially vicious feedback loops.

One might be concerned, however, that success here comes at the cost of making the anxiety affect program uninteresting—it no longer seems to contribute in a substantive way to our everyday anxious experiences. But this worry is misplaced for two reasons. First, we need to countenance

---

is affected by "emotion schemas"—roughly, dynamic interplays between basic emotions, situational appraisals, and higher-order cognition. Emotion schemas can thus be understood as combinations of appraisal templates and behavioral scripts that operate on underlying basic emotions. As such, they have a significant shaping effect on emotion-generated thought and action.

something like the anxiety affect program if we are to be able to make sense of phenomena like repressors and the automatic threat-detection biases discussed in chapter 2. Second, in addition to the cognitively driven example of anxiety we have been working with, there are also everyday cases where anxious experience is better seen as the upshot of the core anxiety affect program. To see this, consider another case:

Dinner Party. You are seated next to a new acquaintance at a dinner party. So far, your conversation has been going quite well. But the mood quickly shifts: the discussion becomes awkward and your dinner partner makes eye contact less frequently. Sensing this, you start to feel anxious. You start to worry that you have said something inappropriate. What could have triggered the change—was it your comments about the election? You become more cautious and deferential as you think about what you could say to restore the earlier tenor of your discussion.

I take it that a case like this is just as familiar as the earlier gala example. But it is also one where your anxiety is not the result of conscious rumination and worry, but rather the automatic detection and appraisal of (e.g.,) the changes in conversational tone or your dinner partner's facial expressions. If so, then we have no reason to think the anxiety affect program has been rendered insignificant. Stepping back, this enriched understanding of the anxiety control system provides us with a more complete understanding of our biocognitive model. This, in turn, helps us see that much—though not all—of what we call 'anxiety' can be captured by our account.

3.6 Taking Stock: Two Lessons for What's to Come

Before moving on to part II, it will helpful to review what we have learned about anxiety so far. Doing this will highlight a pair of lessons that will be important for the discussion of anxiety's significance for social and moral life that's to come.

Lesson 1: Vindicating Anxiety as a Biocognitive Emotion. Our investigation began in chapter 2 with the Puzzle of Kinds. There we saw not only that 'anxiety' picks out a genuine category, but also that anxiety is best understood on the biocognitive model. That discussion, in turn, highlighted the importance of the Puzzle of Diversity. After all, we use 'anxiety' to talk about a wide range of phenomena and this raises questions about both how much of our anxiety talk the biocognitive account captures and what—if anything—unifies and explains the types of anxiety we discuss and experience.

To make sense of this, I showed that the biocognitive model allows us to develop a principled and plausible account of how to individuate anxiety at the macro- and microlevel. I also showed how these tools could be used to mark off varieties of anxiety that capture much of the structure of our use of 'anxiety.' The resulting picture is thus significant because it delivers an empirically grounded account of anxiety that is tolerably revisionary with regard to our everyday talk and experiences.

Lesson 2: Environmental, Punishment, and Practical Anxiety as Genuine Subtypes. The second lesson concerns the three subtypes of anxiety—environmental, punishment, and practical—that we have identified. As we have seen, each brings a distinctive, functionally integrated combination of situational sensitivities, behavioral tendencies, and motivational drives. *Environmental anxiety* is a concern about potential physical harms that brings avoidance/withdrawal tendencies and that engages a self-defense motivation; *punishment anxiety* is concerned with occasions where negative social evaluation is possible and brings deference/appeasement efforts guided by an ego-defensive motivation; and *practical anxiety* concerns difficult or novel choices and prompts epistemic efforts shaped by accuracy motivations. Recognizing this is significant in three ways.

First, the diversity in the sensitivities and responses that we see in these three varieties of anxiety suggests that they serve distinct functions—they are responses that we have developed to address different kinds of uncertainty and the trouble they bring (Kurth, 2016). Second, the cognitive mechanisms that undergird the distinctive features that we see in environmental, punishment, and practical anxiety appear to reside in the (malleable) control systems that shape the inputs to and outputs of the anxiety affect program (sections 3.3.2–3.3.4). This suggests that these varieties of anxiety will be (somewhat) responsive to our efforts to regulate—even cultivate—when and how they manifest themselves.[34] Finally, we should expect to see differences in the extent to which these subtypes of anxiety can be shaped and so differences in the extent to which each can be valuable for social and moral life. After all, we've not only seen that these three

---

34. Recall the Levenson quote from section 2.1: "The control mechanisms are exquisitely sensitive to learning, fine-tuning their operating parameters across the course of life."

varieties of anxiety have different concerns and engage different behavioral responses, but also that the socially oriented varieties of anxiety (i.e., punishment and practical) are likely to be more susceptible to our efforts to shape them (section 3.3).

* * *

A final point. As we have seen (section 2.1.4), if anxiety—and kinds of anxiety—don't count as genuine categories, but rather pick out narrower (culturally bounded) phenomena or jade-like things, then there will be important limits to what we can say about anxiety and its significance. To the extent that 'anxiety' (or 'practical anxiety') does not refer to a genuine (sub)category, there will be less unifying structure undergirding the phenomena we are seeking to categorize and make sense of through our anxiety talk. For instance, there will be limits to what we can say to justify and explain why anxiety is valuable and when it can contribute to, say, progressive moral inquiry. Thus, it is significant that our biocognitive account provides us with a rich, empirically informed account of anxiety and subtypes like environmental, punishment, and practical anxiety. So, with our model of anxiety in hand, we can turn to investigate its relevance for social and moral life.

II Anxiety's Relevance to Moral Psychology and Ethical Theory

4 Value: The Ways Anxiety Matters

Any kind of creative activity is likely to be stressful. The more anxiety, the more you feel that you are headed in the right direction. Easiness, relaxation, comfort—these are not conditions that usually accompany serious work.
—Joyce Carol Oates

In the argument of chapters 2 and 3 we have the beginnings of an answer to the Puzzle of Value—the challenge of understanding how an emotion that seems, at least at first pass, to be wholly pernicious, might nonetheless be deeply valuable. After all, that discussion paints a picture of anxiety, or at least central varieties of it, suggesting it can be a moderate and beneficial emotion. Though anxiety can sometimes go awry, it is also an important feature of our psychology: by making us more aware of, and sensitive to, a wide range of potential physical and social threats, anxiety can better enable us to navigate life's complexities. But the claim that anxiety can be a valuable emotion will strike many as odd, if not just ridiculous. Anxious individuals, even nonpathologically anxious individuals, are often consumed by intense, debilitating cycles of worry. And because their anxiety is so unpleasant, they will sometimes do just about anything to make it go away. What could be valuable in that?

These claims aren't just bits of folk wisdom—they have psychological and philosophical backing. On the empirical side, for instance, one review of research investigating the effects of anxiety in evaluative settings notes that it is "predominantly harmful to task performance" (Zeidner & Matthews, 2005, p. 147). And among philosophers, there's a long tradition that views anxiety, and negative emotions more generally, as problematic for virtuous thought and action. For instance, Stoics like Seneca (1995) saw negative emotions as problematic because they are "obstinate and intent on anything once started, closed to reasoning or advice, agitated on pretexts without foundation, [and] incapable of discerning fairness or truth" (p. 18). Though Seneca's focus here is anger, he took his observations to apply to negative emotions as a whole. Speaking more generally, the ancients saw negative emotions, psychological conflict, and stress as signs that something had gone wrong—a sharp contrast with the harmony of thought, feeling, and action characteristic of the virtuous (Annas, 1993, p. 54).[1] We find something similar in Kant (1797/1996). As he sees it, for an individual to be truly virtuous, he must "bring all his capacities and inclinations under his (reason's) control and so to rule over himself" (p. 536). In this respect, emotions—especially negative emotions like anxiety—are problematic insofar as they make reflection "impossible or more difficult" (p. 535); for Kant, the "true strength of virtue is a *tranquil mind* with a considered and firm resolution to put the law of virtue into practice. That is the state of *health* in the moral life" (p. 536, original emphasis).[2] In short, we have a rather unflattering picture of anxiety: it is impairing, inherently unpleasant, and inconsistent with virtue.

I reject this skepticism. Contrary to the folk, psychological, and philosophical wisdom, anxiety is a very important emotion. Not only can it be instrumentally valuable, it can also be aretaically, perhaps even intrinsically, valuable—that is, anxiety isn't just valuable because of the behaviors and consequences it brings, but also because of what it reveals about the emotional and evaluative attunement of those who experience it. To show this, I will challenge three broad objections that we find in the above observations from Seneca and Kant: (i) Anxiety cannot be valuable because it is never fitting—that is, there is a systematic misalignment between what anxiety is about and what has value. (ii) Anxiety, even when fitting, is not instrumentally valuable because it is too likely to do more harm than good. (iii) Anxiety cannot be aretaically (or intrinsically) valuable because the unease and psychological conflict that characterize anxiety are incompatible with the "tranquil mind" of the virtuous person. In each case, I will

---

1. We find a similar assessment in the proposals of contemporary philosophers working in the Aristotelian tradition—for example, Annas (2011), Foot (1978), Hursthouse (1999, pp. 92–93), and McDowell (1998). More on this below.
2. Korsgaard (2009) might be read as making a similar point. On her account of agency as self-constitution, without the rational endorsement that affirms and creates agency we are mere heaps of discordant impulses and emotions.

show not only that these objections are misplaced, but that understanding why highlights the various ways anxiety matters. The result will be an account of anxiety's value that shows it to be an emotion whose distinctive concern—problematic uncertainty—makes it a fitting response to a wide range of life's predicaments. We will also see that anxiety's tendency to sensitize us to uncertainty makes it an emotion with significant instrumental value. Moreover, the feelings of anxiety we experience in the face of a difficult or a novel (moral) choice manifest an admirable form of concern— one that speaks to anxiety's aretaic value. Not only will these conclusions provide answers to the Puzzle of Value, they will also set an important foundation for a broader understanding of anxiety's role in moral and practical thought. In so doing, it will prepare us for our investigation of the Puzzles of Virtue and Progress in chapters 5 and 6.

Before getting started, two comments on the scope of the investigation in this chapter. First, I am most interested in a notion of virtue applicable to ordinary humans, not ideal or perfect agents (recall chapter 1). Here I take myself to be operating in the same manner as the ancients (see, e.g., Annas, 1993, pp. 83–84) and many contemporary value theorists (see, e.g., the citations in note 1).[3] Second, in what follows, I focus primarily on the ways environmental, punishment, and practical anxiety have value. This will allow us to better understand the suggestion from chapter 3 that certain varieties of anxiety—especially practical anxiety—are likely to be more valuable than others. Along the way, we will also draw some conclusions about the value of other negative emotions—particularly anger and disgust. We will see that the case for anxiety's value is just as good as—likely better than—the cases made for the value of these and other emotions (e.g., Bell, 2013; D'Arms & Jacobson, 2006; Plakias, 2013).

4.1 Is Anxiety Ever Fitting?

A familiar charge against certain emotions—anxiety, envy, vengeance, lust, and the like—is that they cannot be valuable because it is never fitting or appropriate to feel them. To flesh this out, some background will be

---

3. In contrast with the ancients, Kant appears to have been principally concerned with a notion of full or ideal virtue—though I will have more to say about the nuances of his account at the end of the chapter.

helpful. This "fittingness objection" starts from the common assumption that emotions are intentional states in the sense that they have content (or aboutness): fear is about danger, anger is about insult and offense, sadness is about loss, joy is about success.[4] Moreover, and as these examples suggest, the aboutness or content of an emotional experience is evaluatively loaded. To fear the dog is to see the dog as dangerous—as something to be avoided; to be happy about the talk you just gave is to see the talk as a success—as a commendable performance. But notice: if emotions are intentional states with evaluative content, then they're the kinds of things that can have accuracy conditions. That is, they're states that can be (un)fitting or (in) appropriate in virtue of (mis)representing the evaluative content of their targets (D'Arms & Jacobson, 2000, 2006). So, for instance, your fear of the dog is fitting when the dog really is dangerous; being happy about your talk is fitting when the talk actually was a success.[5]

As suggested by the above examples, the accuracy conditions of a particular emotion (fear) are a function of the content (dangerousness) that it attributes to its target (the dog). For the discussion that follows, it will be helpful to be a bit more precise. First, we can distinguish between the particular and formal objects of an emotion (de Sousa, 1987, pp. 115ff.; Helm, 2002, pp. 15–16; Prinz, 2004, pp. 62–63). *Particular objects* are the events, persons, or things an emotion is directed toward; they are the emotion's

---

4. I intend my use of 'intentional state' to be neutral with regard to details about the nature and structure of the associated content—for example, whether it must be propositional or conceptual. For a narrower view, see Scarantino (2010); cf. Wringe (2014). Relatedly, the examples of a particular emotion's content in the text are meant merely as familiar glosses; I aspire to neutrality on the exact formulations—ditto for debates about whether there is a canonical, non-emotion-vocabulary invoking way to articulate the content of a particular emotion (see, e.g., D'Arms & Jacobson, 2003).

5. There is a broader use of 'fitting' or 'appropriate' emotions that not only takes a fitting emotion to be one that accurately represents the emotion's target as having the evaluative features (danger) associated with the emotion in question (fear), but also that the intensity of the emotion is properly proportional to those evaluative elements and that the resulting behaviors (flight) are also appropriate to the situation at hand. Since there's reason to want to keep these different dimensions of an emotion's match to its object distinct, I will use 'fitting' or 'appropriate' in the narrow sense articulated in the text; I will use 'well-regulated' to capture these other dimensions (e.g., proportionality, behaviors). More on this below.

target (e.g., the dog is the particular object of my fear). *Formal objects*, by contrast, are the general (evaluative) properties distinctive of particular emotions. For fear, the formal object is something like danger; for sadness, it's loss; for joy, it's success. With this distinction in hand, we can see formal objects as articulating the general categories that circumscribe the fittingness conditions for particular emotions. But since formal objects are formal, they can only specify broad contours for what counts as an (un) fitting emotional response. To get further substance about what counts as (e.g.,) a danger, loss, or success, we must look to particular facts about (e.g.,) individuals' biology and environment (including their social/cultural environment). More specifically, these facts give shape to what Ronald de Sousa (1987) calls a "paradigm scenario"—roughly, an articulation of what makes something (e.g.,) dangerous and how one should respond to it (pp. 182–184). Thus, it is the combination of a formal object and the associated paradigm scenarios that gives substance to the (person-specific) fittingness conditions of a given emotion.[6]

Not only does this picture fit nicely with our earlier discussion of the biocognitive model, it also allows us to see that assessments of fit are *unique* forms of assessment: the assessment that a particular token of an emotion is fitting is the assessment that the emotion's target has the features the emotion attributes to it (D'Arms & Jacobson, 2000; Tappolet, 2016). Assessments of fittingness are thus assessments about the match between an emotion's formal object/paradigm scenario, on the one hand, and the emotion's target on the other (I will come back to this point shortly).

With this background in hand, we can return to the fittingness objection. The core concern is that emotions like envy, vengeance, lust, and anxiety cannot be valuable because they are never fitting: given what these emotions are about—that is, given the evaluative content they attribute to their targets—they are never appropriate responses to their situations. To draw this out, first consider common ways of characterizing the formal objects associated with lust and envy:

To lust after another is to see that individual merely as an opportunity for one's own sexual gratification. (Paul, 1980)

---

6. See D'Arms and Jacobson (2006) and Helm (2002, pp. 15ff.) for a similar account of the appropriateness conditions of emotions (though without the talk of formal objects).

To envy someone is not just to see her as superior to you in some respect, but to want that superiority relation reversed. (Roberts, 2003, p. 262)

Given these characterizations of the formal objects of lust and envy, the objection then maintains that these emotions are never fitting because they are, at their core, about things that cannot be valuable—roughly, a positive evaluation of, respectively, making someone your sexual object and wanting to gain status at another's expense.[7]

Applying this framework to anxiety, one might maintain that it too is never fitting because it too is about something that could never be valuable. However, while I agree that there's a potential difficulty in the vicinity of this worry, it's not one that concerns the *unfittingness* of anxiety. Anxiety, as we have been understanding it, is an emotion that is about problematic uncertainty. Thus, the unfittingness charge amounts to the claim that such a negatively valenced sensitivity and responsiveness to uncertain threats is never appropriate. But that is implausible. Some situations we face are clearly safe, others clearly dangerous; but there are a range of cases in between where the nature of the threat is uncertain. It's in situations like these that anxiety is fitting. Witness some of the examples we have been working with: walking through the streets of an unfamiliar city late at night; negotiating a conversation with someone you want to impress; and needing to make a novel or difficult decision (e.g., get a PhD in philosophy or head to law school). In situations like these, one faces problematic uncertainty. So these are situations where, *pace* the objection, anxiety is fitting. It is fitting because given the uncertainty and the stakes, these situations really are worrisome—they are situations where it's fitting to feel anxious. Moreover, recognizing this reveals that the objection confuses the behavioral tendencies of anxiety—things like ruminating, fretting, and avoidance—with the content of its formal object: problematic uncertainty. So while it is true that the discomfort and avoidance that anxiety tends to bring can lead to all kinds of trouble (more on this below), that's not a problem of *fit*. To think otherwise is to conflate unfittingness and having

---

7. One can, of course, respond by objecting that the above characterizations of lust and envy are inaccurate—properly understood, lust and envy can (at least sometimes) be fitting. For replies of this sort see Prinz (2004, pp. 123–124) (on lust) and D'Arms and Jacobson (2006) (on envy).

bad practical consequences (D'Arms & Jacobson, 2000). So we can see that the objection fails. If anxiety lacks value, the reason for this lies elsewhere.

That said, having set the fittingness objection aside, one might reasonably want to know more about both what fitting anxiety amounts to and whether anxiety is fitting often enough to make questions about its value interesting. Taking these in turn, we can start by building on de Sousa's move to understand the fittingness of an emotion in terms of its formal object and paradigm scenario. This allows us to say that anxiety, in general, is about problematic uncertainty—it is a response to potential threats that brings a negatively valenced combination of risk-assessment and risk-minimization behaviors aimed at helping one respond to the threat in question. Moving beyond this gloss, we can say that anxiety is a fitting response to a situation S just in case:

(F1) S involves a potential threat or challenge (broadly construed),

(F2) The precise nature of the threat/challenge in S is worrisome in the sense of being problematically uncertain: it's one that is unpredictable, uncontrollable, or otherwise open to question, and

(F3) Given the uncertainty of the threat/challenge in S, one has reason to be cautious—one has reason to further assess the nature of the threat/challenge and to take steps to minimize exposure to it.

A couple of points of elaboration. First, this account of fitting anxiety is vague in many ways (e.g., how should terms like 'threat' and 'uncertainty' be understood?). That, however, is unavoidable given that fittingness conditions are the product of how an emotion's formal object gains substance from facts about biology, culture, and individual experience, each bringing its own degree of imprecision (cf. section 2.1).

Second, while the above is an account of fitting anxiety in general, it provides a framework for understanding fittingness for the particular subtypes of anxiety we discussed in chapter 3. To get fittingness conditions for environmental, punishment, or practical anxiety, we refine the details of both threat/challenge in (F1) and the response behaviors in (F3). Fleshing this out a bit, we get something like the following:

Environmental anxiety about S is fitting iff (i) S brings the chance of physical harm, (ii) the chance of that harm is uncertain, and as a result one (iii) has reason to (e.g.,) avoid or withdraw.

Punishment anxiety about S is fitting iff (i) S brings the chance of negative evaluation or (social) sanction, (ii) the chance of negative evaluation/sanction is uncertain, and as a result one (iii) has reason to (e.g.,) appease and be deferential toward potential evaluators.

Practical anxiety about S is fitting iff (i) S presents an important decision or choice, (ii) S is such that it provides insufficient guidance about what to do (e.g., the relevant norms are vague or conflicting; one's grasp of the facts about S is incomplete), and as a result one (iii) has reason to (e.g.,) deliberate, gather more information, and (re)assess one's options.

While more could be said about the fittingness conditions for these three varieties of anxiety, we have enough to see their connection to both the above account of fittingness for anxiety in general and the larger discussion of environmental, punishment, and practical anxiety from chapter 3. Moreover, notice that this account of the fittingness conditions for these three central subtypes of anxiety provides answers to the second question from above: anxiety is likely to be a fitting response in a wide range of cases—occasions for potential physical harms, social evaluation, and new/novel decisions are regular features of our lives. Thus, questions about the value of (fitting) anxiety have purchase across much of ordinary life.

4.2 Is Fitting Anxiety Instrumentally Valuable?

One might think the above observations about fitting anxiety are of little importance for our assessment of its instrumental value. Here the quotes from Seneca and Kant earlier in the chapter give a more accurate picture. The problem with negative emotions like anxiety, anger, disgust, fear, envy, and sadness is that these emotions—fitting or not—are so lacking in instrumental value that we would, all told, be better off without them. After all, even when negative emotions are fitting, they can still badly distort our understanding of our situations: though your sadness is fitting because your aunt has just died, your all-consuming grief is inappropriate—the two of you weren't actually very close.[8] Moreover, negative emotions can, even when fitting, motivate us to act in ways that bring problems: anger, for

---

8. Brady (2013), Goldie (2004, 2008), and Sripada and Stich (2004) raise concerns of this sort.

instance, can get us to lash out at others in ways that are disproportionate (e.g., the offense was minor) or misdirected (e.g., they were merely bystanders to a genuine offense).[9]

Along both of these dimensions, anxiety might seem to be in big trouble. After all, there is no shortage of examples of it leading to disaster. Woody Allen is a wonderful case in point—he finds occasion for anxiety everywhere and is a hopeless mess as a result. Consider too what we find in Scott Stossel's memoir *My Age of Anxiety* (2013). There he describes his struggles with anxiety. Public speaking events, for instance, bring such intense, escalating cycles of dread, nausea, and sweating that he must resort to Xanax and vodka to prevent himself from running out on the talk he is supposed to give. Hardly a picture of anxiety contributing to health and well-being—much less one's career prospects.

However, while examples like these represent a rhetorically powerful way to raise concerns about both anxiety's tendency to misfire and its ability to bring serious problems even when fitting, we should pause to ask whether they really make for a convincing case. After all, without specific details on *why* anxiety is so likely to misfire or do more harm than good, the case against anxiety arguably rests on just a cherry-picked set of examples. Is Woody Allen really a good example of how anxiety functions in general, or just some of the ways it can to go awry? Compare: Are manic episodes and instances of rage good models for thinking about the instrumental value of (fitting) joy and anger?

To sort this out, it will be helpful to start by sharpening our focus. In particular, we can ask: Given that even fitting anxiety can badly distort one's understanding and motivation, why think that such distortions aren't the norm? Put another way, is there reason to think fitting anxiety tends to be instrumentally valuable? To assess this question, I begin by drawing on empirical work to make a prima facie case that anxiety is beneficial when fitting. I then draw on clinical work to identify features of anxious episodes that might suggest it's *especially* likely to go awry. In both of these steps, I will make use of two general strategies. The first aims to show that anxiety is a fitting and useful response more often than the folk wisdom suggests.

---

9. For worries of this sort, see Lelieveld, Van Dijk, et al. (2011), as well as Seneca (1995, pp. 17–18). For similar concerns about disgust, see Rozin, Millman, and Nemeroff (1986) and Sripada and Stich (2004).

The second strategy supplements the first by showing that, though anxiety can go awry, the general capacity for anxiety is both valuable and something that we can learn to use more effectively. Moreover, though we will see that anxiety can break down, we will also see that its tendency to do so appears no worse than what we find in other generally valuable emotions (e.g., disgust). In fact, anxiety may be better insofar as its pernicious manifestations seem more susceptible to correction. Thus, on closer examination, the charge that fitting anxiety is unlikely to be instrumentally valuable falls short.

4.2.1 A Prima Facie Case That Fitting Anxiety Is Instrumentally Valuable

We have already seen evidence of fitting anxiety making a positive contribution to our ability to assess and address potential dangers. There is, for instance, the research showing that anxiety brings an enhanced sensitivity to a range of environmental and social threats—snakes, spiders, angry faces, and the like (section 2.3). We have also seen that anxiety tends to bring benefits in performance situations. Recall, for instance, the comments of the anxiety researcher David Barlow (2001) from chapter 1:

> The performance of animals on a simple task [is] better if they [are] made "moderately anxious" than if they [are] experiencing no anxiety at all. ... Similar observations have been made concerning human performance in a wide variety of situations and contexts. Without anxiety, little would be accomplished. (p. 9)[10]

To this we can add the findings of political scientists (e.g., the work of the MacKuen and Valentino teams discussed in section 3.3.2) showing that anxiety about novel or difficult decisions brings open-minded inquiry and improved understanding of the choice at hand.

While the above speaks to fitting anxiety's tendency to bring instrumental benefits, of equal note is research pointing to the problems associated with having little or no anxiety on occasions where it would be fitting. We have seen some of this already. For instance, the psychopharmacological research on anxiolytics indicates that anxiety-free mice are more likely

---

10. Barlow's assessment isn't unusual, but rather is the received opinion among social and clinical psychologists. (See, e.g., Baumeister & Tice, 1990; Carver & Scheier, 1998; Csikszentmihalyi, 1999, pp. 73ff.; Hofmann, Korte, & Suvak, 2009; Horwitz & Wakefield, 2012, chap. 2; Jamieson, Mendes, & Nock, 2013; Leary & Kowalski, 1995, pp. 22ff.; Marks & Neese, 1994; and Zeidner & Matthews, 2011, pp. 12–15.)

to find themselves in mousetraps (see, e.g., the Blanchards' research discussed in section 2.3). We also saw that individuals who do not feel or recognize their anxiety (as the result of misattributions or taking antianxiety drugs) are more likely to engage in immoral behavior when put in (morally) ambiguous or uncertain situations (Jackson, Gaertner, & Batson, 2016; Perkins, Leonard, et al., 2013; section 3.4.3).

Further evidence comes from research examining the relationship between low anxiety and psychopathy. For instance, there is a robust and growing body of work pointing to low anxiety as diagnostic of primary psychopathy (Newman, MacCoon, et al., 2005; Skeem, Kerr, et al., 2007). Moreover, this anxiety deficit is thought to underlie the profound difficulty that these psychopaths have in recognizing and responding to the contextual information that would likely inhibit their impulsive and violent behavior (Zeier & Newman, 2013). While one might think this decreased sensitivity to peripheral information could be instrumentally valuable—it could, say, allow for more efficient pursuit of immediate goals—the fact that 93% of male psychopaths are incarcerated indicates that the overall result is quite costly (Keihl & Hoffman, 2011). But the troubles that come with low anxiety are not unique to psychopaths. Within the normal population (i.e., among those not diagnosed as psychopaths), there is a correlation between low anxiety and both psychopathic traits (e.g., being guiltless, manipulative, unempathetic) and academic misconduct (Hofmann, Korte, & Suvak, 2009)—a result that further supports the idea that anxiety is useful because it functions as a restraint on impulses to break the rules when the rules or their likelihood of enforcement are uncertain (Gilbert, 2001; Kurth, 2016). Taken together, the connections between low anxiety and psychopathy provide more evidence that fitting anxiety will tend to be instrumentally valuable.

* * *

The above observations help make explicit a feature of anxiety that has been in the background of much of our discussion so far: anxiety—especially the consciously experienced anxiety that's a concomitant of novel and difficult situations—plays an important role in learning. More specifically, a central part of how one learns a skill, refines particular talents and capacities, and develops as an agent more generally involves both trying things out on one's own and making adjustments when needed. But notice that one is better able to do this to the extent that one has a capacity for *self-regulation*—that is, a capacity to independently secure feedback about whether one is making progress toward one's goals and to generate a motivational push to stay the course or make corrections. How does this happen? According to standard theoretical models of this type of self-regulation, emotions play a central role. The positive feeling of joy and pleasure functions to signal and reward one's successes. Similarly, and importantly for our purposes, the aversive experience of anxiety and frustration informs one of (potential) failure and prompts a search for better strategies (Carver & Scheier, 1998; Csikszentmihalyi, 1991, pp. 73ff.; Oatley, Keltner, & Jenkins, 2006, chaps. 8–9; Schwartz & Clore, 2007). Importantly, this isn't just theoretical speculation. For instance, from the research of the MacKuen and Valentino teams, we see that (practical) anxiety is a response to novel and difficult decisions, the feeling of which tends to prompt open-minded inquiry and an increased interest in exploring new solutions. As such, and in line with the learning models, it is a tool that can help generate innovation and discovery.[11]

Stepping back, we can put all this into a larger theoretical framework. Developing as an agent—acquiring skills, learning to make good decisions in novel circumstances—requires a distinctive attunement and receptivity to the reasons for acting in a particular way. More specifically, our concepts of effective agency, good decision making, and the like presume that individuals have certain metacognitive capacities, three of which are particularly noteworthy here:

---

11. Research looking at the contribution of affect/emotion—including anxiety—to creativity is mixed (see Baas, De Drue, & Nijstad, 2008, for an overview). This seems to be, in part, a consequence of ambiguities in 'creativity.' Among other things, it can refer to *fluency* (i.e., one's capacity to generate unique, nonredundant ideas or solutions), *flexibility* (i.e., the breadth and depth of the associations one can make within and across semantic categories), or *originality* (i.e., one's ability to generate uncommon or novel ideas and solutions). Within these narrower categories, anxiety appears to contribute to fluency but detract from flexibility. Anxiety also appears to contribute positively to *persistence* (i.e., one's ability to sustain time-consuming, effortful, analytic engagement with a set of alternatives), which can, in turn, bring originality (e.g., once the common solutions have been identified, continued persistence leads to novel ones (Rietzschel, Nijstad, & Stroebe, 2007)). The upshot, then, is that anxiety *does* promote creativity, but how and when it does so depends on context (for further discussion, see Baas, De Drue, & Nijstad, 2008, p. 797; De Drue, Baas, & Nijstad, 2008).

1. The ability to monitor one's cognitions (e.g., beliefs, desires, emotions, and attitudes) as they relate to each other and to the features of the world that they purport to be about
2. The ability to recognize and assess problems with one's cognitions (e.g., inconsistency, falsity, insufficient justification)
3. The ability to bolster, revise, qualify, or even abandon one's cognitions in light of one's assessments of them[12]

The capacities described in (1)–(3) are *metacognitive* in the sense that they are forms of mental processing that—at the conscious or unconscious level—monitor, assess, and regulate other aspects of mental processing. And they are characteristic of *effective* agency and *good* decision making in the sense that they are capacities that help one monitor, assess, and regulate one's thinking and doing (Kurth, forthcoming b).

Recognizing that effective agency and good decision making require metacognitive capacities of this sort helps draw out the importance of fitting anxiety—especially practical anxiety. For it is a psychological mechanism that underlies this trio of metacognitive capacities and so helps explain (e.g.,) how anxiety contributes to learning and why not feeling anxiety when it's fitting can bring trouble. As we have seen, feeling anxiety functions as a signal of problematic uncertainty. It tells us that our cognitions are in tension with one another: the desire to be safe is in tension with the belief that the approaching man seems dangerous; the goal of making a good impression conflicts with the thought that you have just made a faux pas; the aim of making a good choice is challenged by your belief that the underlying norms are in conflict. Thus, anxiety is engaged in the metacognitive functions of (1) and (2). Moreover, anxiety's tendency to prompt epistemic behaviors—information gathering, reflection, reassessment, and so on—indicates that it is also implicated in the regulatory functions of (3).

---

12. While the capacities in (1)–(3) are not generally made explicit, they're clearly presumed in a wide range of theories about practical activity. For instance, these metacognitive capacities underlie the distinctive form of self-consciousness that is central to Christine Korsgaard's (2009) account of agency as self-constitution, the wants/interests mechanism that is key to Peter Railton's (1986a, 1986b) accounts of moral and prudential judgment, Allan Gibbard (1990) and Philip Kitcher's (2011) accounts of the role of normative discussion in practical decision making, and Valerie Tiberius's (2008) virtue-theoretic account of practical reflection.

In short, anxiety is an emotion that is *in the business* of engaging the metacognitive functions that are essential to effective agency and good decision making.[13] Moreover, recognizing anxiety's metacognitive role sheds some light on the earlier discussion of research suggesting that individuals with very low anxiety have psychopathic traits. Part of the difficulty that these individuals display with regard to social functioning may lie in a compromised ability to monitor, assess, and revise their beliefs, desires, attitudes, and intentions (cf. Gross, 2015; Hofmann, Korte, & Suvak, 2009, p. 724).

The upshot of all this is a prima facie case for the instrumental value of fitting anxiety. Understanding what anxiety is, and what it does, reveals that it brings an important, functionally integrated combination of attentional sensitivity and motivation—a combination that can help us work through problematic uncertainty and that can contribute to learning and innovation. Moreover, while we must acknowledge that anxiety can go badly awry—it can be both unfitting and distorting even when fitting—we can also see that this does not appear to be its normal course. Not only is anxiety likely to be fitting across a wide range of situations, but when fitting we have seen that it tends to be a moderate and beneficial emotion. We fail to recognize this, I suspect, because we tend to focus on the more vivid—but less common—cases where anxiety distorts our understanding of our situation or leads to rash behavior. But everyday anxiety is *not* the anxiety of Allen or Stossel: it typically manifests as a twinge of unease that prepares us for a potential threat, not a consuming worry that distracts and debilitates. In this way, anxiety appears no different than say, fear, anger, sadness, or even joy. These emotions are good things to have even though they can at times manifest in unfortunate ways—as phobias, rages, depression, and manic episodes.

4.2.2 Does Fitting Anxiety Do More Harm Than Good?

Given both the above prima facie case for fitting anxiety's instrumental value and the general affinities we have noted between anxiety and other emotions that we find valuable (e.g., anger, fear, joy, sadness), the burden

---

13. I should emphasize that in talking about anxiety's metacognitve role, I am not claiming that anxiety is the only mechanism that undergirds capacities like (1)–(3). Rather, the claim is that our discussion of what anxiety does indicates that it is a central driver of these capacities.

has shifted in a significant way. The skeptic now needs to provide us with a reason for thinking there is something distinctive about fitting anxiety (in general, or specific varieties of it) that makes it particularly likely to do more harm than good. In this context, recent discussions of moral disgust may provide a nice model. So before turning to see what the anxiety skeptic might say, it will be helpful to briefly review some of this work on disgust.

In his book *Yuck!*, Dan Kelly (2011) argues that while disgust, in general, is a useful and fitting emotion—one that helps protect individuals against poisons and parasites—it invariably does more harm than good in the context of moral assessment.[14] As he explains, the very features that make disgust effective as a tool for protecting against *biological* contaminants make it highly problematic as a tool for protecting against *social* "contaminants." For instance, the disgust response is shaped by a learning mechanism that's both quick in its ability to acquire content about potential contaminants and difficult to revise. While such a mechanism is useful in keeping us from again eating something that has made us sick, it also makes it more likely that disgust will quickly attach to mistaken moral beliefs about "contaminated" individuals or actions and makes it more difficult for us to revise our mistaken assessments about who or what is morally disgusting. In a similar vein, Kelly argues that the ballistic purge/rejection response that is helpful for guarding against poisoning will likely bring excessively strong reactions to moral wrongs that disgust us.

As with disgust, one might think the very features that make anxiety effective as a response to situations that are potentially threatening from an evolutionary perspective, make it likely to do more harm than good in other contexts. Here, our understanding of how anxiety functions points to two independent, but potentially reinforcing, possibilities: fitting anxiety could cause trouble (i) by provoking escalating—and so debilitating—cycles of worry or (ii) by prompting impulsive action as one tries to make one's anxiety go away.

To begin to flesh out (i), first recall from chapter 3 that instances of fitting anxiety can be prompted and sustained by conscious rumination.

---

14. For a critical assessment of Kelly's argument, see Plakias (2013). In addition to Kelly's assessment of moral disgust, Sripada and Stich (2004, pp. 150–156) take food taboos to be a further case where disgust tends to lead to systematic, instrumentally disvaluable decision making.

Moreover, while these feedback loops can be helpful by, for example, bringing persistent reflection to the problem at hand (Verhaeghen, Joormann, & Khan, 2005) or preparing us to better address similar situations in the future (Baumeister, Vohs, DeWall, & Zhang, 2007, p. 186), they can also develop into debilitating cycles of worry.[15] Research by Adrian Wells (2000; also see Nolen-Hoeksema, 2000), for instance, suggests that anxiety's tendency to prompt (often helpful) rumination and concern makes it susceptible to being hijacked, amplified, and turned on itself: as we grow worried about our worries, we end up worrying even more. Thus, one might maintain that fitting anxiety is likely to do more harm than good on the grounds that it's just too easy for anxiety's feedback loops to generate crippling spirals of worry out of (initially) benign ruminations. In fact, we saw evidence of this in both the gala case from chapter 3 and in the above discussion of Stossel's experiences with public speaking events: in these cases, the anxiety, though fitting, brings serious problems.

Turn now to possibility (ii). As is all too familiar, anxiety is an inherently unpleasant emotion—an often deeply uncomfortable thing to experience.[16] Moreover, and as we've seen, the fact that anxiety is so aversive is part of what makes it an effective motivational tool: it's in part because anxiety feels bad that we tend to become more cautious and risk averse around things that make us anxious. However, there seems to be little that constrains this motivational push. In fact, one might maintain that because anxiety is so unpleasant, we often respond rashly in an effort to make it go away. The results can be disastrous: impulsive decisions, imprudent efforts to appease, and hasty attempts to escape or avoid the situation at hand. Worries of this sort aren't mere speculation. Again, witness Stossel's (2013) account of his own experiences:

My wedding was not the first time I'd broken down [from anxiety], nor was it the last. ... I've frozen, mortifyingly, onstage at public lectures and presentations, and on several occasions I have been compelled to run offstage. I've abandoned dates,

---

15. Here I follow the clinical literature in distinguishing between rumination and worry. Ruminations are collections of conscious thoughts that revolve around a common theme. Worries, by contrast, are chains of negative, often uncontrollable, conscious thoughts.

16. Witness: Individuals with clinical social anxiety (i.e., social anxiety disorder) report lower life satisfaction than people infected with herpes (Wittchen & Beloch, 1996)!

walked out on exams, and had breakdowns during job interviews, on plane flights, train trips and car rides, and simply walking down the street. (pp. 5–6)

Moving beyond anecdotes, experimental work indicates that some individuals are so averse to feeling anxious that they will opt for a larger shock now rather than enduring the anxiety associated with the anticipation of a milder shock in the near future (Berns, Chappelow, et al., 2006).

There's no denying that fitting anxiety can prompt both vicious spirals of worry and rash actions. But the skeptic needs to do more to explain why these observations about anxiety substantiate the claim that it is *likely* to do more harm than good. On this front, the skeptic might point to work suggesting that features of modern life are making vicious spirals of anxiety and the associated impulsive responses more common. For instance, today we face increased social and economic uncertainty; we also need to make more choices but with less information and structure (Price, 2003; Schwartz, 2004; Slater, 1970). Pressures like these seem the very sorts of environmental factors that could highjack anxiety in ways that could explain the increases in clinical/extreme anxiety we appear to be seeing: according to a World Health Organization survey of 18 nations, anxiety disorders are now the most common mental illness (Kessler, Angermeyer, et al., 2007); in the United States, over 40 million Americans (18%) suffer from anxiety disorders (Kessler, Chiu, Demler, & Walters, 2005) and the anxiety levels of college freshman are at an all-time high (Twenge, 2006, p. 107). Perhaps most strikingly, anxiety prevalence studies indicate that there has been a *fivefold increase* in anxiety disorders from 1980 to 2010 (Horwitz & Wakefield, 2012, p. 2).[17]

Though the above line of thought might at first appear to make a compelling case against the instrumental value of (fitting) anxiety, I believe it ultimately fails. There are three interrelated reasons for this:

(1) Consider the above suggestion that the surge in anxiety disorders supports the skeptic's contention that features of modern living are undermining our anxiety mechanisms so that they're increasingly likely to do more harm than good. While it's true that we find increases in reported cases of clinical/extreme anxiety, it's much less clear whether this is because (i) anxiety disorders are actually becoming more prevalent, (ii) individuals are

---

17. See Stossel (2013, chap. 10) for an overview of, and commentary on, work on anxiety's prevalence.

more knowledgeable about, and willing to acknowledge, their anxiety, or (iii) the diagnostic criteria are being applied more liberally—symptoms that are now taken to be indicative of a clinical case of anxiety would have been insufficient in the past.

In recent work, Allan Horwitz and Jerome Wakefield (respectively, a sociologist of mental illness and a psychiatrist) make a compelling case for (iii) as the central driver of the dramatic spike in reported anxiety disorders (Horwitz & Wakefield, 2012). In particular, they point to significant methodological problems in the survey questionnaires that provided the data for the prevalence rates cited above. As they detail, the questions used to determine rates of general anxiety disorder and social anxiety disorder make no substantive efforts to "screen out people who had experienced anxiety symptoms that were *proportionate responses to actual life situations*" and so, as a result, they were highly likely to overdiagnose these disorders (pp. 153ff., emphasis added). For instance, the diagnostic criteria of the *DSM* require that symptoms of general anxiety disorder be "extreme" or "unreasonable" in at least two different life circumstances as determined from the clinician's professional perspective. The diagnostic questionnaire's prompts, by contrast, dropped the two-instances requirement and take the individual's self-reports of "extreme" or "unreasonable" symptoms to be sufficient.[18]

Compounding these methodological problems (and in line with pernicious versions of explanation (b) above), Horwitz and Wakefield also discuss how both changes in how medications are paid for (i.e., more of the cost is borne by insurance) and the profit motives of pharmaceutical companies (fanned by the media) have contributed to the expansion in reported anxiety disorders. Witness the following excerpt from a pharmaceutical marketing report:

Despite a fifth of the total population across the seven major markets suffering from an anxiety disorder only a quarter of these individuals are diagnosed and therefore treated. As a result, drug manufacturers are *failing to maximize revenues* from the anxiety disorders market. *Investment in awareness campaigns is essential.* (Quoted in Horwitz & Wakefield, 2012, p. 216, emphasis added)

---

18. See Horwitz and Wakefield (2012, chap. 6) for further discussion of these and other methodological problems. Related to the discussion in text, notice that if anxiety disorders are best understood as *mood* disorders (not malfunctions of anxiety the *emotion*) as some maintain (e.g., Watson, 2005; but see Mennin, Heimberg, et al., 2008), then we have further reason to question the relevance of these results.

Taken together, the Horwitz and Wakefield research raises serious doubts about whether the prevalence data help substantiate the skeptic's claim that (fitting) anxiety is likely to do more harm than good. Moreover, even if *clinical* anxiety is becoming more prevalent, this does not vindicate the skeptic's claim that *as a general matter* anxiety lacks instrumental value— there may well be (many) forms of nonclinical anxiety that are both fitting and beneficial and there may be ways to manage anxiety so that it is more likely to be helpful and less likely to misfire. As the next two points draw out, these suggestions aren't mere speculation.

(2) There is a significant body of research examining how anxiety affects performance—be it with regard to test taking, social interaction, creative endeavors, or athletic competitions.[19] Moreover, because the experimental paradigms of this research make use of (e.g.,) situations where individuals are given tasks they've been told they will be evaluated on, they involve situations where (punishment) anxiety would be fitting, so they provide insight as to whether fitting (punishment) anxiety aids or hinders performance. On this front, while much of this work suggests anxiety has an undermining effect on performance, there are also results supporting the opposite conclusion. This raises further problems for the anxiety skeptic. More specifically, the data on anxiety's effects on performance suggest two general patterns (Alpert & Haber, 1960; Zeidner & Matthews, 2005):

Pattern 1: Anxiety harms performance. Anxiety is more likely to bring problems either in situations where the possibility of evaluation/punishment is particularly salient or in situations where the anxiety involves worry (i.e., chains of negative, often uncontrollable, conscious thoughts or images). For instance, a metastudy on the effects of test anxiety showed both that scores on anxiety measures are correlated with poor test performance and that the correlation is twice as strong when the anxiety is accompanied by worry (Hembree, 1988). Social anxiety scores also correlate with peer ratings of poor social interactions—a connection that appears to be enhanced

---

19. See Zeidner and Matthews (2005) and Learner and Tetlock (1999) for reviews of recent empirical work. For more detailed discussion, see (e.g.,) Zeidner (1998) on test anxiety; Cartwright-Hatton, Tschernitz, and Gomersall (2005) and Kashdan (2007) on social anxiety; and Ashcraft (2002) on math anxiety.

by the presence of worry (Bruch, 2001; Cartwright-Hatton, Tschernitz, & Gomersall, 2005).[20]

Pattern 2: Anxiety aids performance. Anxiety does *not* tend to undermine performance—and often enhances it—in situations where concerns for progress or accuracy are particularly salient as well as in situations where the anxiety brings, not worry, but rather a felt tenseness or unease. For example, anxiety of this sort has been shown to contribute positively to performance on a variety of creativity tasks (e.g., De Drue, Baas, & Nijstad, 2008; Matthews, 1986; Spering, Wagener, & Funke, 2005). Moreover, anxiety's beneficial contribution appears to be enhanced when the anxiety is accompanied by rumination (i.e., collections of conscious thoughts revolving around a common, instrumental theme) (Verhaeghen, Joormann, & Khan, 2005). Similarly, anxiety that is associated with felt unease (rather than worry) predicts good athletic outcomes (Hanin, 2007; Hatzigeorgiadis & Biddle, 2001) and has been shown to improve academic performance (Jamieson, Mendes, et al., 2010).

In the present context, results like these are significant because they indicate that whether fitting anxiety tends to bring more harm will turn on particular features of both the situation at hand and the individual involved. Moreover, we have also seen that there is a broad range of situations where anxiety is likely to be genuinely beneficial (section 4.2.1): in particular, situations where considerations of accuracy or progress (rather than, say, evaluation by others) are particularly salient and situations where the anxiety prompts rumination (rather than worry). This suggests that certain varieties of anxiety—especially practical anxiety—are likely to be more useful than others (e.g., social or punishment anxiety).

(3) Even in cases where fitting anxiety brings trouble, there's reason for optimism. For starters, while there's much that we do not know about how anxiety works and when it's likely to generate unfitting or exaggerated

---

20. A couple of important qualifications to these results. First, much of this research focuses primarily on the relationship between performance and *high* levels of anxiety and so—on its own—it does not tell against the possibility that more *moderate* levels of anxiety might be helpful. Second, even when we look to cases of high anxiety, we should be cautious, for "there have been sufficient instances of nonconfirmation of predicted deficits to suggest that high anxiety does not automatically generate lower [test] achievement outcomes" (Zeidner & Matthews, 2005, p. 148).

responses, what we do know suggests that the situations where anxiety breaks down in these ways will be fairly predictable—even manageable. For example, clinical work suggests that the pernicious effects of anxiety are brought on by specific triggers and vulnerabilities. Research on the causes of vicious cycles of worry, for instance, suggests they are the result of feedback mechanisms triggered by (e.g.,) abnormal levels of self-monitoring behavior (Barlow, 2001; Mor & Winquist, 2002; Wells, 2000). Other work suggests a second driver of these cycles: the tendency to adopt an immersed, first-person reflective point of view on one's situation as opposed to a distant, third-person perspective (Kross & Ayduk, 2008). Moreover, individuals who have experienced a history of failures or difficulties in particular situations (e.g., test taking, social interactions) are more likely to view subsequent instances of those tasks/situations as potentially threatening and more likely to fall into the narrowing of focus that anxiety brings (section 3.5). As a result, they are more vulnerable to the increased self-doubt and self-monitoring behavior that can trigger pernicious cycles of worry (Hill & Eaton, 1977; Nolen-Hoeksema, 2000; Wigfield & Eccles, 1989).

This is significant. These findings about when and why fitting anxiety is likely to lead to extreme/destructive results allow us to identify strategies that can help us better manage our anxiety (Gross, 2015). For instance, a common element in the above findings is that anxiety is more likely to bring debilitating cycles of worry when the anxious individual's attention is internally focused on themselves or on their feelings of anxiety. By contrast, anxious individuals who focus, not internally, but rather on the task at hand (e.g., taking the test, delivering the talk) appear better able to avoid these cycles—in fact, their anxiety can even help them work though the threat or challenge they face (Bachrach & Zaurta, 1985; Folkman & Lazarus, 1985; Verhaeghen, Joormann, & Khan, 2005).

Similarly, anxiety appears to interact in interesting ways with goals and expectations. For instance, the psychologist Jeremy Jamieson and his colleagues looked at the effects that reappraising anxiety can have in high-stakes testing situations. In this work, students studying for the GRE exam were put into either a reappraisal group or a control group. Before taking a practice GRE test, students in the reappraisal group read the following passage:

People think that feeling anxious while taking a standardized test will make them do poorly on the test. However, recent research suggests that arousal doesn't hurt performance on these tests and can even help performance. ... People who feel anxious during a test might actually do better. This means that you shouldn't feel concerned if you do feel anxious while taking today's GRE test. If you find yourself feeling anxious, simply remind yourself that your arousal could be helping you do well.

The control group, by contrast, read nothing about reappraisal before taking the practice test. The results of this simple effort to encourage individuals to reappraise their anxiety are striking: students in the reappraisal group not only outperformed controls on subsequent practice versions of the GRE, they also scored higher when they took the actual GRE one to three months later (Jamieson, Mendes, et al., 2010). Similar results have been found with regard to performance in athletic competitions: while viewing one's anxiety as debilitating predicts poor performance, seeing it as (say) a helpful motivator predicts good performance (e.g., Hanin, 2007; Hatzigeorgiadis & Biddle, 2001). Bringing this together, these observations suggest that one might be able to more productively harness one's anxiety by reframing how one interprets the anxiety. If so, then even if one's (fitting) anxiety tends to run awry, one may be able to do something to forestall subsequent troubles.[21]

We can now see that it's certainly true that even fitting anxiety can manifest in problematic ways. But we have also seen that certain varieties of anxiety—especially those, like practical anxiety, that are accuracy-oriented—are likely to be (on the whole) more valuable than others. While these results alone spell trouble for the anxiety skeptic, combining them with the discussion of the last section on the fittingness of emotions allows us to say more. In particular, anxiety, like (e.g.,) anger or fear, is more instrumentally valuable to the extent that it is not just a fitting response, but a *well-regulated* one. That is, emotions like anxiety, anger, and fear are more useful to the extent that we can learn to experience them not just at the right time, but in the *right way*. On this score, anxiety appears importantly different from disgust. As we noted above, and as others have demonstrated, disgust is an emotion that is particularly resistant to cognitive control: once we come to see something as disgusting (be it a food item or a behavior), it is very difficult for us to come to see it differently. Anxiety, by contrast, is more responsive: we just noted some strategies for regulating anxiety in the above discussion; clinical protocols provide further guidance and reason for

---

21. See Gross (2015) for further discussion of reframing as an effective general strategy for emotion regulation. We will return to this in chapter 6.

optimism (more on this in chapters 5 and 6).[22] So given that we are inclined to see disgust as instrumentally valuable even though it badly misfires in certain contexts, and even though is resists cognitive control, we should be willing to acknowledge the instrumental value of anxiety as well. In fact, it is arguably a more useful emotion to have.

4.2.3 Summing Up

We started this section with two worries: anxiety will not be fitting in an interesting range of cases and, even when fitting, it will do more harm than good. But these concerns fall short: we have seen that there is good reason to think both that anxiety will be fitting across an important range situations and that, when fitting, it brings real benefits. While anxiety can (badly) misfire in many ways, the skeptic appears to err in taking these problematic cases as the norm rather than the exception. But to say this, is to invite a parallel charge: the above defense of anxiety works only because it builds on a cherry-picked set of cases. Though I feel the force of this concern, I believe it to be mistaken. My argument for the instrumental value of fitting anxiety does not rest on anecdotes or a small range of cases. Rather, it's grounded in a broad, empirically informed account of what anxiety is, how it works, and why it breaks down. In particular, we started with the biocognitive model of anxiety from chapter 1; we then enriched this by looking at a wide range of research in clinical and social psychology, psychiatry, cognitive science, and the social sciences (chapters 2 and 3). This investigation allowed us to not only identify three subtypes of anxiety (environmental, punishment, and practical), but to develop an understanding of what they do and how they work—an understanding that undergirds the above observations about when anxiety is likely to be valuable and the ways it can break down. While this may not suffice to eliminate lingering cherry-picking worries (but what

---

22. Given the above conclusion that practical anxiety is likely to be a particularly instrumentally valuable variety of anxiety, Jonathan Abramowitz's research on treatment protocols for scrupulosity are of particular interest (e.g., Abramowitz, 2001). After all, and as we have noted (chapter 2), scrupulosity appears to be a clinical manifestation of practical anxiety, so treatment success with regard to scrupulosity suggests that practical anxiety can also be effectively managed. Further support comes from research indicating that cognitive-behavioral therapy is an effective treatment for a range of anxiety disorders (for further discussion, see Hofmann & Smits, 2008; Kurth, forthcoming a).

would?), I believe the thoroughness of our investigation of anxiety seriously diminishes the force of the charge. With this concern set aside, we can turn to investigate whether anxiety has noninstrumental value.

4.3 More Than Just Instrumentally Valuable?

Might anxiety have more than just instrumental value? There's reason to think not. For one, anxiety, like any "negative" emotion, seems to be an essentially aversive response—something inherently unpleasant to experience. So building from hedonistic intuitions, one might object that anything inherently unpleasant is, for that reason, *intrinsically* disvaluable. There is also the worry, captured in the quotes from Kant and Seneca at the beginning of the chapter, that negative emotions like anxiety and anger undermine one's character and so lack *aretaic* value: the mind of an anxious or enraged person, after all, fails to exhibit the tranquility characteristic of virtuous thought and action.

To assess these worries, we can explore the role that certain emotions—anxiety and anger, in particular—play with regard to the moral concern distinctive of human virtue. As we will see, looking at this pair of negative emotions together helps us understand the ways each is more than just instrumentally valuable. More specifically, I will argue that anxiety and anger have aretaic value because these emotions bring the *emotional attunement* that is a constitutive part of moral concern. I then make a more tentative case that, for similar reasons, these emotions might also have intrinsic value.[23]

4.3.1 Anxiety and Aretaic Value

The core of my argument for the aretaic value of anxiety and anger goes like this:

1. Virtues are excellences of character.
2. Virtues are constituted by integrated packages of beliefs, motivations, and feelings, each of which is valuable as a dimension of the overall virtuous character trait.

---

23. As suggested by the focus on anxiety's role in virtuous thought and action in the text, my focus here is on *practical* anxiety, not anxiety in general. For ease of presentation, I will suppress the "practical" modifier—unless I indicate otherwise, my use of 'anxiety' refers to 'practical anxiety.'

3. Moral concern is a virtue.
4. With respect to its emotional dimension, moral concern is constituted by emotions including anxiety and anger.
5. So, anger and anxiety are valuable as dimensions of the virtue of moral concern.
6. The value that accrues to (a dimension of) character is aretaic value.
7. So, anxiety and anger are aretaically valuable.

Getting into the details, I take (1) and (6) to border on truisms, so let's focus on (2)–(5). Taking these in turn, consider premise (2). While the claim that virtues are constituted by integrated combinations of beliefs, motivations, and feelings is contested by some, it is the received view about virtue.[24] The underlying idea is that virtues must involve more than just occasions where one's actions or habits happen to bring (morally) good outcomes.[25] Rather, a virtue is an excellence of character that has cognitive, conative, and affective dimensions, each of which is valuable in the sense that the resulting action would be less admirable were one of these elements missing. So, for example, instances of benevolence are not merely cases where one is prompted to help another in need. Rather, they are situations where the assistance one provides is undergirded by both the belief that the person needs help and a feeling of sympathy for her plight. The belief is necessary because we do not (typically) give credit to those who blindly manage to do good.[26] The affective component is also necessary: to not act from sympathy in this case would be aretaically deficient—you would be emotionally out of tune with those around you. In short, when acting virtuously, one's thoughts, motivations, and feelings must form a cohesive, admirable whole.

Premises (3) and (4) require more discussion. To draw out the plausibility of (3), first notice that the virtuous individual is someone who displays a distinctive type of concern: she stands up for what's right and good in the sense that she will *defend* that which she sees as valuable when it's in danger

---

24. See, for instance, Annas (1993, pp. 47–83; 2011, chap. 2); Aristotle (1925, VI.13, VII.8); Hursthouse (1999); and Swanton (2003, pp. 19ff.). Kant (1797/1996) is a prominent dissenting voice (but see Baxley, 2010, chap. 4).
25. Hume (1888) would likely disagree—he defends a deflationary account of virtue in which the degree of virtue of an action is a function of the consequences it brings.
26. I remain neutral with regard to whether this belief must take the form of an explicitly conscious state or something less robust (e.g., a disposition to affirm and defend).

or under threat (Aristotle, 1925, IV.5; French, 2001; Leighton, 2002). The virtuous individual is also *sensitive to uncertainty* in that she understands and respects both the limits of her knowledge and the extent of her fallibility (Arpaly & Schroeder, 2014, pp. 241–245; Slote, 2014, pp. 175–176; Stohr, 2003). Call this sort of sensitivity and responsiveness *moral concern* (where 'moral' is used in the broad sense typical of virtue theory). Notice as well that the virtuous behaviors and features characteristic of moral concern—to defend what's valuable and to be sensitive to uncertainty—are (given premise (2)) undergirded by particular combinations of beliefs, motivations, and feelings. This leads to premise (4): moral concern is constituted by emotions including anxiety and anger.[27]

To substantiate this, first consider anger. As we have seen, anger has a distinctive phenomenology and functional role: it's a response to affronts and slights that brings inter alia negatively valenced feelings and a motivational tendency to defend oneself, one's interests, or one's standing. So we have a nice fit: our understanding of anger meshes with the dimension of moral concern that involves the defense of what one sees as valuable. But anger's importance runs deeper than just this functional fit. To see this, consider a person who discovers that they have been lied to by someone they trust but doesn't feel at all angry about it. Or someone who has just found out that they have been cheated on by their romantic partner, but who doesn't feel mad in the slightest. Individuals like these strike us not just as odd, but as deficient—they strike us as failing to fully appreciate the moral violation that has just occurred (on this, witness Aristotle (1925): "Those who are not angry at the things they should be angry at are thought to be *fools*" (IV.5, emphasis added)). Moreover, recognizing anger as a constitutive feature of the defense dimension of moral concern explains our reactions to unperturbed individuals like these. The feeling of anger not only helps one stand up for oneself as an individual who has value and merits respect; it is also an *expression* of the moral significance that one takes oneself to have. Thus,

---

27. Anxiety and anger are unlikely to be the only constituents of moral concern. For instance, there is presumably also a dimension of moral concern that is focused on nurturing what one sees as valuable, and making sense of this would seem to require something like compassion. However, since the task at hand is to examine the aretaic value of anxiety and anger, and not to give a complete account of moral concern, I will set this discussion aside.

to not feel angry in the face of betrayal is to evince a lack of emotional and evaluative attunement to what matters.

We find something similar for anxiety. It, as we have seen, is an emotion that is concerned with problematic uncertainty and that prompts a combination of caution and epistemic behaviors (information gathering, deliberation, reflection, etc.). Thus, anxiety has a nice functional fit with the dimension of moral concern that involves a sensitivity and responsiveness to the possibility that one might be mistaken. But here too, there's more than just a functional fit. To draw this out, consider some difficult moral decisions. (i) It's becoming increasingly hard for you to properly care for you aging mother. Her doctors have suggested that it's time to put her in a nursing home, but you know she is terrified of those places. What should do you do? (ii) Your colleague has just been mistreated by your mutual boss. Should you stand up for her even though you know it will come at a significant cost to your own career? (iii) You are a senior professor and have a talented graduate student looking for a job. You have written her a very strong recommendation. But should you do more—say, contact departments where she is applying to try to give them a nudge? Or would that be to take advantage of the system?

In situations like these, one faces a decision that involves complex and potentially competing considerations. Worse, the cases at hand are ones where the existing (moral, professional) norms and your own prior experiences provide insufficient guidance about what to do. To be unfazed—to not feel uneasy or uncomfortable about decisions like these—strikes us not just as odd, but deficient. Such individuals are troublingly disconnected from the significance and complexity of the choice they face. Again, seeing anxiety as constitutive of the uncertainty dimension of moral concern helps explain our reaction. Feelings of anxiety don't just bring an awareness of, and sensitivity to, the problematic uncertainty we find in cases like these; they are also *expressions* of one's appreciation of the complexity of the choice at hand. They evince one's emotional and evaluative attunement.[28]

With premises (1)–(4) in hand, we get the first conclusion (5): anger and anxiety are valuable as dimensions of the virtue of moral concern. If we then

---

28. Helm (2001) makes a similar but more general point about the connection between the emotions we feel toward things and the import those things have for us.

add that the value that accrues to dimensions of character is aretaic value (i.e., (6)), we get the conclusion that anxiety and anger have aretaic value.

But here one might respond with what I will call the Xanax objection. Suppose you could take a pill—a new version of Xanax—that would bring all the instrumental benefits associated with anxiety (e.g., sensitivity to uncertainty, caution, reflection) but without the felt unpleasantness. If you had such a pill, would you take it? A yes answer raises two worries. First, it suggests there's nothing aretaically valuable in anxiety. It's only valuable because of the virtuous concern it helps bring about. But a yes response also suggests that there may not be anything valuable in anxiety *itself*— what we really care about is being properly attuned to potential threats and responding to them with the appropriate mix of risk-minimization and epistemic behaviors. Thus, the Xanax objection poses a twofold challenge to the claim that anxiety is aretaically valuable.

Taking these concerns in reverse order, first notice that the thought that we would be better off with just the sensitivity and responsiveness to uncertainty characteristic of anxiety relies on two presumptions: (i) we can reliably secure these benefits across the wide range of situations in which anxiety does what it does, and (ii) we can get these anxiety-free benefits at little or no cost. While I take the truth of these presumptions to ultimately be an empirical matter, I believe we should be skeptical that we can get the benefits of anxiety without it (or its costs) for two reasons.

First, appreciating the role that anxiety plays in our lives suggests it will be very difficult (perhaps impossible) to excise. As the above discussion draws out, part of what is distinctive about *human* agency—in contrast with agency simpliciter—is that we have a deep emotional tie to the world. Emotions, both positive and negative, are central to how we perceive, learn about, and assess the people and things that surround us. So while it may be possible for a Spock-like creature to perceive, learn, and assess without emotion, that's not how we do it. These general observations about the importance of emotion in human psychology work to undermine the thought that we could rid ourselves of our emotions without incurring a significant cost. Moreover, this general point is arguably stronger when we focus on anxiety. As we have seen, anxiety is something we experience across a wide range of situations: potential physical dangers, occasions where we might be negatively evaluated by others, and situations where we are uncertain about what to do or what will happen. Moreover, while treatments like cognitive-behavioral therapy can be effective in helping us manage the anxiety we feel, they don't typically eliminate it and require substantial effort to implement. Similarly, while anxiolytic drugs can be an effective treatment for some anxiety conditions, they do not appear to work across the board and can have serious side effects (e.g., sedation, memory impairment).[29] So not only does anxiety shape much ordinary life, it does not appear to be something that we could (easily) get rid of.[30]

Second, it is also doubtful that the traits and skills that one might look to as "better" replacements for what anxiety does—humility, open-mindedness, curiosity, concern, and the like—are up to the task. Though they might free us of the felt unpleasantness that anxiety can bring, they also seem less effective in their alarm and motivating functions because—unlike anxiety—they are *not experienced as aversive*. This, of course is not to deny that these traits/skills are important. Humility and open-mindedness bring an important degree of caution and a willingness to consider new or conflicting evidence (Arpaly & Schroeder, 2014, pp. 241–245). Similarly, curiosity and concern motivate us to work through challenges and to explore issues we find puzzling (Morton, 2010). Rather, the point is that (practical) anxiety provides something that we do not seem to get from these traits/skills alone. As we have seen, feelings of anxiety function as a distinctive kind of *alarm*—namely, one that disrupts our current behavior and prompts reassessment. So while traits like humility, curiosity, and concern play an important epistemic role, they are unlike anxiety in that they are not inherently unpleasant and so are not disruptive epistemic mechanisms. Rather, they are capacities that manifest only *after* we have come to see that we face a puzzle or problem (more on this in chapter 5). Thus, (practical) anxiety's distinctive value is twofold: it is an aversive response that makes us aware of the need to engage the deliberation and inquiry that humility, open-mindedness, curiosity, and concern help guide, and it gives us a motivational push in this direction. Taken together, these considerations provide good reason for doubting that creatures with psychologies like ours could reliably, by some other means, get the range of benefits that anxiety can provide.

---

29. For an overview, see LeDoux (2015, chaps. 9–11).
30. For a similar point, see the discussion of wide and deep psychological roles in D'Arms and Jacobson (2006, pp. 216–217).

Let's now turn to the first worry from above: the thought that the anxiety pill shows that there's nothing aretaically valuable about (practical) anxiety—it's merely valuable because of benefits (the moral concern) it helps bring about. To counter this thought, we need a case where anxiety is neither fitting nor provides any instrumental benefits, but where we nonetheless deem it valuable. Such a case would provide a situation where taking the pill would prevent us from realizing that noninstrumental value—it would indicate that something important gets lost in taking the pill.

So consider a revised version of the earlier example of your Alzheimer's-stricken mother. Her disease has now run its course and, tragically, each day only brings her more pain and suffering. You promised her that when this moment came, you would give her a euthanizing dose of morphine. So you must now decide whether to keep your promise. You are anxious—is this the right thing to do?—and, as a result, think hard about both your promise and your mother's condition. After much reflection, you conclude that you ought to do what you promised. And you do. But days later, you are still anxious. Though you keep rethinking your decision, you keep coming to the same conclusion: it was the right thing to do. Yet your anxiety about the choice remains.[31]

What can we say about your anxiety? First, given that it's anxiety about a difficult decision that prompts reflection and reassessment, we can see that we are dealing with an instance of practical anxiety. So, in light of the above discussion of practical anxiety's fittingness conditions, your anxiety is fitting as you contemplate whether to keep the promise: you face a difficult choice and have reason to reflect and reassess (section 4.1). But your anxiety is unfitting after you have come to your conclusion and have administered the morphine: since you no longer face a hard choice and since the choice you made cannot be reversed, you have no reason to revisit or reassess it. Moreover, your postdecision anxiety is not just unfitting, it also lacks instrumental value: not only is your lingering anxiety unpleasant, but the reflection it prompts does nothing either to change your conclusion or to enrich your understanding of what was at stake—each new round of

---

31. In this example, I presume that though euthanasia is legal (you're in Denmark, say), its moral status is ambiguous—so there's uncertainty about what's morally permissible.

anxiety-induced reflection leads you back to the same considerations and the same conclusion.

However, your lingering feeling of anxiety—though unfitting and devoid of instrumental value—still *reflects well on you*. It's the manifestation of your admirable sensitivity to the difficult, morally ambiguous choice you faced. Someone who had no lingering unease in a situation like yours would be disconcerting; a quick transition back to an anxiety-free orientation would prompt worries about their *character*—it would suggest they hadn't really appreciated the gravity of their choice.[32] But notice what this means: it means we are again seeing the aretaic value of practical anxiety.

In this way, the assessment of anxiety's value that we have here is analogous to what we find in Bernard Williams's (1976) famous lorry-driver example. In this case, a lorry driver runs over a child who darted in front of his truck. By stipulation, there was nothing the driver could have done to prevent the tragedy. But, as Williams notes, we still expect the driver to feel guilt and regret. As Dan Jacobson (2013) analyzes the case, the driver's guilt and regret are unfitting and unhelpful, but admirable nonetheless. Guilt and regret are emotions that are fitting as responses to a tragic outcome for which you have made an error or done something wrong. Since there was nothing the driver could have done to avoid this, he made no mistake and did nothing wrong—any guilt or regret is thus unfitting. However, the driver's response is admirable nonetheless: the guilt and regret he feels are "a reassuring sign that he takes his agency seriously" (p. 115). So here too we have a situation where emotional expressions are aretaically valuable despite being unfitting and unhelpful.[33]

Though these two cases involve different emotions, they both point to the same conclusion: the aretaic value of these emotions is independent of their fittingness or instrumental contributions. Anxiety, regret, and guilt are important not just because of the benefits they can bring, but also because of what they say about the character of the individual who experiences

---

32. You yourself might also become quite troubled were you to recognize that you were able to seamlessly bounce back to your carefree self.

33. Williams and Jacobson disagree over whether the lorry driver's guilt/resentment is fitting. Though I have sided with Jacobson, not much turns on this: even if the guilt/regret is fitting, we still have a case where it has *noninstrumental* value. A similar point applies to the previous case: even if your anxiety was fitting, it would still reflect well on you and so be noninstrumentally valuable.

them: as emotions that are (partly) constitutive of virtues like moral concern, they manifest one's appreciation of life's complexity and uncertainty. Moreover, given that emotions like these are so central to human agency, they are features of our (moral) psychology that, if eliminated by popping some special pill, would come at real cost to how we understand and assess ourselves and others. So while the Xanax objection might have initially seemed to cause trouble for our claims about the aretaic value of anxiety, its plausibility fades on closer examination.

4.3.2 Anxiety and Intrinsic Value

Can the argument be pushed further? Might anxiety and anger be not just aretaically valuable, but also *intrinsically* valuable? Perhaps. There are two ways one might try to establish that these negative emotions have intrinsic value. As we will see, whether they work turns on (among other things) what one takes 'intrinsic value' to be.

First, one might attempt an indirect argument for the intrinsic value of anxiety—its intrinsic value is something it, in a sense, inherits from something else that is intrinsically valuable. Fleshing this out, one might maintain, following William Frankena (1973, pp. 87–88), that morally good dispositions and virtues have intrinsic value. Combining this Frankena premise with both the above account of moral concern and the claim that the constituents of something intrinsically valuable are themselves intrinsically valuable leads to the conclusion that well-regulated anxiety and anger are *intrinsically valuable* in virtue of being partly constitutive of moral concern:

1. Virtues are intrinsically valuable.
2. Moral concern is a virtue.
3. Moral concern is constituted, in part, by anxiety and anger.
4. The constitutive elements of something intrinsically valuable are themselves intrinsically valuable.
5. So, anxiety and anger are intrinsically valuable.[34]

But this argument—premise (4) in particular—invites a Moorean objection. From the fact that X is intrinsically valuable, it does not follow that

---

34. Bell (2013, pp. 163–164) makes an argument of this sort for the conclusion that contempt is an emotion with noninstrumental value. As such, it is vulnerable to the objections that follow.

the things that comprise it—a, b, c—are also intrinsically valuable. After all, it may be that it's only through the *combination* of a, b, and c that we get something intrinsically valuable; the elements *themselves* have no intrinsically value (Moore, 1903, pp. 27–29). I suspect this concern is fatal. If so, then we need to give up premise (4) and argue more directly for the intrinsic value of anxiety.

On this front, one might look to relational accounts of intrinsic value (e.g., Kraut, 2007; Railton, 1986a; Rosati, 2006). That is, one might maintain that the claim "X is intrinsically valuable" is incomplete. What one is really saying when one makes such a claim is that X is intrinsically valuable *for Y*; an intrinsic value claim only makes sense against the backdrop of an account of the sort of thing X is claimed to be intrinsically valuable for. With this schema in hand, one could then add that to assess whether X is intrinsically valuable for Y, one needs to ask whether X matters to Y for its own sake and not merely as a means for something else. If X matters to Y for its own sake, then X is something with intrinsic value. Applying this to anxiety, one could maintain that (well-regulated) anxiety matters to our character not merely because it helps us recognize and respond to uncertainty about what to do, but also because it is the manifestation of our emotional attunement to the difficult choice we face.

While I think there is something to this line of reasoning, two significant qualifications are needed. First, the argument is only as plausible as the relational account of value on which it rests. Second, even if one is comfortable about relational value, one might still worry that if we accept the claim that anxiety has intrinsic value in virtue of its mattering for our character (our emotional attunement), we lose (or at least cloud) the distinction between aretaic and intrinsic value. I for one am uncomfortable on both fronts—a discomfort that I suspect is rooted in my deeper uncertainty about what, exactly, intrinsic value is. But for those who do not share my unease, there will presumably be a greater willingness to take anxiety as intrinsically valuable. Regardless, I stand by the initial argument that anxiety has aretaic value and thus that anxiety is more than just instrumentally beneficial.

Stepping back, we have not only learned that anxiety and anger are aretaically valuable. We have also sharpened our understanding of why this is so. It's because anger and anxiety are unpleasant that they are able to express the distinctive moral attunement that they do: respectively, the outrage of a moral violation and the unease of a weighty or difficult choice. This is something Kant and the ancients appear to have missed.

4.4 Two Implications

Recapping: Anxiety is a valuable emotion. To say this, however, is not to deny that anxiety can go awry. Rather, it is to emphasize that anxiety, in its more typical and moderate manifestations, plays an important role in helping us recognize and respond to a range of potential threats and dangers. In fact, anxiety's ability to bring this distinctive sensitivity and responsiveness makes it aretaically, perhaps even intrinsically, valuable. Appreciating this has two significant implications. First, it reveals that anxiety—particularly practical anxiety—is an emotion *we ought to cultivate*. Not only does it play an instrumental role with regard to effective agency and good decision making, it is also partly constitutive of the psychology that underlies virtuous moral concern. Second, we see that effective agency and good decision making are often the product of *psychological conflict*—a conclusion that challenges existing accounts of virtue and agency. In what follows, I say more about these two implications.[35]

4.4.1 Anxiety: An Emotion We Ought to Cultivate

The argument that we ought to cultivate (practical) anxiety is straightforward. It begins with the plausible premise that we ought to cultivate emotions and other capacities that make distinctive and important contributions to our ability to be virtuous agents and to engage in good decision making. It then draws on observations of the sort we have been looking at as evidence of anxiety's ability to make contributions of this type. The upshot then is that anxiety is an emotion we ought to cultivate. To be clear, in saying this, I am not suggesting that we want to just experience anxiety more often or more intensely. Rather, the point is that (practical) anxiety is something we should learn to feel at the right times and in the right ways. In this respect, the situation with regard to the cultivation of anxiety is no different than what we find with other emotions that play a distinctive and important role in social and moral life: we want to cultivate sympathy and

---

35. I make similar points with respect to moral anxiety in Kurth (2015). The discussion that follows can be seen as a more general version of those arguments.

anger, not in the sense of getting ourselves to experience these emotions more often or more intensely, but in the sense of getting ourselves to feel them at the right time and in the right way. In short, we want *well-regulated* sympathy and anger. And, as with anxiety, the reason for this lies in the central role that these emotions play: the capacity for sympathy underlies our ability to act benevolently and the capacity for anger (as we have seen) underlies moral concern. This, of course, raises questions regarding how best to cultivate anxiety—a topic we will return to in chapter 6.

4.4.2 A Challenge to Existing Accounts of Virtue and Agency

The conclusion that anxiety is something that should be cultivated comes with a novel, empirically grounded picture of the psychology of the virtuous agent. On this picture, good decision making and virtuous agency are a function of, among other things, one's tendency to feel anxious in the face of novel or difficult choices. This in turn indicates that good decisions are (often) the product of emotion-based *psychological conflict*—conflict and unease that lead one to consciously explore, evaluate, and reject possible challenges to the decision that one is contemplating. This is not to deny that much (good) decision making and agency is the product of automatic processes.[36] But it is to insist that any account of decision making and agency must acknowledge that decisions will often benefit from feelings of anxiety that get one to consciously explore and assess possible objections to the decision one is contemplating. The picture of the psychology of the virtuous agent that comes out of this account of anxiety is significant in its own right. But it also brings a challenge to some prominent proposals. In what follows, I consider three examples.

The Stoics While the Stoics are often characterized as viewing emotions as devoid of value (e.g., Roberts, 2014, chap. 2), their view is actually more sophisticated. To draw this out, I begin with a brief review of the Stoics' moral psychology. This will better position us to understand the nature of the Stoics' complaint against emotion—an understanding that will, in turn, draw out what they would say about anxiety's value.[37]

---

36. See, for example, Arpaly and Schroeder (2014, chaps. 1–3); Railton (2009). More on this in chapters 5 and 6.

37. The sketch that follows glosses over much richness in the Stoic position. See Brennan (2003), Brown (n.d.), and Graver (2007) for more detailed discussions.

At its core, the Stoic theory of mind takes emotions to consist of two elements: an appearance and an assent to that appearance.[38] For the Stoics, *appearances* are not mere sense data but rather representational states with propositional content. In the context of emotions, appearances present features of a person's situation (e.g., having money, experiencing disgrace) as being unconditionally good or bad for them. Turning to the form of *assent* constitutive of emotion, the Stoics understand this as a cognitive act whereby one gives one's unqualified, motivationally laden endorsement to an appearance: one takes its content to be true and forms an action tendency (an "impulse") that accords with the content of the appearance (e.g., to pursue what one takes to be good; to avoid what one sees as bad).

With this overview in hand, we are positioned to see the Stoics' problem with emotions. First, because emotions are partly constituted by appearances that present indifferent objects like money (or disgrace) as being *unconditionally* good (bad), they have content that is false or "weak" (weak in the sense of failing to enhance the overall coherence of one's epistemic state). Second, because the assent distinctive of emotion is *unqualified* and *motivationally laden*, one's resulting actions are likely to be rash. Avoiding these problems—becoming a Sage—involves using one's rational capacities to protect against such errors. With greater understanding, one comes to recognize that only virtue, and the wisdom it manifests, is unconditionally good. Similarly, one comes to see that one should only accept appearances, and so form motivations, with "reservation." Put another way, part of becoming a Sage is learning how to appraise one's situation *without* forming emotion—emotional responses are to be transformed into unemotional assessments.[39]

While the above might seem to affirm the common idea that the Stoics saw emotion as valueless, or even inherently pernicious, such a conclusion would be too quick. Granted, since the Stoic axiology deems only virtue/wisdom to be unconditionally good for a person, emotions will lack

---

38. Here I follow Graver (2007) in using 'emotion' rather than 'passion' to refer to what the Stoics termed 'pathē.' As we will see, though the Stoics took pathē to be deeply problematic, they allowed that other, related affective states—what they called 'eupatheiai'—were valuable.

39. Recalling the previous note, an 'unemotional assessment' needn't be one that is dispassionate or devoid of affect. More on this shortly.

aretaic or intrinsic value. That said, their account allows that emotions can be instrumentally valuable. To see this, recall that part of the problem with emotions is that they tend to track indifferents—things that are only conditionally good (bad). But the Stoics also recognized that indifferents tend to co-occur with what is unconditionally good (bad). For instance, while pride presents glory as good (though it is really just an indifferent), occasions where one feels pride tend to also be occasions where one can realize something of unconditional value—namely, honor. Thus, emotions are instrumentally valuable, at least for the non-Sage, insofar as they tend to point—both cognitively and conatively—toward what is unconditionally good. Moreover, though the Sage does not experience emotions (and so cannot profit from them), the Stoic account allows that they can benefit from a kind of *proto*emotion. The basis for this lies in the Stoic notion of a "first movement." In brief, first movements are felt physiological changes that accompany the appearances that, when assented to, become emotions.[40] They are interesting for our purposes for several reasons. For starters, first movements are, phenomenologically speaking, very similar to the felt experience of the emotions they are associated with. Second, since first movements are not emotions, but precursors to them, they are things that the Sage experiences. Thus, on the Stoic account, there are nonemotion forms of affect that Sages feel. Moreover, since the Stoics take first movements to be *natural* parts of human psychophysiology, and since they see the constitutive elements of a being's nature as existing for a good reason, they are committed to first movements being useful: according to the Stoics, Sages use first movements to make assessments about what courses of action to pursue. For example, the positive feeling that comes in the face of a financial opportunity provides the Sage with information that this opportunity is likely choiceworthy; the negative feeling that one feels in the face of a potentially disgraceful action indicates it would likely to be a mistake to do it. Thus, even the Sage can secure instrumental benefits from emotion-like affective states.

Combining the above observations with the fact that the Stoics recognized anxiety as a negatively valenced emotion felt in the face of uncertain

---

40. Whether first movements are essential elements of these appearances, or just common features of them, was a point of controversy among the Stoics. For discussion see Cicero (1927, 3.82–3.83); Graver (2007, chap. 2); and Seneca (1995, II.4).

threats,[41] they could agree that anxiety can have instrumental value for the non-Sage. Moreover, given what we just learned about first movements, the Stoics could also agree that protoanxiety is an ineliminable and valuable part of the Sage's moral psychology.[42] However, given their very narrow understanding of virtue—whereby only wisdom is good for a person—they would deny that anxiety can be aretaically valuable. Relatedly, the Stoics deny that the point of applying reasoning to emotions is to cultivate them; rather, the point is to transform emotions into something else—namely, unemotional assessments. However, we have seen that there is good reason to resist such a restrictive account of virtue and its development. And so we have good reason to reject the Stoics' narrow account of anxiety's value.

Kant Turn now to Kant's account of virtue. As we saw in the introduction, Kant took *full* virtue to require the presence of a "tranquil mind"—a proposal at odds with the picture that comes out of our investigation of the role of anxiety. But the contrast with Kant grows more subtle when we look to his remarks about the role that emotions play in the *development* of virtue (1797/1996, pp. 528–530; 1997, pp. 130–137, 241–242). For instance, according to Kant, virtue is its own reward in the sense that morally good individuals, and those predisposed to be morally good, will experience feelings of pleasure on having acted from duty. Moreover, and more importantly, such individuals will also feel pain when they fail to act from duty. So, unlike the Stoics, Kant believes that negative emotions themselves can play an important role in moral development. Moreover, and more significantly given our purposes, Kant identifies a role for *anxiety* in his account of how conscience drives moral self-regulation (1797/1996, pp. 559–562). On Kant's picture, conscience is an innate moral capacity

---

41. More specifically, based on Graver's (2007) articulation of the Stoic taxonomy of emotion, they appear to recognize anxiety (as we have been understanding it) as either a subtype of fear or a subtype of distress (pp. 56–57).

42. That Sages would only experience protoanxiety is a result that follows from the Stoics' highly intellectualized account of what emotions are—appearances one cognitively assents to (for critiques of cognitivist accounts of this sort, see Griffiths, 1997, chap. 2; Scarantino, 2014; cf. Nussbaum, 2001). On the biocognitive account of emotion that we have been working with, first movements would (likely) be part of emotions themselves and so emotions like anxiety would be things that even Sages could experience—and so benefit from.

that functions in three ways: (i) it warns one that one might be making a decision that is contrary to moral law, (ii) it acts as a "prosecutor" as it investigates whether, after the deed is done, one has in fact violated moral law, and (iii) it operates as a "judge" who levels an acquittal or a condemnation based on the prosecutor's findings. Moreover, as Kant explains, on occasions where conscience determines that we *did* follow moral law, our "anxiety" about our fate subsides. Fleshing this out, his idea seem to be that given the possibility that we might have done wrong, we have a negative emotional experience—we feel anxious. But when we subsequently learn that we have actually done right, we "rejoice" at having avoided the possibility of being found punishable: "Hence the blessedness found in the comforting encouragement of one's consciousness is not positive (joy) but merely negative (relief from preceding anxiety)" (1797/1996, p. 562).

In the present context, Kant's account of the role of negative emotions and psychological conflict is noteworthy in several ways. First, not only does he acknowledge a role for anxiety in practical decision making, but he also takes it to play an important role in moral development: because anxiety is an aversive response to situations where we may have done wrong, it acts as a corrective mechanism—it makes us sensitive to (the possibility of) violating the moral law. However, in contrast with the role that we have identified for anxiety (and psychological conflict more generally), Kant focuses exclusively on its *instrumental* value with regard to our development as moral agents. Moreover, on Kant's picture, anxiety functions primarily in a backward-looking manner: it signals that we have (likely) violated the moral law. As such, his picture neglects the more positive and forward-looking roles that we have identified: anxiety functions both to bring epistemic behaviors that help us figure out what the correct thing to do is, and to express the moral concern that we take to be (partly) constitutive of virtuous agency. So while Kant's account of the moral psychology of nonideal agents like us improves on the proposal we get from the Stoics, we see that he too fails to fully appreciate the importance of anxiety and psychological conflict more generally.[43]

---

43. David Velleman (2003) has developed an account of (fitting) guilt that focuses primarily on guilt as an emotion concerned with being "normatively vulnerable." I believe his proposal has significant affinities with Kant's account of conscience. In brief, Velleman takes guilt (or at least a dominant version of it) to be an emotion that

Neo-Aristotelians More recently, philosophers working in the Aristotelian tradition—Philippa Foot (1978), John McDowell (1998), Rosalind Hursthouse (1999), Julia Annas (2011), and others—have developed proposals that see virtuous action as *harmonious*. Though the details get fleshed out in various ways, the core idea is that while learning to be virtuous can bring frustration and psychological conflict, this is *not* the case for virtuous individuals. McDowell (1998), for instance, sees genuinely courageous behavior as action that "combines a lively awareness of risk, and a normal valuation of life and health, with a sort of *serenity*" (p. 92, emphasis added). Similarly, Annas (2011) maintains that for the virtuous, thought and action are "effortless" and "unimpeded by frustration and inner conflict" (p. 73).[44] But this account of virtuous action as a harmonious, conflict-free experience clashes with the picture we have been developing. As the case of your decision about whether to place your Alzheimer's-stricken mother in a nursing home makes plain, there are clearly occasions where anxiety is part of what makes for virtue (more on this in chapter 5). In that example, your anxiety about how best to reconcile your mother's needs and wants, and the deliberation this brings, express an admirable moral sensitivity—an attunement that reveals your understanding of the complexity of moral life. So while these neo-Aristotelian proposals are right in acknowledging the importance of anxiety (and psychological conflict more generally) in our development as virtuous agents, they (like Kant) are wrong to maintain that anxiety is incompatible with virtue once it has been attained. Fleshing this point out will be a central part of our work in the next chapter.

---

we experience when we (may) have acted in a way that calls into question our trustworthiness. As such, we feel normatively vulnerable in the sense of both being anxious and having a diminished sense of self-worth. As in Kant's account, Velleman's proposal emphasizes more backward-looking features: guilt/anxiety signals that we have done something wrong and brings the associated negative reinforcement in the form of one's diminished self-worth. As such, he too neglects the more forward-looking benefits that we find in (practical) anxiety.

44. An important point of difference between these neo-Aristotelian proposals concerns whether the resulting account of harmonious, conflict-free virtue is attainable by ordinary human agents. Annas, for one, maintains that it is (e.g., 2011, pp. 30–32); whether this is also the case in McDowell's view is less clear.

4.5 Conclusion

We have seen that anxiety is a valuable emotion. Moreover, we have seen that practical anxiety plays a particularly important role in helping us understand and navigate the complexities of moral and social life. Not only does practical anxiety help us recognize situations where we are confronted with particularly novel or difficult situations, it also kicks us into the deliberation, reflection, and information gathering that can help us work through the challenging decision we face. But this picture relies on two important assumptions—assumptions that have recently come under attack. First, emotion theorists have challenged the idea that emotions like anxiety can be reliable forms of evaluative awareness. Second, empirically minded moral psychologists have challenged the thought that we ever really engage in deliberation and reflection—what might seem like genuine conscious deliberation is really nothing more than a post hoc confabulation. The next two chapters take up these skeptical challenges in a way that not only shows them to be misplaced, but enriches our understanding of how and why anxiety matters.

5   Virtue: Anxiety, Agency, and Good Decision Making

Fear is the main source of superstition, and one of the main sources of cruelty. To conquer fear is the beginning of wisdom.
—Bertrand Russell

This chapter tackles the Puzzle of Virtue. More specifically, it further develops our investigation of the instrumental and aretaic value of (practical) anxiety by looking more closely at the role that it plays in virtuous human thought and action. To get started, recall that a central conclusion from the last chapter was that anxiety, especially practical anxiety, is an emotion we ought to cultivate because it plays a central role in engaging the epistemic behaviors—for example, reflection, deliberation, information gathering—that are essential to good (practical, moral) decision making and agency.[1] In particular, we saw that a good decision will (often) be the product of *psychological conflict*—conflict that leads one to consciously explore, evaluate, and reject possible challenges to the decision that one is contemplating. This is not to deny that much (good) decision making results from automatic processes alone. But it is to insist that any account of human agency must acknowledge that thought and action will often benefit from the practical anxiety that gets one to consciously explore and assess possible objections to the decision one faces. In fact, the previous chapter's discussion of practical anxiety's aretaic value suggests something stronger: that deliberation, reflection, and the like are *essential* to good decision making and virtuous agency.

---

1. As in the previous chapter, I will continue to use 'good decision making and agency' and like phrases quite broadly so as to capture both the moral and practical domains.

This idea—that deliberation is, in some way, necessary for virtuous thought and action—captures a central tenet of much of our thinking about agency, responsibility, and ethical theory more generally. There's good reason for this. After all, deliberation seems essential to our ability to appropriately work through inconsistencies in our moral beliefs and judgments. It also seems to be essential to our ability to understand, and wisely navigate, the complexities of moral and social life. Granted, there is disagreement about how exactly to understand deliberation's role in all this. That said, the basic picture—call it the standard deliberationist model—is widely endorsed.[2]

But is this tenable? There is reason to be suspicious. After all, even a little reflection reveals that many virtuous acts proceed without conscious deliberation. If so, then how essential can deliberation really be? Recent work in moral psychology brings further trouble. In particular, this work suggests an account of decision making and agency that, if true, would undermine the standard thought that deliberation matters for virtue. On this alternative picture, emotions and other automatic mechanisms—not conscious deliberation and reflection—drive practical decision making. What seems like genuine deliberation is really nothing but a post hoc rationalization (e.g., Arpaly & Schroeder, 2014; Doris, 2009, 2015; Greene, 2008; Haidt, 2001; Prinz, 2007; Wegner, 2002). Stepping back, then, we can see that if we want to vindicate the thought that deliberation has an important—even essential—role to play in good decision making and virtuous agency, we need to answer this antideliberationist challenge.

In what follows, I will argue that accounts of the moral psychology underlying human agency that incorporate what we have learned about practical anxiety are uniquely well placed to answer the antideliberationist challenge. To show this, I will begin by looking at Julia Annas's neo-Aristotelian account of virtuous agency—a proposal that models the development and exemplification of virtue on the development and exemplification of athletic, musical, and artisanal skills. As we will see, Annas's skill-based account appears to provide a forceful reply to antideliberationists. I will argue, however, that her proposal ultimately falls short. But appreciating

---

2. See, for instance, Brink and Nelkin (2013); Kennett and Fine (2008); Fischer and Ravizza (1998); Frankfurt (1971); Gibbard (1990); Tiberius (2008, 2013); Korsgaard (2009, 2010); Wallace (1994); Watson (1982); and Wolf (1990).

why it fails points us to a better understanding of both the role of deliberation in virtuous thought and action and the importance that practical anxiety has for a viable response to antideliberationists. In short, practical anxiety is a feature of human psychology uniquely well suited to engaging conscious thought and reflection in the face of novel and difficult decisions—the very situations that reveal deliberation's essential role for virtuous agency. I then show that a similar appreciation of practical anxiety's significance can also enhance Humean and Kantian replies to antideliberationists. The upshot will be a better understanding of the moral psychology that underlies good human decision making and agency. In short, if you want to vindicate the importance of deliberation, you need a moral psychology that takes seriously the role that practical anxiety plays.[3]

5.1 The Antideliberationist Challenge

Two lines of research in moral psychology—one theoretical, one empirical—combine to generate a significant challenge for the standard deliberationist model (the 'SDM'). To draw this out, I will begin by saying a little more about the SDM. I will then introduce the two lines of research that undergird the antideliberationist challenge.

The central claim of the SDM is that our thoughts and actions are virtuous only if they are tied (in some suitable way) to conscious mental processing—deliberation, reflection, and the like. Moreover, while the claim that deliberation is essential to virtue can be fleshed out in a variety of ways, the most prominent and plausible versions share two features: (i) they tie virtuous agency, not to actual conscious reasoning, but to our *capacity* for conscious deliberation (or, as it is sometimes put, our capacity to respond to reasons *as reasons*), and (ii) they aim to provide accounts of what virtuous decision making amounts to for ordinary humans, not perfect or ideal agents as such.[4]

---

3. The discussion that follows builds on Kurth (forthcoming b).
4. Accounts of ideal agency can be found in (e.g.,) McDowell (1998); Rawls (1971, pp. 416–424); and (perhaps) Korsgaard (2009). Though one can go this route, it has familiar and significant problems. For instance, given the high degree of idealization these proposals involve, how can agents of this sort serve as normative standards for ordinary individuals who have no hope of ever realizing them (e.g., Doris, 2009, 2015; Enoch, 2006; Rosati, 1995)?

Much of the appeal of the SDM lies in the thought that deliberative capacities are essential not just to human agency in general, but also to the exemplification of virtuous thought and action. Intuitively, it is (in part) because normal adults can consciously assess, regulate, and act for reasons that we view them as agents. Moreover, we take our development as agents—our ability to become virtuous—to go hand in hand with the development of our deliberative capacities. Similarly, for our responsibility intuitions: it is (partly) because of our capacity for deliberation—our ability to recognize and work through deficiencies in our beliefs and goals—that we take ourselves to be subject to praise, blame, and an expectation of becoming better. So, for instance, David Brink and Dana Nelkin (2013) maintain that

> our paradigms of responsible agents are normal mature adults with certain sorts of capacities. We do not treat brutes or small children as responsible agents. Brutes and small children both act intentionally, but they act on their strongest desires or, if they exercise deliberation and impulse control, it is primarily instrumental reasoning in the service of fixed aims. By contrast, we suppose, responsible agents must be normatively competent. They must not simply act on their strongest desires, but be capable of stepping back from their desires, evaluating them, and acting for good reasons. This requires responsible agents to be able to recognize and respond to reasons for action. (p. 292)

Similarly, Jeanette Kennett and Cordelia Fine (2008) state that

> genuine moral judgments must be made by moral agents and ... moral agents must, as matter of conceptual necessity, be reasons responders ... [i.e., creatures who, like us, have the] capacity to respond to reasons as reasons and to guide their behavior accordingly. (pp. 85–86, 81)

Here's Christine Korsgaard (2010) making a similar point:

> moral action is not mere behavior that is altruistic, cooperative, or fair. It is action governed by a conception of the way that you ought to act. To be a moral being is to be capable of being motivated to do what you ought to do because you believe you ought to do it. And that requires reason. (p. 25)

And, finally, Valerie Tiberius (2008) holds that "a well-lived life is a life we endorse or approve of upon reflection. In other words, paraphrasing David Hume, to live well is to live a life that can bear your reflective survey" (p. 12; also 2002).[5] Thus, making sense of what it is to be an agent, much

---

5. For additional defenses of versions of the SDM, see the citations in note 2. Cf. Hieronymi (2014).

less a virtuous agent, seems to require vindicating the importance of deliberation for human thinking and doing—a conclusion that, as the above quotes indicate, is endorsed by ethical theorists of all stripes.[6]

But the SDM's commitment to taking our capacity for conscious deliberation to be essential to virtuous thought and action leaves it open to theoretically and empirically motivated lines of skepticism. On the theoretical side, antideliberationists maintain that the SDM's central commitments (i.e., (i) and (ii) above) entail a vicious regress.[7] This is easiest to see if we focus on Tiberius's version of the SDM. On her account, a good practical judgment requires a type of (mental) action: it is a judgment one would (continue to) endorse on reflection. So consider a particular subject S and judgment J. Given Tiberius's proposal, J is a good practical judgment if and only if J would be endorsed were S to reflect on it. Put another way, J's status as a good practical judgment is a function of a further (possible) practical judgment—namely, the reflective endorsement S would make were she to reflect on J. Now suppose that were S to reflect, she would affirm J. Does this fact about S's counterfactual reflection on J mean that J is a good practical judgment? Not necessarily. After all, the reflection that would result in S's endorsement of J—call it D1—is itself a (possible) practical judgment. So D1 would count as a good practical judgment only if it were reflectively endorsed by S. But this means that for it to be the case that J is genuine, it must not only be the case that

D1: were S to reflect on J, she would approve of it,

but also that

D2: were S to reflect on D1, she would approve of it.

Moreover, D2 is itself a (possible) practical judgment and so is good only if S would reflectively endorse it. And thus the series continues with

D3: were S to reflect on D2, she would approve of it.

---

6. For the discussion that follows, I intend my talk of *good* practical/moral decision making, *virtuous* agency, and the like to be neutral with regard to metaethical debates about (e.g.,) the nature of moral properties and facts.

7. Broadly similar versions of the regress argument that follows can be found in Arpaly and Schroeder (2014, pp. 31–32) and Railton (2009).

This is significant. It reveals that according to Tiberius's version of the SDM, facts about whether J is a good practical judgment are grounded in facts about an *infinite* set of embedded counterfactuals (D1, D2, D3 ...) about what S would endorse were she to reflect. But the reliance on this infinite set of embedded counterfactuals about what S would do is problematic. After all, claims about what S would reflectively endorse are claims about S's mental capacities and actions. Moreover, since the goal is to give an account of agency that matters for ordinary humans (recall (ii) above), we must assume that S's mental capacities and ability to act are finite. But this means Tiberius's proposal specifies a set of conditions for something to count as a good practical judgment that cannot be realized: for it to be the case that J is a good practical judgment, it must be possible for a *finite* mind to ground an *infinite* set of embedded counterfactuals.[8]

There are a variety of ways an advocate of the SDM might respond. She could, for instance, idealize away from the limitations of actual human deliberative capacities. But as we noted above, and as is captured in commitment (ii), this is not likely to be the preferred route. Alternatively, she could back off Tiberius's move to understand the essential role of deliberation and reflection in terms of endorsement. Something like this is presumably what the talk of "reasons responsiveness" in the above quotes is trying to get at. But until more is said to unpack this metaphor, it is hard to understand—much less assess—the proposal.[9] In short, without a substantive proposal, we cannot assume that the SDM can avoid the regress problem.

While that alone is bad, recent work in psychology and cognitive science supports two claims that reveal further problems for the SDM.[10] First, work on dual-process theories of mind supports a picture in which practical

---

8. One might think the regress problem could be avoided if one were to adopt a decision-making rule of the following sort: endorse any higher-order judgment (D1, D2, ... Dn) only if you have endorsed the preceding lower-order judgment (J, D1, ... Dn-1). But there are two problems with this proposal. First, the rule seems to trivialize the reflective endorsement that deliberationists like Tiberius are interested in. Second, and more significantly, to adopt such a rule would itself be a practical judgment—and so something in need of reflective endorsement. Thus, it could help only if we already had a solution to the regress problem.
9. Below (section 5.6.1), I will develop a proposal of this sort on Tiberius's behalf.
10. Versions of the arguments that follow can be found in, for example, Doris (2009, 2015); Greene (2008); Haidt (2001); Haidt and Bjorklund (2008); Prinz (2007).

judgment starts from, and is largely driven by, automatic—not conscious—mental processes.[11] More specifically, antideliberationists begin by pointing to work that supports the idea that there are two general types of mental processing: type 1 processes that are quick, effortless, unconscious, and (often) affectively valenced; and type 2 processes that are slow, effortful, conscious, and (largely) affectively neutral. They then draw on research regarding various kinds of framing effects in order to argue that type 1 processes dominate practical decision making. As one example of this strategy, consider John Doris's appeal to work on "pronoun effects." He points to experiments (in, e.g., Gardner, Gabriel, & Lee, 1999) that

> asked participants to circle the pronouns in a written paragraph about a visit to the city. When they later completed a values questionnaire, people given a version featuring first personal plural pronouns (e.g., we, ours) were more likely to report that interdependent values (e.g., belongingness, friendship, family security) were a "guiding principle in their lives" than were people given a version featuring first personal singular pronouns (e.g., I, mine). (Doris, 2009, p. 63)

He then argues that this result suggests—contra the SDM—that type 1, not type 2, processes drive practical judgment and decision making. After all, if something as trivial as circling "I" rather than "we" can affect the value judgments one makes, then can these judgments really be the product of conscious deliberation and reflection (much less *good* decisions)? A better explanation, say antideliberationists, is that practical judgment is the product of type 1 processes—even if we have the capacity for type 2 processing, it doesn't seem to play a substantive role in our practical decision making. Moreover, notice that a move to avoid this problem by holding that the subjects' value judgments are not genuine (because, say, they wouldn't reflectively endorse them) comes at a significant cost: it suggests that many of the value judgments we make and take to be genuine actually aren't.

The second worry comes from work on confabulation. This research indicates that we are generally unaware of the causal processes responsible for our behavior—be it picking up a certain object or making a particular practical judgment. But our lack of awareness does not stop us from confidently

---

11. Though the skepticism that follows usually builds from dual-process theory, the worry itself does not require this—what is crucial for the objection is that there be a sufficient degree of modularity or independence between automatic, unconscious processes and conscious deliberation/reflection.

offering (typically false) explanations for why we did what we did—we are unaware of our lack of awareness (Nisbett & Wilson, 1977; Wilson, 2002). Antideliberationists take this to undermine the thought that our reason-giving behavior amounts to genuine deliberation: given our tendency to confabulate, for all we know, our "deliberation" is nothing more than a post hoc rationalization of a judgment we have already made.[12]

The overall picture of agency suggested by this work quite disconcerting. These skeptical worries, if well founded, reveal that deliberation does not—perhaps cannot—play the role in decision making and agency proposed by the SDM. Importantly, antideliberationists need not (and do not) claim that we never engage in genuine deliberation. Rather, they need only maintain that the deliberation we engage in fails to plays an interesting—much less essential—role in shaping virtuous thought and action (e.g., Doris, 2015, pp. 22–23; Haidt & Bjorklund, 2008, pp. 194–196). But if that is correct, if there is no interesting or essential role for deliberation, then much of what we take to be distinctive about humans as rational and moral agents is threatened: our intuitions to the contrary, deliberative capacities are irrelevant for things like identifying normal adults (but not children or brutes) as agents, understanding what is involved in becoming virtuous, and making sense of responsibility. Such revision to ordinary thought is quite radical. As Kennett and Fine (2009) observe:

> If it should turn out that human agency is of the minimal kind suggested by [antideliberationists] then our moral concepts will lack application, and *moral discourse and practice will be systematically in error* since they are irreducibly predicated on the assumption that we are reason responders [i.e., creatures that have the capacity to respond to reasons as reasons and to guide their behavior accordingly]. (p. 85, emphasis added)[13]

In light of all this, one should feel the force of the antideliberationist challenge: Can there be a substantive place for deliberation given the

---

12. It is worth noting that the antideliberationist claim that what seems like genuine deliberation is really post hoc rationalization can be forcefully made *without* appeal to the work of Jonathan Haidt and others on "dumbfounding" (i.e., the phenomenon where individuals appear to affirm a judgment even after acknowledging that the evidence they cite in favor of it is incorrect). This is good news since there are excellent reasons to question the soundness of these findings. See, for example, Jacobson (2012) for an insightful critical assessment of Haidt's work on dumbfounding.

13. Tiberius (2013, p. 223) and Sauer (2011) express similar sentiments.

empirical and theoretical arguments that undergird the antideliberationists' objections? More specifically, if we are to resist the antideliberationists' skepticism, we must (i) establish that deliberation plays a substantive and essential role in good practical decision making and agency, while (ii) granting that practical judgment is a process that starts from, and is largely driven by, automatic processes.[14] In the discussion that follows, I take up this challenge. I will argue that antideliberationists are wrong in thinking deliberation plays (at best) a trivial role.

5.2 Deliberation and the Skill Model of Virtuous Agency

In the face of the above skeptical challenge, skill-based models of virtuous agency have much appeal. These proposals take the fluid performances of accomplished athletes, musicians, and craftspeople as the paradigm of human excellence and use them as a model for understanding virtuous agency more generally. This move is significant. If we can understand virtuous thought and action as akin to skilled performances, then we have a model of agency that can secure an essential, but limited, role for deliberation in our understanding of virtue. After all, musical and athletic skills require conscious effort to acquire; but once one has become proficient, one can perform automatically, without conscious thought or reflection. Thus, the focus on skills gives us a proposal that's both applicable to ordinary humans, and well equipped to answer the challenge that proponents of deliberation face.[15]

To give this sketch more substance, we can turn to Julia Annas's (2011) proposal. There are several reasons for focusing on her account. Not only

---

14. One might reasonably hold that responding to antideliberationists needn't involve granting (all) the data on which their arguments rest (for arguments of this sort see Fine, 2006; Jacobson, 2012; and Pizarro & Bloom, 2003). While I am quite sympathetic to this move, it is important to see if the antideliberationists' conclusions can be resisted *even if* we grant them their starting place.
15. While the skill model is defended most often by contemporary Aristotelians (e.g., Annas, 2008, 2011; Bloomfield, 2000; Dreyfus & Dreyfus, 2004; Foot, 1978; Hursthouse, 1999), elements of it can also be found in non-Aristotelian accounts of agency (e.g., Kennett & Fine, 2009; Railton, 2009; Suhler & Churchland, 2009; Tiberius, 2008; and Velleman, 2008). In what follows, I will say more about the limitations of these alternative versions of the skill model.

is she explicit about wanting to secure an essential place for deliberation in virtuous agency (pp. 16–19, 76–77),[16] but she also wants her account of virtue to be something ordinary human agents can attain (pp. 30–32).[17] Moreover, and as we will see, in comparison with other versions of the skill model, Annas's account emphasizes features of virtue and its development that make for a particularly forceful reply to the skeptic.

According to Annas, there is a strong analogy between the development and exemplification of skills and the development and exemplification of virtues:

> The kind of practical reasoning found in the development and exercise of virtue is like the kind of reasoning that we find in the development and exercise of practical expertise. ... Virtue is habituated, built up over time and from experience by a process of learning. ... The virtuous person acts by way of immediate response to situations, but in a way that exhibits the practical intelligence of the skilled craftsperson or athlete. (p. 169)

As this quote suggests, Annas's proposal has two elements. First, like a skill, virtuous agency is *learned*. In particular, to count as the form of learning that is necessary for the acquisition of skills and virtues, one's development must be something that meets two conditions: it's development that (i) proceeds via explicit instruction whereby one comes to recognize the reasons for doing one thing rather than another, and that (ii) involves one exhibiting a drive to aspire. As Annas explains, this "drive" consists of the

---

16. In turning to empirical work, Annas is principally concerned to respond to situationist critiques of virtue—critiques that use work in social and personality psychology to raise doubts about whether there are character traits of the sort presupposed by (some) virtue ethicists (e.g., Doris, 2002; Harman, 1999). I take this situationist debate to be orthogonal to the present investigation of the role of deliberation in virtuous thought and action. So, for instance, while I endorsed an account of virtue in chapter 4 of the sort challenged by situationist, the discussion of virtue here need not be understood that way. More generally, if one is skeptical of talk of virtuous agency, one could reframe the discussion here in terms of an investigation of the role that deliberation plays in good decision making.

17. While Annas (2011) is primarily concerned with giving an account of virtue applicable to ordinary human agents, she also acknowledges that there is a notion of virtue as a regulative ideal—though ordinary humans can never secure this "full" virtue, it is something they can "aspire" to (pp. 64–65). Following Annas, my focus will be on the primary, nonidealized notion of virtue, though I will return to the idealized notion at the end of section 5.3.

combination of three interrelated motivations: a desire to understand why the teacher does what she does, a desire to be able to execute the skill in a self-directed way (rather than exhibiting a mere mimicking capacity), and a desire to improve (pp. 17–18).

Second, and again like a skill, once the underlying capacities have been acquired, the subsequent exemplification of virtue is automatic, but nonetheless intelligent. The core idea here is that virtuous thought and action are akin to the "flow" experiences that Mihaly Csikszentmihalyi (1991) and others have used to characterize optimal human performance. Such performances are paradigmatic examples of practical intelligence: they are cases where one demonstrates the reasons responsiveness that's characteristic of virtuous agency, but does so without consciously deliberating about what to do. As Annas (2011) explains,

Honest actions will be experienced by the mature honest person in the 'flow' way; however complex and hard to navigate the circumstances are, there is no felt resistance to acting honestly, no interference with the direct having of honest responses. (p. 75)

More specifically, the flow experiences of both skilled and virtuous agents involve engagement that is "unmediated by deliberation" and "unimpeded by frustration and inner conflict" (pp. 71–73).

To see how Annas's skill model helps address the antideliberationist challenge, first consider her account of learning and development. Unlike versions of the skill model that take learning to typically involve explicit instruction that appeals to reasons,[18] Annas's account requires it. As such, she is better placed to locate an essential role for deliberation. Moreover, because Annas takes virtuous agency to be on a par with the flow experiences of athletes and artisans, she can capture the data underlying the empirically motivated skepticism. After all, since the exemplification of virtue once acquired is a flow experience, it's action that is both automatic and intelligent. So Annas can maintain that virtuous agency is driven by automatic processes, while still insisting that it's not just mindless habit. Finally, because developing one's agential capacities is, like becoming

---

18. See, for example, Dreyfus and Dreyfus (2004) and Stichter (2016). We find a sharper contrast in Railton's (2009, 2014) version of the skill model: he takes learning via automatic mechanisms—not explicit instruction—as the paradigm for skill/virtue acquisition.

a skilled musician, a process that requires developing understanding via explanations that appeal to the underlying reasons, one will be able to accurately explain why one did what one did (p. 20). Because other versions of the skill model avoid tying virtuous action to the ability to provide such explanations (e.g., Bloomfield, 2000; Dreyfus & Dreyfus, 2004; Stichter, 2011), we again see an advantage to Annas's proposal: given her explanation requirement, she seems particularly well placed to respond to the skeptics' charge that what appears to be "reasoning" is nothing but a post hoc rationalization.

5.3 Two Problems with the Skill Model

With this understanding of Annas's skill model in hand, I will now argue that her proposal offers an account of the moral psychology of the virtuous agent that is overintellectualized in its account of how virtue is acquired, but underintellectualized in its insistence that conscious deliberation is unnecessary once virtue has been acquired. But since Annas's version of the skill model seems the one that's best equipped to answer the skeptic, the result will be real cause for concern regarding the ability of the skill model in general to provide a response to the antideliberationist challenge. The balance of the chapter develops a better way forward.

5.3.1 Problem 1: Overintellectualized

As we have seen, Annas takes skill and, by analogy, virtue acquisition to *require* learning that involves both (a) explicit instruction that appeals to the underlying reasons and (b) a drive to aspire. In fact, it's this intellectualized account of learning that allows her to secure an essential role for conscious deliberation in virtuous thought and action. Thus, her proposal would be in trouble if it were possible for individuals to develop sophisticated skills without either (a) or (b). On this front, things like language acquisition seem problematic: while learning a language might be facilitated by explicit instruction and a drive to aspire, neither appears necessary, as evidenced by immersion methods. Moreover, even if we grant that language learning requires instruction (Annas, 2008, p. 23), why think it must be the highly intellectualized learning Annas's account demands—namely, instruction that highlights the underlying reasons for (say) using one verb form rather than another?[19] Similarly, consider the culinary arts. One can become a skilled cook even if one's talent results, not from explicit instruction that appeals to reasons, but rather from a combination of mimicking others (e.g., recipes, cooking shows) and one's own trial-and-error efforts.

In response, Annas might reply that a closer look reveals that language acquisition and the culinary arts demand both her requirements be met. While I'm skeptical that this move works (it's hard to really assess without an actual proposal), we need not pursue that issue here—for work in anthropology and primatology provides us with examples of sophisticated skills being acquired despite a clear lack of either of Annas's two conditions. Moreover, working through these examples in light of potential replies will help us better understand why her version of the skill model is overintellectualized.

Consider, for instance, the flake-and-core knapping technology of Oldowan toolmakers or tool use among chimps. The consensus among anthropologists and primatologists is that the learning of these sophisticated skills is *not* well explained on an account of explicit instruction, much less the highly intellectualized picture we get from Annas. Rather, these instances of learning are best accounted for by a "seeding" model (de Beaune, 2004; Sterelny, 2012a, pp. 31–33; Tennie, Call, & Tomasello, 2009). On this model, an individual develops a new piece of practical expertise—say, a flaking technique that allows for a sharper edge. The inventor then leaves the tool where others will likely find it. Though this "seeding" of a prototype is not meant to help others acquire the skill, it tends to have this effect: because of the seeding, others can "reinvent" the flaking technique on their own or in combination with observation of others' efforts. But—importantly—this reinvention does *not* involve instruction or correction by the original inventor. This is trouble for Annas. For starters, it gives us an actual case of sophisticated skills being acquired without explicit instruction or explanations that appeal to reasons. Moreover, we also have, especially in the chimp case, skill acquisition that appears to lack central elements of the

---

19. Consider that novelists like Mark Twain and William Faulkner dropped out of school at (respectively) age 12 and 14. They seem to be examples of literary exemplars despite (presumably) lacking either the explicit instruction or drive for understanding Annas takes as essential.

drive to aspire: at most, the chimps seem to want to do what they see others doing—but that is merely a desire to mimic, not the deeper desire for self-direction and understanding that are essential to the drive to aspire.

As I see it, Annas could respond in three ways: she could argue that acquired behaviors like these do not amount to (sophisticated) skills; she could grant they are skills, but insist that they are not of the sort relevant to understanding virtue; or she could maintain that the acquired behaviors do not come via the right kind of learning. But there's trouble with each line of defense. Moreover, understanding why these replies fail will help us understand the limits of her intellectualized account of skill/virtue acquisition.

Fleshing out the first strategy, Annas might maintain that these examples do not involve particularly sophisticated skills: they are more like learning to tie shoelaces in that, unlike the skills relevant to virtue, they do not involve a competency that manifests in a variety of ways across a variety of situations (2011, pp. 21–22). However, this move fits poorly with the empirical data. For instance, the evolutionary psychologist Andrew Whiten and colleagues, when summarizing a wealth of field research on tool use by chimps, note that

> the chimpanzee repertoire exemplifies a *flexibility unique among primates in the range of different tools, techniques, and targets exploited*, implying a correspondingly rich grasp of the functional parameters of ... these tools. (Whiten, Schick, & Toth, 2009, p. 423, emphasis added; also Tennie, Call, & Tomasello, 2009, p. 2406)

In light of this, it is hard to see how the "too unsophisticated" reply could stick: if a rich and flexible competency is the mark of the type of skill acquisition relevant to virtue, then chimpanzees appear to have it.[20] We find a similar sophistication in the blades, spear points, and axes produced by the Oldowan toolmakers (Sterelny, 2012a, pp. 31–33).

The second line of defense grants that flaking technologies and tool use amount to genuine (and sophisticated) skills, but insists that they are nonetheless of the wrong sort for thinking about virtue and its acquisition. Why, one might ask, are the capacities and skills acquired by hominins and chimps relevant for understanding human virtue? But notice that if this reply is to have force, we need to identify a significant difference between

---

20. This is all the more so given Annas's (2011) desire for an account of skilled and virtuous action that is *relativized* to the individual's capacities and level of development (p. 65).

the two sets of skills that can substantiate the disanalogy. But it's hard to see how this could work. After all, the skills in our examples—making and using tools—are of a piece with the ones that Annas herself points to as relevant for understanding virtue: they are all examples of *craftspeople* at work. Put another way, if the skills of a carpenter, woodworker, or stonemason count, then why not the Oldowan stone knapper?

Turning to the final strategy, Annas might maintain that the kind of learning relevant to the development of skilled and virtuous agency is learning that brings a true appreciation of the underlying reasons—it's learning that allows the individual to explain why she did what she did. Without this ability to explain, we have a mere "knack," not genuine practical expertise (2008; 2011, pp. 19–20). But this move comes at a big cost. Granted, by requiring the rich understanding that would allow one to explain why one acted as one did, Annas can rule out that the Oldowan and chimp cases as counterexamples. However, the requirement that one be able to explain one's reasons also appears to rule out the artisans, athletes, and musicians that she points to as paradigmatic instances of individuals who have acquired their expertise in the right way: as accomplished as they are, these experts are typically unable to provide explanations for what they have done.[21] In short, in intellectualizing learning in order to rule out the skill acquisition of Oldowan/chimp toolmakers, Annas ends up undermining her ability to use these skilled experts as a model for virtue.[22]

---

21. Brownstein (2014) develops a powerful argument of this sort against Annas. One of his examples is the following quote from the Hall of Fame running back Walter Payton: "People ask me about this move or that move, but I don't know why I did something. I just did it." Also see Bloomfield (2000); Dreyfus and Dreyfus (2004); and Stichter (2011).

22. At this point, Annas might try to draw on empirical work suggesting that skilled athletes *can* explain their actions (e.g., Christensen, Sutton, & McIlwain, 2015, regarding expert mountain bikers; Sutton, 2007, on professional cricket batters). But there's reason to be concerned about the effectiveness of this move. First, showing that some skilled athletes can articulate their reasons does not mean all can—witness Walter Payton. So, unless more can be said, the objection in the text stands. Second, it's unclear whether this empirical research even does the work Annas needs it to do. More specifically, the research supports the claim that (some) skilled athletes display a distinctive capacity for higher-order, top-down cognitive control. So it provides evidence that these individuals rely on type 2 processing. But since not all type 2 processing is conscious (e.g., Price & Norman, 2008), it's unclear whether we get

Stepping back, we get a more general lesson. If the practical expertise of these paradigms of human excellence fail Annas's explanation requirement for learning, then it's strange to think that skill or virtue acquisition *must* be so intellectualized. This, in turn, suggests that while Annas may be right that skills (and so virtues) are acquired more efficiently when they come via explicit instruction and a drive to aspire, she errs in thinking these features are essential to the learning process. Thus, if we are to vindicate deliberation, we need to look elsewhere.

5.3.2 Problem 2: Underintellectualized

As we noted, Annas (2011) takes the harmonious, automatic performances of artisans, athletes, and craftspeople as evidence that virtuous thought and action will be similarly free of unease, struggle, and deliberation: "Honest actions will be experienced in the 'flow' way; however complex and hard to navigate the circumstances are, there is no felt resistance to acting honestly" (p. 75). Moreover, this strong analogy with flow experiences provides a forceful reply to the skeptic: if virtuous action is both *automatic* and *intelligent*, then there is no need to give—much less substantiate—a role for deliberation once virtue has been acquired. But Annas recognizes that this psychological picture may seem dubious in light of our own personal experiences with difficult (moral) choices. Thus she identifies two ways that feelings of unease and struggle, as well as conscious reflection and deliberation, can be consistent with her account of virtuous agency.

First, there are cases where the virtuous agent struggles and feels unease because she's faced with a challenge she cannot control: she, say, gives generously but feels regret and discomfort because she cannot do more—there are just too many who need help. What makes unease in a case like this consistent with virtue is that it results from difficult *external* circumstances, rather than an *internal* conflict in one's desires and values (e.g., one gives but regrets one's self-interested resistance to giving more) (p. 78). Second, there are cases where the virtuous agent must think through how to address a complicated situation. Such cases of deliberation and reflection are consistent with virtuous agency because the "activity is harmonious in the

---

evidence for the further claim that Annas needs—namely, that skilled athletes can *articulate* their reasons for doing what they did in a manner that doesn't collapse into a mere post hoc rationalization.

sense that there is no disruption of intent" (p. 77); like a skilled surgeon who comes across an unexpected complication, one's reflection proceeds "easily and without internal struggle" (2008, pp. 32–33).

However, while Annas is right that an account of virtue applicable to ordinary human agents needs to make room for instances of unease, struggle, and deliberation like these, virtuous human agents do—and should—feel uneasy and deliberate in more ways than Annas's account allows. To better draw this out, consider the following case:

Refugees. You provide assistance to a group of refugees and do so from sympathy. But your decision is a source of unease, not because you feel guilt or regret, but rather because your decision to give so much strains your other goals and values (e.g., regarding your commitments to your family)—it gets you thinking about whether you are making the correct choice.

Intuitively, this is an instance of virtue. Not only do you provide assistance from sympathy for the refugees but—through your unease—you evince a broader emotional attunement that, as we have seen (chapter 4), matters for virtuous agency. More specifically, the anxiety you feel about your decision, and the deliberation this provokes, reflects an admirable form of concern: a sensitivity that evinces your appreciation of the significance and complexity of the decision you are making.[23]

But notice: the refugee case provides an instance of virtuous action that's at odds with the psychological picture Annas presents. In particular, we have virtuous agency that involves both *internal* struggle and *disruptive* deliberation: not only are you concerned about whether your sizable contribution to the refugees will put too much strain on your other commitments, but this concern interrupts your decision making—it gets you to

---

23. Following Williams (1981), one might think that the unease experienced in the refugee case is not anxiety, but rather the residual guilt or regret that we (typically) experience when we make a difficult decision: though we see that our decision is correct, we nonetheless feel guilty or regret the value foregone in the unchosen option. I grant that residual feelings of this sort are possible in the face of a hard choice. But they are not plausible ways of accounting for the unease of the refugee case. If the emotion experienced was guilt or regret, we should expect to see evidence of their characteristic response behaviors—efforts to make amends for guilt and an intention to change one's standing policy for how to act in situations of this sort for regret (Jacobson, 2013). But we don't. Rather, we see the epistemic behaviors (reflection, reassessment) characteristic of practical anxiety. Thus, this worry can be set aside.

pause and assess things more closely. Moreover, and in a more normative vein, the case reveals the *value* we attribute to someone who not only feels uneasy or anxious in the face of difficult and novel decisions, but who—as a result of this unease—also stops to reassess the situation at hand.[24] To be clear, I am not denying that the unease- and deliberation-free agency of Annas's (above) surgeon example is admirable.[25] Rather, my point is that such cases do not exhaust our understanding of virtuous agency. As the refugee example reveals, the virtuous agent is someone who feels uneasy about how to act and who reassesses—even revises—her plans as her situation becomes less familiar. An individual who finds herself in a novel or difficult situation like this—but who is not even the slightest bit worried and does not reassess—strikes us as flawed or deficient in an important way (recall chapter 4).

Annas might respond that this case only reveals the rather obvious fact that some individuals are more virtuous than others: while it might make sense for an internally conflicted individual to feel uncertain and deliberate, a more virtuous person would not be conflicted—though problems may arise that require reflection, the virtuous individual will proceed fluidly and without disruption.[26] However, so long as we are focusing on a notion of virtuous agency applicable to ordinary—not ideal—agents, it is hard to see how this move helps. After all, for *any* level of actual human development, there will be situations where even the most experienced individuals face novel situations—situations quite unlike what they have seen before. When this happens, past experience will be insufficient to guide automatic action, so one must have the ability to recognize that one faces a novel situation in a way that prompts one to pause and consider whether one's initial thought about what to do is correct. What makes the unease of someone in

---

24. This point has been recognized by others—for example, see the discussion of open-mindedness in Arpaly and Schroeder (2014, pp. 241–245) and Slote (2014, pp. 175–176); also see Stohr (2003).
25. That said, we also admire *anxious* surgeons: recall the discussion of the neurosurgeon Henry Marsh from section 1.1.
26. For the makings of a reply along these lines, see, for example, Annas (2011, p. 77); Foot (1978) also makes a move of this sort.

the refugee case admirable is that such a person evinces this attunement—her worry signals a novel or difficult situation and prompts reassessment.[27]

Moreover, the claim that skilled/virtuous action involves a tendency to feel uneasy and reassess in the face of uncertainty finds support in empirical research on the decision making of experienced firefighters (Klein, 1999). For these individuals, initial decisions about how to fight a fire come automatically based on intuitive assessments grounded in past experience. But unnoticed features or changing conditions can reveal problems in the initial plan—the situation fails to unfold as expected. These anomalies can in turn spark feelings of "discomfit" that signal trouble and motivate reflection, reassessment, and changes in plans (p. 33). So while Annas (2011) is right that the expert is attuned to "what is happening and respond[s] appropriately to feedback" (p. 77), she is mistaken in thinking that this process is harmonious, easy, or free of disruption. In fact, the firefighter research suggests that a consciously experienced unease, disruption, and reassessment will sometimes be exactly what is needed.[28]

The Upshot Stepping back, one might think the above difficulties would be avoided by versions of the skill model that are both less intellectualized in their account of learning and less restrictive regarding the role of

---

27. That anxiety plays this role in sensitizing us to novel situations is consistent with the need for anxiety to do this diminishing as one acquires (practical) understanding and experience.

28. In response, Annas (2011) might repackage the claim about disruption- and conflict-free agency as a claim, not about *ordinary* human virtue, but rather about what *full* virtue amounts to as a regulative ideal. So understood, the claim would be that we should "aspire" to be like the fully virtuous agent: figure out what reasons the fully virtuous agent follows, and work to inculcate that new knowledge so that we can come to respond fluidly and automatically (pp. 22–23, 64). The problem with this strategy, however, is that it fails to demonstrate that virtuous agency should be free of disruption and conflict. After all, one could agree that we should use the ideal of the fully virtuous agent as a tool for figuring out what to do without also thinking that we must emulate the fully virtuous person's fluid and automatic performances. That is, if the function of the regulative ideal is to help the less-than-fully-virtuous agent figure out what she ought to do, then we can secure this normative function without the further claim that her resulting actions should also be fluid and harmonious. In fact, as we'll see, for *ordinary human agents*, there is real value in the disruptive signal and motivational push to reassess that come with anxiety.

deliberation once skill/virtue has been acquired (e.g., Dreyfus & Dreyfus, 2004; Railton, 2009; Velleman, 2008). However, we have seen that these alternative proposals lack the resources needed to respond to skeptics (section 5.2; more on this in section 5.5). But in addition to this negative conclusion, a positive lesson also emerges. The refugee case and the firefighter research suggest that virtuous thought and action involve both a tendency to feel uneasy about how to act as one's situation grows increasingly unfamiliar, and a tendency for that unease to prompt a reassessment of one's initial intentions. I take this, in turn, to motivate the idea that practical anxiety—particularly in its consciously experienced form—is central to a plausible account of the psychology that undergirds virtuous agency. That is, it is a psychological mechanism that gets us deliberating about novel and difficult situations—situations where automatic processes alone are unable to provide guidance about what to do. In what follows, I show how building on what we have learned about practical anxiety allows us to develop a better skill-based defense of deliberation. With this in hand, we will be positioned to see how a moral psychology that incorporates practical anxiety also provides Humeans and Kantians with the makings of a reply to the antideliberationist challenge.

5.4 Vindicating Deliberation

To understand how practical anxiety can help a neo-Aristotelian like Annas demonstrate that there is a genuine and essential role for deliberation, recall from chapter 3 that practical anxiety differs from other varieties of anxiety in important ways. Of particular note for present purposes are the differences between practical anxiety and social anxiety (or punishment anxiety more generally). As we have seen, practical anxiety is an emotion that integrates an awareness of situations where you face a novel or difficult choice with epistemic behaviors—deliberation, reflection, information gathering, and the like—that are geared toward helping you work through your uncertainty about what to do. Here a paradigmatic example is the anxiety you felt about your Alzheimer's-stricken mother (chapter 4). Social anxiety, by contrast, is an emotion that combines a sensitivity to occasions where one might be evaluated or observed by others with a broad set of risk-minimization behaviors—deference, caution, preemptive apologies, and the like. This combination can help individuals manage a wide range of social challenges and complexities. Here a paradigmatic example is the anxiety you felt at the dinner party: you wanted to make a good impression on those at the party, but the sudden change in rapport during your exchange with a new acquaintance made you anxious (section 3.5). It both signaled that you might have said or done something silly, and prompted you to become more deferential (e.g., apologizing for an earlier, potentially embarrassing comment).

We have also seen that these two varieties of anxiety bring different motivational orientations (section 3.3.1). In the case of practical anxiety, you are uncertain about what the correct thing to do is, and so tend to engage in epistemic behaviors driven by a concern to get it right. By contrast, social anxiety is elicited in situations where you might be evaluated by others, and so tends to rely on more defensive and self-interested behavior—for example, deference, preemptive apologies, and efforts to make excuses for your faux pas. This reveals an important contrast: in practical anxiety one is oriented toward concerns for *accuracy*, while in social anxiety we see a more *ego-defensive* motivational orientation. Moreover, that these two varieties of anxiety engage different underlying motivational tendencies makes sense: practical anxiety's accuracy orientation fits well with our understanding of it as a sensitivity to novel or difficult choices; social anxiety's ego-defensive orientation meshes with our account of it as a sensitivity to being evaluated by others.

We get further support for this account of practical anxiety's distinctive motivational orientation from the research investigating the effects that different emotions have on political decision making discussed in chapter 3. Recall, for instance, the work of the MacKuen team. They investigated how feelings of anger and anxiety in response to a challenge to one's political policy preferences affect one's subsequent attitudes and actions. To explore this, they presented individuals with a fake news story that challenged their views about the appropriateness of affirmative action policy. This challenge not only provoked distinct emotions—anger in some, anxiety in others—but also brought emotion-specific differences in behavior. Individuals for whom the fake news story provoked anxiety displayed a greater tendency to seek out more information about affirmative action policy, a greater interest in learning more about both sides of the issue, and an increased willingness to explore new solutions. By contrast, those who experienced anger were less interested in informing themselves, and when they did seek out more information, they tended to just look for things in line with their initial views about affirmative action policy. The Valentino team not only replicated these results but also showed that anxiety (but not anger, fear, or enthusiasm) had positive effects on knowledge and understanding. In the present context, these results are significant because the different patterns of behavior we find between the anxious participants and those who experienced anger suggest that these emotions engage different underlying motivations. The open-minded inquiry and enhanced understanding that we see in the anxious individuals point to an accuracy motivation—a concern to get it right. The more biased search of the angry subjects, by contrast, suggests a more defensive orientation.

With this refresher on practical and social anxiety in hand, we can turn to the antideliberationist challenge. The task for proponents of deliberation, recall, was twofold: demonstrate that there's an essential place for deliberation in our account of virtuous thought and action, and do so while accommodating the empirical data that underlies skepticism about the possibility of genuine practical deliberation. The response, in brief, is this. Deliberation is essential to our ability to choose (and so behave) virtuously in the face of difficult and novel situations. However, observations of the sort we just reviewed suggest that we can engage in such deliberation in large part because of emotions like practical anxiety. In fact, practical anxiety seems uniquely well-suited to play this role—it's an emotion that both automatically signals that we face a difficult or novel choice and engages the genuine reasoning that helps bring good practical judgment.[29]

Let's start with the question of why deliberation is essential. As the cases we have been looking at reveal, deliberation is crucial when we face novel or difficult practical decisions. There are at least two reasons for this. First, in the face of a hard or novel choice—Should I give more to those in need? What should I do about my Alzheimer's-stricken mother?—we lack the knowledge and experience necessary to be guided by automatic processes, hence the need to think and gather more information about what the best course of action is. Second, hard and novel cases involve increased uncertainty as well as a greater chance of error. So they are situations where we

---

29. See Tappolet (2016, chap. 5) for a complementary discussion of the (positive) role that emotions can play in guiding practical thought.

demand the cautious, (re)evaluation that comes with careful deliberation (sections 5.3 and 4.3).

These observations help us better understand both the importance of deliberation and the role of practical anxiety. For instance, while Annas is correct that deliberation can help us develop more efficiently as agents, we can now see that its real value lies in helping us figure out what to do when we face the uncertainty of a difficult or new situation—situations where automatic mechanisms and past experience provide insufficient guidance about what to do. Moreover, given that the situations where deliberation is needed are ones involving both uncertainty about what to do and a demand for caution, we should expect practical anxiety to be a central part of the explanation for how this deliberation is engaged. Practical anxiety, after all, is an emotion that is in the business of engaging deliberation in the face of novel and difficult decisions.

With this in mind, we can turn to the second chore: providing an account of how deliberation is engaged that both (i) fits with the skeptics' observation that practical judgment starts from and is (largely) driven by automatic processes, and (ii) explains why the resulting reason-giving behavior should be understood as genuine, open-minded deliberation and not a motivated, post hoc rationalization of a decision one has already made.

Consider task (i). As we saw, when confronted with the doctor's recommendation to put your mother in a care facility, you started to deliberate. Moreover, you did so *because* of the anxiety you felt. Given our account of how practical anxiety signals problematic uncertainty, we can now see both why this is and how it allows us to respond to antideliberationist skeptics. In short, practical anxiety is an emotion—an automatic mechanism—that helps us see that we face a difficult decision and that kicks us into conscious deliberation to help us figure out what to do. In the language of dual-process theory, it is a type 1 mechanism that detects novel/difficult situations and engages type 2 processes to address what type 1 mechanisms alone cannot accomplish. Thus, we can agree with the skeptics that practical decision making is grounded in, and driven by, automatic processes while nonetheless insisting that there is an essential place for genuine deliberation—namely, in helping us work through difficult choices when automatic mechanisms alone are not enough.

Turning to task (ii), does practical anxiety bring genuine deliberation? The cases we have been looking at suggest it does: the anxiety you felt both about whether you were giving too much to the refugees and what you should do for your mother brought genuine epistemic behaviors—information gathering, reflection, deliberation, and the like—that were aimed at helping you work through those difficult decisions. But one might be skeptical. After all, as intuitive as these cases are, they can only do so much to establish that the reason-giving behavior that practical anxiety tends to bring represents, not post hoc rationalization, but rather the type of genuine deliberation conducive to good decision making. To address this concern, we can return to the research from the MacKuen and Valentino teams. As we saw, individuals made anxious by the challenge to their beliefs about political policies displayed a greater interest in learning more about both sides of the issue, an increased willingness to consider alternative proposals, and improved understanding. Open-minded inquiry of this sort suggests these individuals are engaged in a genuine effort to think through the challenge to their policy preferences, and not a motivated search for evidence that will help support their preexisting views. That latter kind of behavior seems a better description of the individuals who became angry in response to the challenge—they were not only less willing to explore new solutions, but also tended to only seek out information in line with their antecedent beliefs.

By bringing additional empirical support to our account of practical anxiety as a psychological mechanism that kicks us into genuine deliberation, the results from MacKuen, Valentino, and others help undermine the thought that our reason-giving behavior is, for all we know, just a post hoc rationalization. But we can do better. To see this, recall the differences in motivational orientation that we observed between social and practical anxiety. Unlike the ego-defensive motivations associated with social anxiety, practical anxiety—as a response provoked in the face of a novel or difficult decision—tends to bring a concern for *accuracy*. As such (and in contrast to social anxiety), it is more likely to generate genuine, open-minded inquiry rather than motivated, post hoc rationalizations. In fact, recognizing this helps us explain in a principled and empirically grounded manner both *when* purported instances of anxiety-provoked deliberation will bring genuine reasoning, and *why* this is. Deliberation provoked by practical anxiety will tend to be genuine because it is driven by accuracy motivations. By contrast, "deliberation" provoked by social anxiety will more often take the form of self-serving rationalizations because it is shaped by a desire to make a particular impression on others. So while the skeptic may be right that we confabulate and engage in motivated, post hoc "deliberation," he is wrong to think we cannot explain when and why our reason-giving behavior is doing genuine, substantive work.[30]

So, with this, we have an answer to the twofold challenge facing deliberationists. The antideliberationists are wrong to think that deliberation is of little or no consequence. As we can now see, deliberation is essential to our ability to work through novel and difficult choices, and we can engage in it because of emotions like practical anxiety. In fact, given its distinctive functional profile (section 3.3), practical anxiety is uniquely well equipped to engage the reflection and reassessment one needs in situations like these—situations that highlight why deliberation is essential to virtuous human agency. However, one might worry that the above vindication of deliberation is too hasty. After all, implicit in this defense is the assumption that practical anxiety can contribute to the *good* decision making that makes for virtuous agency. This claim may seem suspect given the trouble we know anxiety can bring—cycles of unproductive rumination and worry, avoidance, impulsive responses, and the like.

But recall that we have seen worries of this sort before (chapter 4). And we have seen that they fall short for two reasons. First, they fail to appreciate the difference between practical anxiety with its accuracy orientation, and things like social and punishment anxiety with their more ego-defensive motivations. So while it is true that anxiety can lead us astray, this is more likely to happen when we are dealing with social/punishment anxiety. In fact, given its focus on accuracy, practical anxiety is likely to engage the constructive epistemic practices we are looking for. On this front, we find support from recent empirical work showing that, while moderate levels of anxiety appear to affect how one goes about solving complex problems (e.g., more initial information gathering, narrower focus), it does not produce inferior results (Spering, Wagener, & Funke, 2005; also De Drue,

---

30. The claim in the text about the differences in motivational orientation that we find between practical and social anxiety, and the associated differences in behavior they bring, fits nicely with empirical work investigating the ways different underlying motivations (e.g., motivations for accuracy or ego defense) affect decision making and other behavior. See, for instance, Chen, Shechter, and Chaiken (1996). This, of course, is consistent with (practical) anxiety also engaging less epistemically virtuous behavior. I take this issue up below.

Baas, & Nijstad, 2008) and can even improve performance (recall, e.g., the discussion of Jamieson's research on harnessing anxiety in the context of GRE testing from section 4.2.2).

Second, and more significantly, practical anxiety is a psychological capacity we can learn to use more effectively. In this regard, it is no different from anger or fear—the value of these emotions is enhanced as we learn to experience them at the right times and in the right ways. In the context of practical anxiety, effective emotional regulation will involve learning to recognize, for instance, when our unease is the result of uncertainty about what the correct thing to do is (as opposed to uncertainty about, say, whether we will be evaluated or embarrassed). This cultivating of practical anxiety will also involve developing the ability to appropriately channel the unease we are experiencing. In the face of a difficult decision such as what to do about your Alzheimer's-stricken mother, you could relieve your anxiety by heading to the corner bar for a drink or trying to dump the decision off on a relative. But doing that would amount to just avoiding the source of your anxiety. Appropriately addressing your anxiety will involve things like working through your uncertainty about how best to satisfy your mother's needs and wishes, and resisting your inclination to just duck the decision you face. On this front, effective reappraisal strategies can help—as we have seen, one does better when one sees one's anxiety as energizing or enhancing rather than debilitating and destructive (section 4.2.2).

Developing a better understanding of how to cultivate anxiety (and emotion in general) is an important, largely empirical project. While I will have more to say on this front in chapter 6, three general points merit emphasis here. First, providing an account of emotion regulation is essential to *any* account of virtuous agency—so in noting that we need to do this with regard to practical anxiety, we are not adding anything new. Second, Annas's skill model gives us a start on how to proceed with cultivating our anxiety—namely, through explicit instruction and the use of examples. Finally, and most significantly, with regard to practical anxiety, we are likely in a *better* position to develop a plausible, substantive account of what this cultivation involves—for we can draw on the significant work that's already been done in clinical and social psychology.

At this point, however, one might raise a related worry. Empirical work by the psychologist Tim Wilson and colleagues suggests that reflection on one's reasons can, at least in certain circumstances, lead us to make worse decisions. For instance, individuals asked to think about their reasons for preferring one kind of strawberry jam in a taste test were less satisfied with their choice than those who did not reflect (Wilson, 2002; Wilson & Schooler, 1991). One might take results like these to suggest that, even if we do engage in genuine deliberation—anxiety provoked or otherwise—it's likely to bring bad results.

In response, I make three points. First, this research does not specifically target anxiety-provoked deliberation. Rather, it suggests that deliberation and reflection *in general* can undermine decision making in certain situations. Thus, it does not raise a special problem for anxiety. Second, it is not clear whether these results regarding one's decisions about the best-tasting jam are relevant to the kinds of situations we are focused on—namely, situations where one faces problematic uncertainty about what to do.[31] Finally, and most significantly, Wilson's own work suggests that the negative effects deliberation can have diminish as one acquires expertise with the kind of decision at hand (e.g., Halberstadt & Green, 2008; Halberstadt & Wilson, 2008; also Tiberius, 2013). Thus, we can acknowledge Wilson's experimental results, but still insist that they fail to undermine our understanding of the role that deliberation plays in virtuous agency: even though practical anxiety can go awry, this does not mean that it always will (in fact, it won't) or that there is nothing we can do to address its failing (there is: recall, e.g., the discussion of chapters 3 and 4).

5.5 Toward a Better Skill-Based Account of Virtuous Agency

We now have our response to the challenge: deliberation is essential because automatic mechanisms alone are not enough to help us work through novel and difficult decisions. This is where antideliberationists go wrong—they fail to fully appreciate the limits of automatic mechanisms and so overlook the crucial role deliberation plays. That said, practical decision making is still very much grounded in, and driven by, automatic processes: routine decisions often do not require conscious deliberation. But when deliberation is needed, it is engaged via automatic mechanisms—and, as we've

---

31. The experiment on reason-reflection and questions about whether one should stay in a romantic relationship might be an exception, though the generality of the experimental set up make it hard to say. See Wilson and Kraft (1993) for details.

seen, given its distinctive functional profile, practical anxiety is uniquely suited to do this. Moreover, we needn't deny that much of our reason-giving behavior is mere confabulation. But we can insist that, whether it is, will turn in important ways on our underlying motivations—is it driven by a desire for accuracy or something else?

It is also worth emphasizing that in acknowledging the significance of practical anxiety, we also do not need to deny that Annas's skill model captures important features of virtue and its development: learning is more efficient when it comes via examples and a drive to aspire; virtuous thought and action can (often) be fluid, harmonious, and free of psychological conflict. The problem lies in thinking that her version of the skill model captures all that matters. We have seen that it does not. Emotions—both ones that are pleasant to experience and ones that aren't—matter for our ability to (learn to) be virtuous. We are virtuous, at times, because of the psychological conflict and anxiety we experience.

Recognizing this suggests that if we are interested in a skill-based account of virtuous agency, we are likely to do better if we move away from the two assumptions that bring trouble to Annas's proposal: (i) skills and virtue acquisition must be the product of explicit instruction that gives a person the ability to explain why they did what she did, and (ii) once skills and virtue have been acquired, all subsequent action is fluid, harmonious, and deliberation-free. In this regard, the skill-based accounts we find in work by Peter Railton (2009), David Velleman (2008), and Herbert Dreyfus and Stuart Dreyfus (2004) look quite promising. These proposals rely on less intellectualized accounts of skill/virtue acquisition and they acknowledge that virtuous action can require deliberation and reflection.[32]

However, while these proposals may certainly avoid some of the problems that undermine Annas's version of the skill model, they also lack the resources to answer antideliberationists. The problem, in short, is that while Railton, Velleman, and the Dreyfuses acknowledge the need for

---

32. Brownstein (2014) argues that, like Annas, Railton and Velleman are committed to skilled/virtuous agents *always* being able to articulate their reasons for acting one way rather than another, and so are just as vulnerable to the charge of overintellectualization. But Brownstein's argument relies on an uncharitable reading of the Railton and Velleman proposals. They qualify their claims about the extent to which agents will be able to explain their actions in a way that Annas does not, and so are not susceptible to Brownstein's charge of overintellectualization.

genuine deliberation, they say almost nothing about how it's engaged. For instance, Railton (2009) identifies "the ability to detect, without reflecting and deliberating, conditions calling for reflection and deliberation" as a competency that we must have if we're to exhibit the reasons responsiveness that is characteristic of human agency (p. 108). Similarly, Velleman (2008) maintains that much human agency is automatic in the sense of being free of conscious self-regulation. Yet he also holds that our "capacity for [conscious] self-regulation remains in reserve in case it is needed" (p. 188). For their part, the Dreyfuses (2004) note that "an expert facing a novel situation ..., like a beginner, must resort to [deliberation via] abstract principles" (p. 241). But in all three cases, we get little beyond the providing of examples where it seems intuitively plausible that mechanisms of conscious deliberation/reflection have been engaged.

But merely pointing to such examples is not enough. Because these examples provide no details about the underlying psychological mechanisms—much less how they are engaged—what we get is less an answer to our question than an illustration of what needs to be explained in the first place. Thus, the proposals provide little that could be used in response to antideliberationists who maintain these examples aren't really examples of conscious deliberation, but rather just instances of confabulation and post hoc rationalization.

Notice, however, that these difficulties go away if we incorporate a role for practical anxiety into the moral psychology of these proposals. After all, it is an automatic mechanism that is in the business of engaging conscious deliberation and reflection when automatic processes alone prove insufficient. So it is something Railton, Velleman, and the Dreyfuses can point to to explain—as we just did—how genuine, nonconfabulatory deliberation can be engaged. The upshot, then, is that if you are interested in a skill-based account of virtuous agency that can silence antideliberationist skeptics, you should build from a psychology that takes seriously the work that practical anxiety can do.

5.6 Further Implications: Humean and Kantian Virtue

The discussion so far might leave the impression that practical anxiety only matters for (neo-Aristotelian) skill-based accounts of good decision making and virtuous agency. That's not the case. Humean and Kantian proposals also have trouble explaining how, in the face of the antideliberationist challenge, genuine deliberation is possible. And, as we will see, these proposals do better if they acknowledge the importance of practical anxiety.

5.6.1 Humean Virtuous Agency

As we noted above (section 5.1), Valerie Tiberius presents, in a Humean spirit, a procedural account of virtuous agency and its development. At a gloss, living well—making wise choices about what to do—involves acting in accordance with the values that you reflectively endorse. Let's take a closer look at the details of her proposal.

A central feature of Tiberius's account is her move to understand virtuous agency in terms of action that accords with one's values—where one's values are the ends, commitments, goals, and so on that one reflectively endorses. So, for instance, the judgment that I ought to honor my promise is a good decision (in the sense of being appropriately responsive to my reasons) just in case it accords with a value—promise keeping—that I reflectively endorse. Elaborating, Tiberius (2008) explains that "in order to take our commitments to have the authority to guide us, we must have the conviction that there is something good about them. This conviction requires confidence in the value of the commitment" (p. 31). Moreover, we have confidence in our convictions "when we take ourselves to be justified in pursuing [them] ..., which in turn means that we have something to say in answer to the question 'Why go for that?' A justification in this context is a set of considerations or a story that fosters confidence, prevents undermining doubt, and contributes to stability" (p. 27).[33]

Thus, for Tiberius, the reflective endorsement of a particular end is a matter of one's conviction: one's belief that a justifying set of considerations (a "story" in the above sense) could be provided to explain why the end in question (promise keeping, say) is valuable. Moreover, the strength of one's conviction—what she calls *confidence*—is a function of the stability

---

33. It is important to recognize (especially in the context of the antideliberationist challenge) that while conviction requires that one believe one's values to be justified, the substance of this belief—the kind of story one needs—is thin. As Tiberius (2008) explains, "Taking yourself to be justified, in my view, means that you *think* a story could be told, not that you are actually prepared to tell it. More importantly, this story need *not* be one that is philosophically illuminating" (p. 28, emphasis added; cf. p. 36).

and coherence of one's story: when the overall set of ends, commitments, beliefs, and so on that underlie one's story about why (say) promises are valuable forms an integrated whole (i.e., when it exhibits sufficient coherence), one become defeasibly disposed not to reconsider the various pieces of that story (i.e., it becomes stable).

To this picture of reflective endorsement, Tiberius adds an account of learning that explains how individuals can bring greater coherence and stability to their values and commitments. On her account, learning "is a dialectic process that takes seriously the verdicts of critical reflection and the teachings of experience" (p. 84). More specifically, she maintains that, on the one hand, we must occasionally reflect on our values, and must take the resulting conclusions seriously: our assessments of particular ends and commitments, "insofar as they are justified, must at some point be grounded in a reflective conception of the good life" (p. 85). But, on the other hand, since she is sensitive to the antideliberationist challenge, she is hesitant to place too much weight on reflection: "A wise person must be guided by her reflective values in some sense, but being a reflective agent does not mean engaging in deep contemplation and justification of one's projects at all times" (pp. 65, 77). Rather, it means having "the capacity to use what we learn from experience and to judge when our being engaged in a particular way manifests a problem with our character or with our ability to pursue other values" (p. 88).

Tying this together gives us the following. For Tiberius, there is a series of causal connections that lead from (i) the coherence of one's ends, commitments, beliefs, and so forth (one's "story"), to (ii) the stability of one's disposition to not reconsider them, to (iii) one's confidence, and ultimately to (iv) one's conviction (or doubt) in a particular end. Moreover, as we have seen, the coherence of one's overall set of ends, commitments, beliefs, and so on is the product of one's experiences and critical reflections. Thus, we get a picture in which reflection and experience bring changes in (i), which in turn bring corresponding changes in (ii)–(iv). The resulting model looks something like what is depicted in figure 5.1.

But while Tiberius's model provides a Humean picture of how deliberation and reflection can play a role in helping individuals become more responsive to the reasons they have, it is (like the neo-Aristotelian proposals considered above) vulnerable to antideliberationist skeptics. This is because, as figure 5.1 makes plain, her proposal provides no account of how

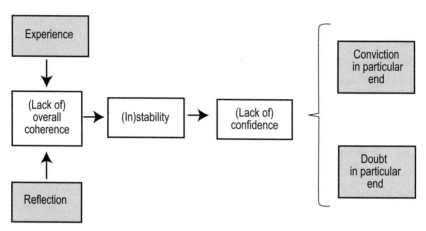

Figure 5.1
Model of Tiberius's Account of Reflective Endorsement. White boxes represent unconscious processes, gray boxes involve (possibly) conscious ones.

reflection is engaged. It—quite literally—just dangles free in her account. So there is reason to worry that the regress problem has not been adequately addressed,[34] or for that matter whether we have an account of why the resulting reflection and deliberation are genuine, not confabulatory.

To better see this, consider the following example that Tiberius provides as an illustration of her dialectical account of learning through reflection and experience:

> Ideally, as we develop and continue to reflect, our reflection has more influence over the judgments we make when we're not being reflective. For example, as one's judgments about what counts as selfish change in response to more mature reflection on the needs of others, the automatic judgments one makes about what counts as selfish without engaging in reflection will also change. (p. 84)

While this example helps explain how much decision making and agency can be reasons responsive even if they are not the product of explicit reflection, it does not provide an account of how one can engage reflection without reflecting on when to engage reflection. How is it, for instance, that one comes to recognize the need for "more mature reflection on the needs of others"?[35]

---

34. Arpaly and Schroeder (2014) press a related worry against an earlier version of Tiberius's account.
35. Elsewhere, Tiberius (2013) points to a conceptual connection between justifying a claim and articulating the reasons for it. As she explains, one "cannot make an

Based on Tiberius's comments regarding a similar issue, her answer seems to be that, through experience, one develops an ability to *just see* when reflection is needed: "The wise person is open to the intuitions, feelings, and perceptions that draw her attention to the relevant reasons without fully engaging her rational capacities. ... This appreciation of reasons is not an explicit rational acknowledgement, but *something more like an intuition or impression*" (p. 81, emphasis added). While this reply makes some progress, it raises the worry—one that Tiberius herself is sensitive to (p. 15)—that the move just switches one puzzle for another: we wanted to know how reflection is engaged without regress, and now we want to know whether this claim about our ability to "perceive" reasons is anything more than an appeal to "the bogus epistemology of intuitionism" (McDowell, 1998, p. 162).[36]

---

assessment that [one is] being directed by the right values without talking about reasons, and we therefore cannot make an assessment that we are being directed by the right values without some kind of reflection on reasons" (pp. 229–230). She is right to note that this connection provides important resources for explaining to antideliberationist skeptics how we resolve conflicting judgments in a principled manner. But it adds little with regard to the issue at hand—namely, explaining how we come to recognize the need for reflection in the first place. For notice that her proposal just starts from our having become consciously aware of a conflict in our judgments. So until we have a better understanding of both how we become aware of this conflict and why such recognition leads to genuine reflection, we have no response to antideliberationists who question whether our "assessment" of our reasons represents genuine reflection or merely self-serving, post hoc rationalization.

36. We find a similar difficulty in the Humean proposal developed in Arpaly and Schroeder (2014). Like Tiberius, they are wary of the antideliberationist challenge, but they want to show that deliberation can play an important role in virtuous agency. Their account of deliberation's role takes the form of the example of Harold. Because of poor memory, Harold recognizes that he is uncertain if agreeing to meet his son at the airport will lead him to break a promise to be elsewhere. Given his uncertainty, Harold begins to consciously reflect on the question of whether he has a prior commitment. Unpacking this, Arpaly and Schroeder explain that Harold's uncertainty about what to do, in combination with his desire not to break promises and his "desir[e] to know what to do ... leads him to begin deliberation" (p. 48). In a way, this is progress. Arpaly and Schroeder's focus on desire and uncertainty implicates a specific psychological mechanism as the driver of Harold's deliberation: his deliberation is brought about by the combination of his *desire* to know what to do and his *uncertainty* about what to do. But this proposal is inadequate for the same sort of reason that Tiberius's is—for it just starts from the assumption that Harold

Here's where things stand. We need a way to get genuine regress-free reflection into Tiberius's model. The key lies in incorporating practical anxiety. As we saw in the above discussion of Annas's skill model, practical anxiety functions as an alarm: it is an emotion (a type 1 mechanism) that functions to disrupt current behaviors and prompt reassessment (type 2 processing). Thus, it's a mechanism of the very sort that Tiberius needs.

Recognizing the importance of practical anxiety, we can revise Tiberius's proposal as follows. First, and as in her account, changes that undermine coherence trigger instability that in turn triggers a reduction in confidence. But, contra her proposal, this reduction in confidence does not lead to an automatic reduction in conviction. Rather, that link is mediated by practical anxiety. More specifically, since one's reduction in confidence introduces uncertainty, it can—if sufficiently robust—trigger practical anxiety. This anxiety, as we have seen, disrupts current behavior and prompts reassessment (via epistemic behaviors like reflection, deliberation, and information gathering). This reassessment may, in turn, reveal evidence or insights that restore coherence and thus stability and confidence. But it might not, in which case confidence is (further) reduced and conviction is undermined (at least to some degree). The resulting model of anxiety-induced reflective endorsement (AIRE) is depicted in figure 5.2.

The AIRE model brings two benefits. First, it shows us how regress-free reflection is possible. After all, since, on this model, reflection is triggered via a type 1 process—namely, practical anxiety—the worry that engaging reflection will launch a regress disappears. Second, our discussion to this point provides us with a rich understanding of practical anxiety as a psychological mechanism that generates genuine (nonconfabulatory) reasoning. As such, we have the kind of detailed explanation of how reflection and deliberation can be engaged that Tiberius's Humean proposal requires.

---

is aware of his uncertainty. But until we have an understanding of how he becomes aware of that, skeptics can plausibly maintain that we have no reason to think the case is best described as one where Harold consciously deliberates about what to do rather than one where he is merely rationalizing a conclusion he has already (unconsciously) come to.

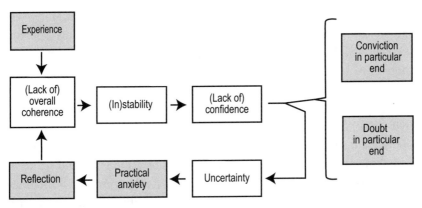

Figure 5.2
Model of Anxiety-Induced Reflective Endorsement. White boxes represent unconscious processes, gray boxes involve (possibly) conscious ones.

5.6.2 Kantian Virtuous Agency

While it might not be surprising that an emotion like practical anxiety could play an important role in a Humean account of virtuous agency, the thought that it also has a place in Kantian proposals might seem less plausible. The Kantian, after all, gives primacy to the rational—not the emotional—dimension of human psychology. Recall Kant's (1797/1996) claim that the virtuous individual is one who "bring[s] all his capacities and inclinations under his (reason's) control and so to rule over himself" (p. 536). But this thinking is too quick. Kant's account of moral education is more nuanced—it allows that emotions, both positive and negative, have an important role to play in the development of virtue (section 4.4.2). This is important because, as we will see, Kant and Kantians are also vulnerable to antideliberationist skeptics—and bringing in emotions like practical anxiety can help them avoid this.

To draw this out, it will be helpful to turn, not to Kant's rather cryptic remarks on emotion and virtue, but rather to Barbara Herman's (1993) sophisticated account of Kantian moral agency. Two features of her proposal are noteworthy for our purposes. First, and in line with our previous conclusions, her account specifies an essential but limited role for conscious deliberation: she notes that deliberation is not something we are always engaged in, but rather something we need to do only when we face a novel or difficult moral situation (pp. 77–78, 145–146, 157). Moreover, she recognizes that a significant aspect of a person's moral development involves acquiring the moral knowledge that "enable[s] him to pick out those elements of his circumstances or of his proposed actions that require moral attention" (p. 77). This knowledge—these "rules of moral salience" (RMS)—are pieces of content that "constitute the structure of moral sensitivity [that] indicate when certain sorts of action should not be taken without moral justification" (p. 78). As such, they "[flag] circumstances of moral conflict (or uncertainty)" for which moral deliberation is needed (p. 157). As Herman explains, "When the rules of moral salience are well internalized, they *cause* the agent to be aware of and attentive to the significance of 'moral danger'" (p. 78, emphasis added). So, for example, what gets the individual in Kant's lying-promises example to deliberate about whether he should make an insincere promise is "his feeling" that, in so doing, he may be making himself an exception to the moral rule that one ought not to make lying promises for personal gain. This, Herman tell us, "is the mark of his 'conscience'" (pp. 77–78, quoting Kant, 1785/1996, p. 74).

In the present context, Herman's proposal is significant in several respects. First, in line with our conclusions from sections 5.3 and 5.4, she notes that deliberation's essential function lies in helping individuals work through novel and difficult circumstances. Moreover, she also emphasizes the role of moral education in helping one develop the sensitivity and attunement necessary to recognize when moral deliberation is needed. Finally (following Kant), she identifies conscience—understood, for her, as an affective capacity: a "feeling"—as the operative mechanism that kicks one into conscious deliberation about whether one's proposed action is in line with moral law. However, despite these virtues, there is still room for antideliberationists to introduce their skepticism. For instance, why think that the individual in the lying-promises case is actually deliberating? More specifically, what reason do we have to take this talk of "conscience" as picking out a mechanism that prompts genuine thought and reflection and not, instead, as mere window dressing on his confabulations?

In response, a Kantian like Herman would do well to draw on what we have learned about practical anxiety. In particular, she could replace her vague talk of a "feeling" that one's action might not be morally correct (and the associated gestures toward "conscience") with our account of practical anxiety.[37] More specifically, the suggestion is that through moral education, one comes to internalize a set of rules of moral salience—rules that give shape to one's practical anxiety. With this in hand, she could then add that the resulting practical anxiety makes one attuned and responsive to occasions of moral conflict and novelty: when one feels anxious about whether the action one is contemplating is morally justified, one is kicked into conscious deliberation to assess the decision at hand.[38] Thus, Herman still could maintain that what is distinctive about "the Kantian agent's moral sensibility" is that his "responsiveness is shaped by moral knowledge (from the RMS), and his attendant motivation includes a higher-order (or regulative) concern for the permissibility of his actions and projects" (p. 83). But she now has the additional resources that come with our account of practical anxiety. And so she has what she needs to answer the antideliberationist challenge.

5.7 Conclusion

The key insight from the investigation of this chapter is that practical anxiety has a central role to play in our understanding of the psychology of virtuous human agency. A wide range of views about what good moral and practical decision making involves—Aristotelian, Humean, and Kantian—maintain that conscious deliberation and reflection are essential to virtuous thought and action. But, as we have learned, they have trouble responding to a set of skeptical challenges to the claim that deliberation matters for virtuous agency. Silencing this skepticism requires a psychological account of how genuine deliberation can be engaged, given the data indicating that practical judgment starts from and is largely driven by nondeliberative mechanisms.

Enter practical anxiety. It is a nondeliberative mechanism that functions to kick us into conscious deliberation in the face of novel or difficult

---

37. More cautiously (given the discussion in chapter 4), the Kantian could draw on our conclusions about the *instrumental* value of practical anxiety, but set aside the further claims about its aretaic and (possible) intrinsic value.

38. In fact, the strategy is something that, as we saw in chapter 4, Kant may have been (imperfectly) wise to, given his comments about the connection between conscience and anxiety.

decisions—situations where automatic mechanisms alone provide insufficient guidance about what to do. So by incorporating anxiety into our understanding of the psychology that undergirds virtuous agency, we get an account with the resources needed to answer the skeptics. Moreover, practical anxiety is a mechanism that can also be tuned in ways that promote good moral decision making and virtuous agency. But notice: all this suggests that anxiety is likely to have an important role in driving moral progress. This next chapter pursues this thought.

6 Progress: Anxiety and Moral Improvement

Nothing in human affairs is worthy of great anxiety.
—Plato

A central conclusion of chapter 5 was that we are better able to make sense of virtuous human agency and good decision making to the extent that we recognize the important role that practical anxiety plays in our psychology. This is significant. If practical anxiety is crucial to our ability to make good decisions, then we should expect it to be a central driver of moral progress—not just progressive changes in an individual's moral beliefs and attitudes but also larger-scale, societal-level progressive changes. The discussion that follows assesses this prediction. In so doing, we will be tackling the Puzzle of Progress. That puzzle, recall, asks whether anxiety is an impediment to, or facilitator of, progressive moral change. It also raises questions about what a better understanding of anxiety might tell us about the nature and prospects of moral progress more generally.

My strategy is as follows. I begin by looking at historical examples where practical anxiety—or better, a moralized version of it—can be seen as playing an important role in effecting large-scale change in moral beliefs and attitudes. In particular, we will see evidence that practical anxiety is a central feature of the psychology of moral reformers and so in moral reform (section 6.1). But we will also see that anxiety can be a driver of resistance to moral change (section 6.2). Recognizing this raises questions about when and why anxiety contributes to progressive change, as well as questions about the extent to which we can influence anxiety's impact on moral decision making and assessment. Here I will argue that practical anxiety can contribute to moral progress, though the extent to which it can will turn on (empirical) questions about our ability to cultivate our anxiety. Here I draw on lessons from part I regarding our understanding of anxiety as a biocognitive emotion in order to defend a modest optimism about our ability to shape (practical) anxiety for the better (sections 6.3 and 6.4).

6.1 Anxiety and Moral Improvement

If practical anxiety is central to good decision making and agency, then we should see evidence of it contributing in distinctive and important ways to instances of moral reform. I believe we do see evidence of this and so have support for the prediction that comes out of the discussion of chapter 5—namely, that anxiety matters for moral progress. However, in claiming that practical anxiety is an important driver of moral progress, I am not claiming that it is a moral elixir—a feature of our psychology that has an outsized ability to bring beneficial moral change. Clearly it is not. Any plausible account of moral progress will need to identify a range of social and psychological features that are important for explaining the occasions of moral progress we find in the historical record—expansions in civil rights, greater economic justice, a move away from "an eye for an eye" forms of punishment, and the like.[1] Thus, the project here is the more modest one of showing that a plausible account of the drivers of moral progress must acknowledge anxiety's role.

To do this, I will begin by presenting a pair of historical examples that provide initial support for the claim that anxiety has played a role in driving moral improvement. In particular, I look to autobiographies and the historical record to develop a picture of the moral psychology of moral reformers like John Woolman and Martin Luther King Jr.—for it's here that we see practical anxiety playing a distinctive and important role. A benefit of this method is that it allows us to focus on the part these reformers played in shaping actual instances of moral progress. This will, in turn, position us for a more detailed examination of anxiety's role in progressive and regressive moral change. That said, there are obvious limitations to what historical accounts can reveal about an individual's psychology. However, as others have shown, there's also much that a careful investigation

---

1. In what follows, I assume that there has been moral progress. For recent discussions of some of the social and psychological drivers of (progressive) moral change, see Campbell and Kumar (2012); Kitcher (2011); and Pinker (2011). Cf. Mackie (1977, chap. 1).

of the historical record can tell us about moral change and its moral psychological drivers (e.g., Anderson, 2014, 2016; Campbell & Kumar, 2012; Kitcher, 2011; Nussbaum, 2001; Pinker, 2011). With these methodological preliminaries in hand, let's turn to the cases.

Case 1: John Woolman and the American Abolition Movement. Recall the case of the eighteenth-century American abolitionist John Woolman introduced in chapter 1. Woolman is considered to be one of the most influential abolitionists of his time (Cady, 1966; Kitcher, 2011, pp. 158–162; Plank, 2012). Through his writings—principally, his *Some Considerations on the Keeping of Negroes*—and his travels in colonial America and abroad, Woolman convinced many of his Quaker peers to free their slaves. Part of what makes Woolman so interesting is that his posthumously published *Journal* (1952) provides a window into the evolution of his thinking about the evils of slavery. Consider, for instance, the following passage (repeated from chapter 1) where Woolman recounts one of his early—and formative—experiences with the institution of slavery:

> My employer, having a negro woman, sold her, and desired me to write a bill of sale. … The thing was sudden; and though I felt uneasy at the thoughts of writing an instrument of slavery for one of my fellow-creatures, yet I remembered that I was hired by the year, that it was my master who directed me to do it, and that it was an elderly man, a member of our Society, who bought her; so through weakness I gave way, and wrote it; but at the executing of it I was so afflicted in my mind, that I said before my master and the Friend that I believed slave-keeping to be a practice inconsistent with the Christian religion. (pp. 26–27)

Woolman's account of his experience is particularly relevant for our discussion of anxiety and moral progress. For starters, though he wrote the bill of sale in this case, the event had a lasting effect on his beliefs and attitudes. For instance, the next time Woolman was asked to write a similar document, he refused. And the memories of the incident gave shape to much of his subsequent efforts as an abolitionist (p. 27).

More importantly, his account of this experience suggests that anxiety was a central driver of his doubts and concerns. He tells us, for instance, that he felt "*uneasy* at the thoughts of writing an instrument of slavery" and that his role in consummating the transaction left him "so *afflicted* in [his] mind" that he was moved to revise his initial thinking and protest the sale. That is, Woolman's emotions have the marks of practical anxiety: he experiences a strong feeling of unease that both *signals* that his initial inclination to write the bill of sale may be incorrect, and *prompts* his subsequent epistemic behavior—his reflection, reassessment, and ultimate decision to reverse course and protest. As further evidence that anxiety is the emotion Woolman is feeling, notice that the functional profiles of other seemingly plausible candidate emotions—guilt, embarrassment, shame—fit poorly with his account. In particular, we do not find mention of the reparatory and withdrawal behavior that we would expect to see if he was feeling one of these emotions (more on this in section 6.3.2).

Case 2: Martin Luther King Jr. and the Vietnam War. The second example concerns Martin Luther King Jr.'s decision to start publicly protesting the Vietnam War. Though King was a long-standing opponent of violence, for much of his career he was hesitant to publicly denounce the war. As he explains in his autobiography (King, 1998, pp. 333–335), his hesitation was grounded, in part, in a concern that if he were to speak out against President Johnson's foreign policy, he would undermine the administration's willingness to enact—and enforce—civil rights legislation. King's hesitation was also driven by pressure from his peers in the civil rights movement: they worried that if King started protesting the war, he would be distracted from his efforts to fight for racial and economic equality at home.

But as the Johnson administration backed away from its previously stated interest in negotiating for peace in Vietnam, King grew increasingly uncertain and concerned about his decision to remain silent: "I began the agonizing measurement of government promising words of peace against the baneful, escalating deeds of war. Doubts gnawed at my conscience. ... I agonized a great deal over this problem" (p. 334).

The result of this uncertainty and unease—and the reflection they spurred—was King's decision to speak out against the U.S. involvement in Vietnam. In a speech in Chicago on March 25, 1967, one of his first public statements against the war, he explained, "I speak out against it not in anger but *with anxiety* and sorrow in my heart" (King, 1967, emphasis added).

Like Woolman, King's decision to publicly protest the war appears to be an instance of anxiety-driven moral progress. As the war dragged on, he became increasingly "uncertain" and uncomfortable about his initial decision not to speak out: his conscience gnawed and he agonized about the problem he faced. As King explains, because of this unease and uncertainty, he started to reflect: "I went away for two months to do a lot of thinking. ... I thought about civil rights and I thought about the world situation and I thought about America" (pp. 334–335). These comments suggest King's unease about his silence—and the reflection and reassessment it brought—were undergirded by anxiety about what he was doing. He affirms this suggestion in the Chicago speech when he points to anxiety as a central driver of both his recognition that he was mistaken about the need to be silent on the war and his subsequent decision to speak out against it. While I believe this is the correct way to understand King's moral psychology, this example is not as straightforward as the Woolman case: guilt is not as easily ruled out as the emotion King was experiencing, and his change of heart seemed to come gradually in a way that suggests the anxiety he felt was a consequence, not a cause, of his decision to start protesting the war. That said, we will see (section 6.3.3) that on closer examination these concerns fade: King's case provides another example of anxiety-driven progressive change.[2]

6.2 Anxiety and Resistance to Moral Change

While the previous section pointed to an important role for anxiety in driving progressive moral change, this cannot be the whole of it. We are, after all, anxious about change and the uncertainty it brings—and these anxieties can contribute to *resistance* to moral reform. For instance, and in sharp contrast to Woolman, consider the remarks that the Duke of Wellington made before Parliament in 1833 regarding pending emancipation legislation: "Who can regard the change from a State of slavery to a state of freedom, of a population of no less than 800,000 persons, otherwise than with feelings of *anxiety*?" In saying this, the duke was expressing his worries about the speed with which the institution of slavery was being

---

2. For additional examples of anxiety-driven progressive change, see the suffragist Elizabeth Cady Stanton's account of her efforts to reconcile getting married (in an era when marriage entailed—socially and legally—accepting subordination and inferior status) with her commitment to women's equality (Stanton, 1898/1993, chaps. 2–5) and Minnie Bruce Pratt's discussion of the "vertigo" she experienced as she, an affluent, white Christian mother, started to participate in feminist consciousness-raising discussions—discussions that led her to divorce her husband, come out as a lesbian, and move into a racially mixed neighborhood (Pratt, 1984; also Harbin, 2016).

dismantled: he was concerned that slaves would be freed before "they had become civilized" (*Debates in Parliament*, 1833, pp. 533–534).

In fact, that anxiety can operate this way—as an impediment to progressive moral change—is a feature of our psychology that politicians try to manipulate. Recent immigration debates are a case in point. Setting aside the (ethical) merits of immigration in general, these debates are disconcerting in that whether or not there's opposition to immigration often turns on what the race and ethnicity of the immigrant group is.[3] Moreover—and more importantly for our purposes—anxiety appears to play a significant role in amplifying race/ethnicity-based opposition to immigration. On this point, remarks that Donald Trump (2016) made in June 2015 (when announcing his intention to run for U.S. president) are particularly striking:

> When Mexico sends its people, they're not sending their best. They're not sending you. … They're sending people that have lots of problems, and they're bringing those problems with us [*sic*]. They're bringing drugs. They're bringing crime. They're rapists. And some, I assume, are good people.

Provocations like these have been taken to be a way of garnering support by playing to underlying anxieties about the effects immigrants (at least immigrants from certain places) might have on American culture (Porter, 2016). More generally, the 2015 Public Religion Research Institute (PRRI) Survey found that Americans who report being "bothered" about immigrants who do not speak English increased notably from 40% in 2012 to 48% in 2015. Moreover, in 2015, the percentage of Americans who think immigrants are a burden on society because they take jobs, housing, and healthcare rose from 35% to 46%. Additionally, while 60% of blacks and 54% of Hispanics believe cultural change since the 1950s has mostly been for the better, 57% of whites think the change has largely been for the worse—and these views about cultural change are strongly affected by political affiliation: 59% of Democrats (and 61% of white Democrats) say America's best days lie ahead, while only 41% of Republicans and 33% of Tea Party members agree. The conclusion of the PRRI survey's authors is succinctly put in its title: "Anxiety, Nostalgia, and Mistrust"—in other

---

3. Empirical work indicates that one's level of ethnocentrism predicts whether or not one will be opposed to immigration (Kinder & Kam, 2009). Similarly, there are robust correlations between harboring negative stereotypes or implicit attitudes about Latinos, and support for more restrictive immigration policies (Burns & Gimpel, 2000).

words, there seems to be a growing tendency for (some) whites in America to resist immigration because they are anxious that allowing more minorities into the country will undermine important social and economic structures (Jones, Cox, et al., 2015).

However, while the above observations and survey results are striking, they only provide suggestive evidence that anxiety magnifies race/ethnicity-based opposition to immigration. On this front, we get more substantive support for anxiety's role from an experiment by the political scientist Ted Brader and his colleagues (Brader, Valentino, & Suhay, 2008). In this study, participants (all of whom were white) were presented with a fake *New York Times* article about a recent governor's conference on immigration. For half the participants, the story gave a positive report about immigration, while for the other half, the story painted a negative picture. The stories also varied in that they focused on either a Mexican named Jose Sanchez or a Russian named Nikolai Vandinsky (aside from the name and nationality changes, the two individuals were described in identical ways). After reading the news article, participants were then asked about how the article made them feel: anxious, proud, angry, hopeful, worried, or excited. The final part of the study asked participants about both their opinions regarding more permissive immigration policy (e.g., did they support it), and their intentions (i.e., were they interested either in receiving more information about pro-/anti-immigration policy or in sending an email to their congressperson).

The results showed that participants who read the negatively toned version of the story (about Sanchez or Vandinsky) were less supportive of immigration than were those who read the positive version of the article. However, the opposition to immigration was twice as strong for those whose negative story focused on Sanchez (in comparison to those who read a negative story about Vandinsky). More importantly, Brader and colleagues analyzed the extent to which the emotions provoked by the story affected the subsequent opposition to immigration. They found that *only anxiety* had a mediating role. In particular, their analysis revealed that (i) the combination of negative news about immigration and cueing of Hispanic stereotypes (i.e., the story focused on Sanchez, not Vandinsky) provoked anxiety, and that (ii) this anxiety caused the subsequent shifts in opinion and intentions—increased opposition to immigration, a greater desire to receive anti-immigration information, and an increased interest in emailing their congressperson. Thus, in sharp contrast to the positive assessment of Woolman and King's anxiety-induced revisions that we made above, what we see here indicates that, at least under certain conditions, anxiety will inhibit moral progress—in fact, it might be a source of regressive changes in moral beliefs and attitudes.

These observations about anxiety acting as an impediment to progressive moral change raise doubts about the optimistic conclusion from section 6.1. More specifically, if we are to vindicate the prediction that anxiety can make important contributions to moral progress, we need a principled explanation of the differences we uncovered in anxiety's effects on moral change. On this front, our discussion of the differences in distinct subtypes of anxiety in chapter 3 suggests a possibility: the anxiety driving progressive moral change of Woolman and King is underwritten by practical anxiety, but the anxiety we see driving both Wellington's resistance to emancipation and the race/ethnicity-based opposition to immigration of the Brader study is not.

In what follows, I argue that this diagnosis is correct. Whether anxiety will tend to facilitate moral progress depends on the kind of anxiety experienced—is it the practical anxiety that has been the focus of part II or something else? Answering this question will not only further validate practical anxiety's importance for moral progress, it will also provide us with a richer picture of the moral psychology that underlies changes in moral beliefs and attitudes.

6.3   Anxiety, Reformers, and Moral Improvement: A Closer Look

Recalling the discussion of chapter 3, if the changes in Woolman and King's views are examples of practical anxiety driving moral progress, then—given our understanding of what practical anxiety is—we should see evidence along the following three lines. First, Woolman and King should show signs of anxiety in the face of a difficult or novel moral choice. Second, we should see evidence that the anxiety they experience brings epistemic behaviors (reflection, deliberation, reassessment, and the like) rather than, say, avoidance, deference, or attempts to appease. Moreover, we should also see evidence that these epistemic behaviors are shaped by their concern to get it right and not (e.g.,) a desire to protect their personal interest or self-image. Finally, we should see evidence that it's their anxiety—not some other emotion—that undergirds their subsequent changes in moral beliefs and attitudes. So, for instance, an account of their experiences that makes no appeal to practical anxiety should strike us as leaving something important unexplained. Similarly, if the resistance to moral change that we saw in the Brader research on immigration is driven by something other than practical anxiety, we should either have difficulty affirming these predictions or find things that conflict with them.

In what follows, I apply these predictions to the cases we have been looking at. The results will give further support to our original assessment that practical anxiety is an important driver of moral progress: while the experiences of Woolman and King fit with our predictions, the participants in the Brader study do not. I then conclude by drawing some more general lessons about the moral psychology of moral reformers and moral reform.

6.3.1 The Brader Cases

Taking the cases in reverse order, let's start by looking more closely at the Brader findings. As we noted above, after reading the fake *New York Times* article, participants were asked to indicate whether the story made them feel anxious, proud, angry, hopeful, worried, or excited. These results were then used in the subsequent analysis showing that only anxiety magnified the participants' subsequent (negative) opinions and behaviors regarding immigration. However, this statement of their findings is a bit misleading. Though Brader and colleagues talk generally about the magnifying role of "anxiety," they also explain that the anxiety scale they used in their analysis was not just created with data from participants who reported feeling anxious after reading the article. It also included data from participants who reported feeling worried and angry (Brader, Valentino, & Suhay, 2008, pp. 967–968). Though they justify this amalgamating of the data by noting that the information associated with the 'anger' and 'anxiety' labels did not generate different results when analyzed separately, that fact is—for our purposes—quite important.

Anger, as we know (section 4.3), is strongly associated with defensive behaviors aimed at protecting oneself and one's interests. Anxiety's behavioral tendency, by contrast, is more complex: it leads to defensive behaviors only under certain conditions (e.g., the possibility of physical harm; potential social evaluation). More importantly, a defensive response tendency is *not* associated with practical anxiety (section 3.3). But notice what this means: it means that the "anxiety" we see in the Brader study is *not* plausibly understood as practical anxiety, but rather as something else (though what, exactly, is unclear).[4] Thus, the Brader findings do not fit with the above predictions (i.e., the results conflict with the expectation that response behavior will be undergirded by a concern to get it right, not a desire to protect oneself). As such, Brader's work, while important in other ways, does not cause trouble for the claim that *practical* anxiety is an important driver of moral progress.

6.3.2 The Woolman Case

Let's now take a closer look at the Woolman case—does it fit with our three predictions? It appears that it does. For starters, Woolman tells us that he "felt uneasy" when his employer ordered him to write the bill of sale. This *unease* is plausibly understood as his practical anxiety kicking in to warn him: initially, he takes the question of what to do to be answered by his obligation to fulfill his professional duties ("I remembered that I was hired by the year …"). But as he continues to think through the decision he's making, he becomes anxious: Might his initial thought about what to do be incorrect? Might this be a situation where his professional obligations and personal needs get trumped by other concerns? So understood, we appear to have practical anxiety prompting Woolman's doubts about the legitimacy of the existing moral conventions and attitudes regarding slavery.

Similarly, Woolman tells us that the act of writing the bill of sale left him "afflicted in [his] mind." We can see his *affliction* here as practical anxiety prompting epistemic behaviors—getting him to reassess and revise his initial thinking. More specifically, because of the anxiety he feels, Woolman comes to see that his initial self-interested reasons for writing the bill of sale (e.g., that fulfilling this professional obligation would help ensure his annual employment contract would be renewed) were inconsistent with his deeper moral convictions. This anxiety-driven recognition then prompted him to rethink his initial decision: it helped bring the changes in moral belief and attitude that led him to protest the sale. Thus, not only

---

4. It is worth emphasizing that the experiments of the MacKuen and Valentino teams were, in this respect, importantly different. In particular, and unlike Brader and his colleagues, these teams found not only that their anger and anxiety measures function differently in their analytic models, but that the ways they function map to our theoretical accounts of anger and practical anxiety.

does Woolman's anxiety provoke his initial doubts, it also underlies his distinctive moral concern—his concern to get it right even though his choice is likely to come (as he recognizes) at a cost to his own interests and well-being. The upshot, then, is support for first two predictions: Woolman experiences anxiety in the face of a difficult decision, which in turn, prompts reflection and reassessment driven by a concern to get it right.

Turning to the third prediction—that practical anxiety makes a distinctive and important contribution—one might worry. In particular, one might agree with the above discussion, but still think practical anxiety is an ultimately unnecessary piece of the above account of Woolman's decision making. To explain his behavior, all we really need to do is take note of (e.g.,) the empathy he feels for the slave (one of his "fellow creatures") and his (de dicto) desire to do what is right.[5] However, while these features of Woolman's psychology are certainly important to explaining why he responds as he does, they alone are not enough. As his own words make plain, his thoughts, values, and feelings were, in the beginning (and largely unbeknownst to him), quite a mess: he felt uneasy about writing the document; he was hesitant to do anything that might jeopardize his continued employment; and he suspected that the sale might be permissible because the purchaser (an "elderly man") was unlikely to do harm to the slave (Woolman, 1952, pp. 26–27; cf. Kitcher, 2011, pp. 160–161). So for him to come to the principled conclusion that he should protest the sale, he needed to recognize (i) that his thoughts, values, and feelings were potentially in tension, (ii) that his initial ideas (or strongest inclinations) about what to do might not be correct, and (iii) that, as a result, he needed to sort this mess out.

Now there are two noteworthy features of (i)–(iii). First, they are *not* things that empathy or a general desire to do right alone can explain. While empathy plausibly underlies Woolman's values and drives his concern for the slave, it is not a mechanism that can, on its own, bring the *responsiveness* to conflicting cognitions that we see in (i)–(iii). In particular, mere empathy for another does not help one recognize that one's thoughts, values, and so on are in tension, nor does it help one to either appreciate that it might not be appropriate to act on one's strongest inclination, or engage

---

5. The locution 'de dicto desire to do right' comes from Smith (1994, chap. 3).

the deliberation and reflection that can help one sort all this out.[6] Similarly, while a general desire to do what's right might help bring changes in thought and action, engaging it requires the *prior recognition* that there may be a problem with one's existing beliefs and attitudes about what the right thing to do is (section 4.3). So, again, we do not have a psychological mechanism that can fully capture (i)–(iii).[7]

But notice (and this is the second point from above) that the awareness of, and responsiveness to, conflict that we have in (i)–(iii) represent the very capacity that's distinctive of practical anxiety. As we know, practical anxiety functions as an alarm: it signals that the decision that one is contemplating might be (morally) suspect and prompts epistemic behaviors geared toward helping one figure out what the right thing to do is. Thus, we are better able to explain Woolman's decision making when we take practical anxiety into account. While other features of his psychology surely played a role in his thinking (e.g., feelings of empathy, a general desire to do right), these alone do not bring practical anxiety's distinctive sensitivity and concern—practical anxiety, in short, can make a distinctive and important contribution to moral reform.

6.3.3 The King Case

Turning to the King example, we get similar support for the thought that practical anxiety undergirds his revisions. In his famous "A Time to Break Silence" speech, King elaborated on why he had changed his mind about speaking out against the war:

> As I have walked among the desperate, rejected, and angry young men, I have told them that Molotov cocktails and rifles would not solve their problems. I have tried to offer them my deepest compassion while maintaining my conviction that social change comes most meaningfully through nonviolent action. But they ask—and rightly so—what about Vietnam? They ask if our own nation wasn't using massive doses of violence to solve its problems, to bring about the changes it wanted. *Their questions hit home*, and I knew that I could never again raise my voice against the violence of the oppressed in the ghettos without having first spoken clearly to the greatest purveyor of violence in the world today—my own government. For the sake

---

6. Additionally, one might worry that empathy is poorly suited as a driver of *moral* doubt and concern—after all, it appears to be an affective response that biases one toward helping intimates over strangers. For further discussion, see Kauppinen (2014) and Prinz (2011a, 2011b).

7. Recall as well that guilt, embarrassment, and shame are also poor fits (section 6.1).

of those boys, for the sake of this government, for the sake of the hundreds of thousands trembling under our violence, I cannot be silent. (King, 1967, emphasis added)

Looking at these remarks, we see that being called out on his silence made King uneasy—it "hit home"—in a way that made him worry about whether his position was really justified. This is significant for two reasons. First, it reveals that though King's change of mind occurred over a period of several months, it was punctuated by the acute feelings of unease he would experience when his position was challenged by others. This, in turn, suggests that the unease King felt at these moments was the "gnawing conscience"—the "anxiety"—that we saw in the passages we looked at earlier (section 6.1): it was the anxiety that helped him recognize that he could not remain silent in the face of the violence he deplored. As a result of this realization, King began to reflect on his priorities and "agonized a great deal over" the choice he faced. He came to see that the pragmatic considerations that supported his initial preference for silence must give way to his deeper commitment to peace, and to a rejection of war and violence. Thus, the earlier suggestion that King's anxiety was merely a consequence of his decision to protest seems misplaced—his change in outlook appears to have been undergirded by the anxiety he felt when called out for being inconsistent.

Further supporting this, we see that King (1998) concluded he should speak out even though he recognized this would come at a cost to his relationship with the Johnson administration and his own peers in the civil rights movement:

When I first took my position against the war in Vietnam, almost every newspaper in the country criticized me. It was a low period in my life. ... It wasn't only white people either; it was Negroes. But then I remember a newsman coming to me one day and saying, "Dr. King, don't you think you're going to have to change your position now because so many people are criticizing you? And people who once had respect for you are going to lose respect for you. And you're going to hurt the budget, I understand, of the Southern Christian Leadership Conference; people have cut off support. And don't you think that you have to move more in line with the administration's policy?" That was a good question, because he was asking me the question of whether I was going to think about what happens to me or what happens to truth and justice in this situation.

On some positions, Cowardice asks the question, "Is it safe?" Expediency asks the question, "Is it politic?" And Vanity comes along and asks the question, "Is it popular?" But Conscience asks the question, "Is it right?" And there comes a time when one must take a position that is neither safe, nor politic, nor popular, but he must do it because Conscience tells him it is right. (p. 342)

The remarks are powerful on their own. But they also reveal that King's driving concern in reassessing the question of whether to remain silent was a concern to get it right. Moreover, this passage further implicates anxiety as the emotion King was feeling. For one, King's remarks, as well as our earlier discussions of Kant and Herman (sections 4.4.2 and 5.6.2), suggest that we should understand King's references to Conscience as pointing to his unease—his anxiety about what to do—as the driver of his reflection and reassessment. This suggestion gains further support once we recognize, given the richer picture of King's moral psychology that we have been developing, that his response is poorly explained in terms of guilt or shame (about, say, being called out as a hypocrite). As in the Woolman case, we do not see the behavior—the efforts to make amends or withdraw from the spotlight—that we would expect to see if these emotions were driving King's thinking.

Taken together, these details about King's decision making provide evidence for our three predictions: (i) King's experience involved anxiety about the appropriateness of his decision to be silent on the war—anxiety that was provoked when he was called out for being inconsistent. (ii) This anxiety prompted reflection and reassessment shaped not by self-interest or expediency, but rather by a concern to do the morally appropriate thing. And (iii) King's comments about the importance of Conscience (as opposed to Vanity or Expediency) in driving his resoluteness in the face of complaints identify a distinct and important role for anxiety in explaining the strength and persistence of his opposition to the war.

6.3.4 Summing Up

We can now see that, on closer inspection, the Woolman and King examples display the features we would expect to see if the changes in moral belief and attitude they depict were driven by practical anxiety. The participants in the Brader experiment on immigration, by contrast, do not. Granted, there are limits to the psychological conclusions we can draw from autobiographical reports of the sort that are the basis of our assessments of Woolman and King. That said, it's worth pausing to highlight the overlap that we see between those two analyses and the empirical findings from the MacKuen and Valentino teams regarding anxiety's role in prompting open-minded inquiry and knowledge acquisition (section 3.3). In both sets of cases, the individuals experience anxiety in the face of uncertainty about whether a position they have taken or are contemplating is justified—uncertainty that, in turn, triggers efforts to learn more and reappraise the situation at hand. These structural parallels thus provide further support for our conclusions that the changes in moral belief and attitude that we see in Woolman and King are plausibly understood as being undergirded by practical anxiety.

6.4 Lessons from the Psychology of Moral Reformers: Cultivating Practical Anxiety

The discussion to this point raises important questions. In some situations—like those of Woolman, King, and the participants in the MacKuen study on affirmative action policy—challenges to one's moral/political beliefs bring the open-minded inquiry of practical anxiety. But in other cases, like what we see in Brader's work on immigration, similar challenges prompt a more defensive anxiety response: one that brings retrenchment and motivated information seeking driven by a desire to shore up existing beliefs. This raises two questions: Why do we see these differences, and what, if anything, might we be able to do to promote morally productive forms of anxiety? In a way, these questions are just a continuation of the earlier discussion of how we might effectively cultivate our emotions. As such, they are questions whose answers will come from empirical work on things like emotion regulation, psychiatry, and clinical psychology (see Gross, 2015, for an overview). While there is much on these fronts that we don't know, this work does provide the makings of an initial answer to our two questions.

First consider why we see the differences that we do in individuals' ability to productively channel their (practical) anxiety. Here a big part of the answer presumably lies in personality-level individual differences regarding both the emotions people tend to experience and their ability to effectively regulate them. Taking these in turn, recall our discussion of Norman Endler's research showing individual differences in the types of anxiety that people tend to feel: some have (e.g.,) a greater tendency to experience practical anxiety, while others more readily feel socially anxious (section 3.3.2). We find similar individual differences with regard to the general capacities thought to underlie our ability to effectively regulate our emotions. For instance, some individuals have more acute interoceptive awareness (i.e., a better ability to perceive changes in physiological states like heart rate or blushing), and as a result, appear to be better able to reappraise—and so effectively manage—emotional episodes.[8] Fleshing this out a bit, research suggests that effective emotion regulation is a function of inter alia one's ability to (i) recognize when one's emotions have been engaged, (ii) identify which emotion one is experiencing, and so (iii) select an appropriate reappraisal strategy for regulating that emotion. Though there's more to emotion regulation than what we see in (i)–(iii), this trio of capacities is important since the reappraisal they facilitate is thought to be a particularly effective mode of regulation (Füstös, Gramann, et al., 2013; Gross, 2015).

Taken together, these observations suggest that part of the difference we see between people like Woolman and Wellington lies in structural differences in their psychological capacities—differences in their tendency to experience practical anxiety and their sensitivity to things like (i)–(iii).

Turn then to the second question: What can we do to cultivate anxiety of the sort that we see in reformers like Woolman and King? On this front, the above observations suggest that some individuals will have a natural advantage with regard to interoceptive awareness and emotion recognition. That said, there's also evidence that these are capacities most of us can learn to deploy more effectively. For instance, mindfulness interventions—training that teaches individuals to observe and accept their affective states—can improve bodily awareness and so help one better identify what one is experiencing (Teper, Segal, & Inzlicht, 2013).

---

8. One study is of particular note in the present context. It used EEG recordings to measure changes in arousal levels as participants were presented with a range of images previously determined to elicit pleasant, neutral, and negative emotional states. For some blocks of images, participants were asked to employ an emotion reappraisal strategy they had been taught earlier. For other blocks of images, they were instructed not to reappraise or otherwise distract themselves. The results demonstrated that individuals who had shown better interoceptive awareness (as measured by their ability to accurately count their heartbeats) were better able to use reappraisal to limit the level of arousal they experienced when viewing the positive and negative emotion-eliciting images. Importantly for our purposes, the images used to prompt negative emotions included standard anxiety elicitors—snakes, spiders, violent death, and angry faces—suggesting that these results are indicative of a connection between interoceptive awareness and *anxiety* regulation (Füstös, Gramann, et al., 2013).

Speaking more specifically about (practical) anxiety, the discussion of the last several chapters provides cause for cautious optimism with regard to our ability to shape it for the better. For starters, the chapter 3 discussion of anxiety as a biocognitive emotion helps us see that though it has a hardwired core (the anxiety affect program), it is also the product of a more malleable set of control mechanisms. So, unlike more rigid, reflex-like emotions such as disgust, (practical) anxiety's cognitive architecture makes it more susceptible to being shaped by learning and experience (recall section 4.2; cf. Kelly, 2011, chap. 5). More provocatively, combining this with the observations from chapter 5 regarding Julia Annas's account of moral development suggests (practical) anxiety might be skill-like—a capacity we can cultivate using techniques of Aristotelian habituation. On this front, we find support along a couple of lines.

First, as we have seen, research in psychiatry and clinical psychology helps us understand when and why anxiety is likely to break down (section 3.3.3 and section 4.2.2). These insights, in turn, have allowed researchers to develop interventions that can help individuals harness anxiety's potential and minimize its liabilities. On this front, consider cognitive-behavioral therapy (CBT). The driving premise of CBT is that anxiety disorders are sustained by cognitive factors (e.g., minimizing the positive aspects of a situation, catastrophizing, overgeneralizing) and so can be treated by helping individuals develop coping skills that allow them to both better identify situations that trigger the problematic emotional response and engage strategies that can help correct the distorting thoughts/attitudes. Not only do the methods of CBT have strong parallels with the techniques that Aristotelians like Nancy Sherman (1989) and Julia Annas (2011) point to as the core tools for effective emotion cultivation (e.g., working with a teacher or mentor to better understand when and why an emotional response is (in)appropriate), they also turn out to be quite successful. For instance, one meta-analysis found "strong support for the efficacy of CBT" as a treatment for anxiety disorders (Hofmann & Smits, 2008). Similar success has been found in the use of CBT techniques to combat scrupulosity (Abramowitz, 2001)—a result that's noteworthy here given our earlier observation that forms of scrupulosity appear to be clinical manifestations of practical anxiety (section 3.3.3). So while CBT is an intervention for anxiety disorders, the success it brings suggests the basic strategy could be enlisted more generally to help individuals channel their (practical) anxiety and protect against false-positives (i.e., feeling anxiety when their situation isn't actually problematically uncertain).

A second line of research suggests anxiety can also be cultivated to help guard against false-negatives—occasions where one feels no anxiety even though it's fitting (i.e., it's fitting because one's situation is problematically uncertain). This work focuses on a common technique used in public health and safety advertisements (PSAs). These ads use graphic images, audio, and text in order to elicit anxiety and related emotions (worry, unease, distress) in an effort to curb smoking, drunk driving, and other harmful behaviors. Not only are these PSAs effective in combating the risky behaviors they target, but the research suggests they are effective, in part, because the feelings of anxiety and unease that they provoke become associated with the recognition that the viewer is vulnerable to being harmed by the risky behavior depicted in the advertisement (Keller, 1999; Lewis, Watson, Tay & White, 2007; Witte & Allen, 2000; cf, Brader, 2006). Thus, this work helps us see how one's anxiety can be enriched so that one becomes sensitive to a broader range of problematically uncertain situations.

Taken together, these observations provide reason for optimism about our ability to get better at regulating, even cultivating, anxiety. Like a skill, anxiety is something we can hone with practice—reducing false-positives and false-negatives as well as learning to better channel the (fitting) anxiety we feel so that we can take advantage of the caution and epistemic behaviors it brings.[9] That said, the research also reveals both that some individuals will be better equipped from the start to do this, and that improvement along these lines will not come easily. But notice that these are conclusions that fit well with the rarity of effective moral reformers like King and Woolman.

6.5 Conclusion

Returning to the epigraph at the beginning of the chapter, it appears Plato was mistaken—much in human affairs is worthy of anxiety. This, of course, has been a recurring theme of our investigation. As we have seen, anxiety

---

9. As another example, recall the earlier discussion of the positive effects that reappraisal strategies have been shown to have on GRE test performance and athletic competitions (section 4.2.2).

is a fitting response to situations where one faces problematic uncertainty. Not only is fitting anxiety a forward-looking emotion that helps us recognize and appropriately respond to potential threats and dangers, it is also central to virtuous thought and action—anxiety, especially practical anxiety, underlies the emotional attunement that's constitutive of moral concern. We can now say more. Practical anxiety matters for moral progress: it makes a distinctive and important contribution to the progressive moral change of the sort that we see in reformers like Woolman and King.[10]

---

10. The conclusion that practical anxiety is an important driver of moral progress might seem a boon for (naturalistic) moral realists. It appears to provide them with resources to defend against objections to their account of moral improvement (e.g., Kurth, 2012; Nichols, 2004, pp. 162–163), and so might seem to provide a better account of moral objectivity than is available from competing antirealist accounts (both Chandra Sripada and David Brink have made this suggestion to me in conversation). This assessment, however, is only half right. It is true that our account of practical anxiety and its relevance as a mechanism of moral progress can help realists bolster their accounts of moral improvement. But it is also true that practical anxiety can bring comparable benefits to antirealists. After all, so long as we don't beg the question by defining moral progress in a manner that is incompatible with antirealism (e.g., progress toward a mind-independent moral reality), the proposal in the text is compatible with (most) antirealist metaethical accounts. Thus, acknowledging the significance of practical anxiety for moral progress provides no (obvious) advantage to the realist. Rather, it is something both sides should be interested in taking on board.

III Conclusion

7 Conclusion: How Did We Get Here?

In this concluding chapter, I draw together some of the insights we have accumulated to this point in an effort to say something about why human anxiety has taken the form it has. My hypothesis is that anxiety looks the way it does because it functions not merely as a defensive response, but also as an important mechanism of social regulation—what began as a mechanism for protecting against potential environmental threats (predators, cliff edges; cf. section 2.3.1) has become a sophisticated tool that helps individuals manage situations where they must act in the face of vague or conflicting norms and expectations (section 3.3). To defend this claim, I build on the discussion of the prior chapters in order to develop a how-possibly story. In so doing, I am engaging in an admittedly speculative (but nonetheless empirically informed) exploration of the evolutionary pressures, both biological and cultural, that may have given rise to the various forms of anxiety—environmental, punishment, and practical—that we have been focusing on.

By way of backdrop, notice that the biocognitive model from part I provides us with an account of anxiety as a mechanism shaped by both natural selection and cultural forces. Notice as well that the investigation of part II has helped us understand the many ways anxiety—especially practical anxiety—can be valuable. This combination is the launching point for my evolutionary proposal.[1]

---

1. The discussion that follows builds on Kurth (2016).

7.1 Chimps, Foragers, and Egyptians: Getting Here from There

In a paper investigating the origins of sophisticated forms of cooperation, Kim Sterelny notes that two "revolutions" were instrumental in giving rise to modern human civilizations (Sterelny, 2013; Kitcher, 2011, offers a similar picture). The first he dubs the "human revolution"—the gradual movement from chimp-like hierarchically organized, dominance-based social systems to the more egalitarian, cooperative social systems of Pleistocene foragers and hunter-gatherers. The second revolution—the "Holocene revolution"—represents a more recent set of changes. This period saw a rapid move from the small-scale, egalitarian social structures of foraging and hunter-gatherer groups to the large-scale, hierarchical organizations of the early civilizations of Mesopotamia and Egypt.

Sterelny is interested in showing that while we know a fair amount about the biological, social, and environmental factors that drove the first revolution, we know comparatively little about the second. Moreover, he argues that the very features of social life that we believe to have been essential to the development and maintenance of Pleistocene social life are absent in the early, large-scale civilizations. The Pleistocene forager groups were small and the individuals in them faced common challenges. This meant that group members were likely to have substantially overlapping interests that allowed for the development of stable cooperative arrangements. Moreover, in these groups, decision making and problem solving were egalitarian and consensus driven. Information flows were also transparent, which made it (fairly) easy to identify the free riders and bullies that, if left unaddressed, could undermine existing cooperative structures (Sterelny, 2013, p. 94; also Boehm, 2012). By contrast, the circumstances of early civilizations were quite different. Not only were the populations much larger, but there were significant differences in wealth, influence, and interests. Cooperation and governance were hierarchically organized; information about who was doing what was less transparent. Yet despite the (rapid) loss of the very structures that had effectively regulated Pleistocene social life, cooperation and social accord did not collapse. Why?

An important part of the explanation for this, I believe, lies in understanding anxiety—in particular, understanding how a response that began as a mechanism that helped organisms (from rodents to primates) recognize and appropriately respond to potential environmental dangers was shaped into an emotion that functions to facilitate social regulation.

7.2 Norms, Punishment, and Uncertainty

To see why anxiety matters for making progress in our understanding of Sterelny's second revolution, it will be helpful to say a little about some of the changes that made the first revolution possible. Two central features of human/hominin social regulation distinguish it from the dominance-based social regulation of chimps and other nonhuman primates: (i) the reliance on *norms* for structuring permissions and prohibitions, and (ii) the use of *punishment* as a mechanism for enforcing norm violations (Boehm, 1999, 2012; Kitcher, 2011; Sterelny, 2012a). However, because punishment is costly both to receive and to administer, it's generally agreed that there would have been adaptive benefits for mechanisms that would allow groups to secure norm compliance without the need to regularly police and punish. That is, social stability and accord would be enhanced if individuals had the ability to *internalize* the norms of their social group.

Emotions—particularly fear—are generally thought to have played an important role in the development of this capacity for norm internalization. Philip Kitcher (2011) provides a nice gloss on fear's contribution:

The simplest models of [the] internalization [of group norms] trade on the ability of programs of socialization to *exploit human fears*. ... The result is a society in which cooperation is more broadly achieved and in which costly episodes of punishment are less frequently needed. (p. 94, emphasis added)

To flesh out Kitcher's observations about fear's role, notice that for this norm internalization to be possible, at least the following pair of cognitive and motivational developments would have been necessary. First, there needed to be a move from the mere expectation of an aggressive response for Φ-ing that is associated with dominance hierarchies, to the ability to recognize that Φ-ing will violate norm N and so merit punishment. As Kitcher explains, recognizing that a behavior merits punishment contributes to stability because it reduces the chance that allies of the punishee will come to his defense, thus escalating the conflict (p. 89). Second, the ability to recognize that Φ-ing will merit punishment needed to be accompanied by a motivational tendency toward compliance with norm N (Chudek, Zhao, & Henrich, 2013, p. 443; Frank, 1988).

Moreover, and as Kitcher notes, fear is likely to have played a role in both of these changes. Recognizing that Φ-ing will violate norm N is initially associated with an expectation of punishment and so with (anticipatory) fear. This fear in turn provides an incentive to comply with N. However, an emotion like fear doesn't just add a new incentive to the ones a person already has. It also tends to bring lasting changes to the very *structure* of one's motivations. As a result, one complies with N, not because one wants to avoid punishment, but because one sees N as independently meriting compliance. In this way, fear plays a crucial role in the development of a capacity for norm internalization.[2] Moreover, notice that fear's role in norm internalization likely brings benefits to both individuals and groups. Fear not only helps individuals avoid the costs of norm violation, it also allows them to signal their trustworthiness as cooperative partners—partners whose cooperation does not depend on a threat of punishment (Frank, 1988). And when norms are internalized, groups are able to secure the benefits of norm adherence without the costs that come with having to (regularly) police and punish. Benefits such as these likely selected for a more sophisticated fear mechanism—one where fear's basic sensitivity to social threats was enriched by an awareness of, and responsiveness toward, the costs of norm violation (Boehm, 2012; Fiske, 2000).

So far, so good. But notice that an important feature of the above account of fear's role in facilitating norm-and-punishment forms of social regulation is the claim that the punishment for some behavior Φ, and the fear that it tends to provoke, reduce the tendency for group members to do Φ. However, for this claim to be plausible, we must assume the norms clearly articulate both what the prohibited (required) behavior Φ is, and what punishment will result from violating the norm. Were this assumption not in place, it would be hard to understand how fear (of punishment) could regulate behavior and foster compliance with norms against Φ-ing (Chudek,

---

2. The idea that emotions like anger, fear, guilt, and disgust change the structure of one's motivations is a central aspect of Robert Frank's (1988) account of emotions as tools that commit individuals to acting in ways they otherwise would not. Additional support for emotions' ability to affect one's incentive structure comes from Paul Rozin's work on disgust: coming to see a food item (e.g., a cockroach) as disgusting keeps one from eating it even after learning that it's completely safe (Rozin, Millman, & Nemeroff, 1986). Moreover, emotions other than fear (e.g., guilt, shame, pride) likely brought further enhancements to the fear-driven dimension of norm internalization (Boehm, 2012; Kitcher, 2011).

Zhao, & Henrich, 2013, p. 443; Cushman, 2013, pp. 351–352). But here's the rub: as societies grew in size and complexity (i.e., as we entered the second revolutionary period), it likely came at the cost of norm clarity. And if so, then appeals to emotions like fear will be poorly positioned to explain how groups managed to secure the stability undergirding the complex social structures and cooperative arrangements that we find in large-scale civilizations.[3] As we will see, groups also needed a tool that could help them manage messy, unclear sets of norms. This tool, I suggest, was practical anxiety.

To begin to flesh this out, first notice that the above puzzle is the upshot of a mismatch between (i) what was involved in the transition from the relatively simple social structures of early hunter-gatherer societies to the complex social life found in later large-scale civilizations, and (ii) what the fear response has evolved to do. First consider (i). As hominin/human groups grew in size and complexity, regulating social life required larger, more complex sets of norms. But these additions and changes to a group's norms were imperfect in the sense that they generated vague, incomplete, and conflicting sets of prescriptions and prohibitions (Kitcher, 2011, pp. 96–98; Sterelny, 2012a, pp. 8–10, 2013). The result was likely to have brought increased uncertainty about how to act and about what would be punished.[4] Some examples will help us understand why:

- *Vague norms.* Small societies are egalitarian and decisions are based on consensus (Boehm, 1999; Kitcher, 2011, p. 96; Knauft, 1991). However, as group size increases, differences of opinion multiply and securing

---

3. Similarly, notice that if one takes the operative mechanisms undergirding cooperation and social accord to involve not fear, norms, and punishment, but rather trust and pro-social emotions (e.g., Sterelny, 2012b), there is still a problem. After all, building and maintaining trust require that the individuals involved have expectations they trust the others to make good on. But as group size and complexity increase, the dictates of these expectations will presumably also grow more complex—and so less clear. Thus, we can ask: How is trust maintained as the expectations from which it grows become less able to clearly articulate what one is expected to do?
4. Work by the anthropologist Bruce Knauft (1991) indicates that increases in group size not only brought greater norm uncertainty, but that this uncertainty also likely contributed to greater violence—especially violence associated with resource access and status. If Knauft's observations are on point, they further highlight the challenges that come with more complex social life and thus the adaptive pressure for tools that could address them.

consensus grows more difficult. Agreement can still be achieved by appealing to more general norms that gloss over points of contention. But this move to generality comes at the cost of clarity.[5]

- *Incomplete norms.* With increased group size came increased specialization (e.g., toolmaking, animal husbandry, farming) and the emergence of an important new class of artisans. These artisans needed time away from communal activities to develop their skills; they also needed access to valuable resources (Kitcher, 2011, pp. 125–129; Sterelny, 2013). This brings new problems: How much reprieve from communal duties should artisans be granted? What responsibilities do they have to make efficient use of the valuable time and materials they have been given? What consequences will there be when resources are squandered?
- *Conflicting norms.* External pressures (e.g., climate change) or migration might force independent groups to combine.[6] The resulting commingling would likely bring one group's norms into conflict with another's. In such situations, whose norms should be followed? More generally, as group size and complexity increase, so do the norms. The resulting codes were unlikely to be free of conflicting prescriptions—especially to the extent that additions and revisions to the codes were ad hoc responses to problems as they arose (Kitcher, 2011, p. 121).

Now turn to (ii). As we have noted, fear can help secure social regulation only to the extent that the group's norms give *clear* guidance about what behaviors are prohibited (required) and so what misbehaviors will bring punishment. This means that fear-based forms of social regulation are ill-suited to dealing with the uncertainty that comes with *unclear* (e.g., vague, incomplete, conflicting) norms. And this leaves us with a puzzle: How did widespread conformity to group norms remain possible as those norms became increasingly unclear?

---

5. This phenomenon is a pervasive feature of the modern legislative process: lawmakers intentionally write vague statutes to secure the votes needed for passage; courts then need to adjudicate the nearly inevitable disagreements over what the law requires.

6. See Richerson and Boyd (2013) for discussion of the significant climatic changes that occurred during the Late Pleistocene—the period in which the transition from small-scale societies to larger ones likely began.

7.3 Practical Anxiety, Norm Uncertainty, and Social Regulation

The makings of an answer to the above question can be found in what we have learned about anxiety. The basic idea is this. As norms grew in complexity, they were increasingly unable to give clear guidance about what to do. So mechanisms that could help address the resulting 'norm uncertainty' would have brought significant benefits: individuals would have a better understanding of what is prohibited; groups would have lower enforcement costs and greater stability. Moreover, since the problem here is one that concerns *uncertainty*, we should expect anxiety to play an important role in the solution. However, given the particular nature of the uncertainty at issue—namely, uncertainty about what to do in the face of unclear norms—the capacity for the physical harm–oriented environmental anxiety that we share with other mammals (chapters 2 and 3) would not be of much help. We would need a more socially oriented, norm-focused form of anxiety—something like practical anxiety. This suggests that the adaptive benefits that would have come from mechanisms that could help individuals (and groups) manage the challenges of increasingly complex social life may have brought (biological and cultural) selective pressures on the basic anxiety mechanism. What originated as a defense mechanism for environmental threats and physical dangers evolved into a sophisticated tool for facilitating social accord.

To begin to flesh out this suggestion, first notice that the central problem is that acting in the face of vague, incomplete, or conflicting norms puts one in a position where one's decision about what to do—whatever it is—can be reasonably viewed as a norm violation. This obviously raises difficulties for the individual who must decide what to do. But because norm uncertainty creates a situation where *any* decision can be viewed as a norm violation, it also tends to undermine social stability and cohesion at the level of the group: as it becomes less clear who can(not) be trusted and who needs to be punished, it becomes more difficult to secure stable cooperative arrangements (Frank, 1988; Sterelny, 2013).

What mechanisms could help reduce norm uncertainty? Better communication and improved information channels would certainly help. But these mechanisms can only do so much: while better information may be helpful when vague norms make it unclear what acts are prohibited, it's of little assistance when the problems arise from incomplete or conflicting norms. Addressing structural difficulties like these requires a mechanism that can spur additions to, and revisions of, the existing (problematic) norms. However, securing such norm revision is easier said than done. Since we are dealing with situations involving established norms—norms that have already been accepted by the community—making revisions is likely to require significant "buy-in" from the community.[7] Mitigating the problems associated with norm uncertainty requires individuals/groups to have ways of both (i) recognizing that there is a problematic lack of clarity in their norms, and (ii) revising those norms so they become interpersonally acceptable.[8]

Enter practical anxiety. As an emotion that is felt in the face of uncertainty about what the correct thing to do is, it's well equipped to function as the kind of social-awareness mechanism needed to meet requirement (i). Moreover, practical anxiety also tends to provoke the deliberation, information gathering, and other epistemic behaviors that are important for securing the interpersonally acceptable norm revisions of requirement (ii).

As we have seen, when one experiences practical anxiety, one comes to see one's situation as providing insufficient guidance about what the correct thing to do is; this awareness, in turn, prompts caution. Moreover, given the source of one's anxiety—namely, a problematic lack of clarity about what to do—one tends to engage in various epistemic behaviors. One's thinking becomes more focused on the challenge that one faces and one's perspective shifts: one is pushed to think about one's choice from the point of view of those who might call one's decision into question. This perspective taking is also accompanied by the open-minded information gathering that practical anxiety tends to provoke—be it reflecting on the situation at hand, consulting with trusted sources and potentially affected individuals, or other forms of investigation.

---

7. While the need for broad community acceptance is, as we have seen (section 7.2), crucial in small-scale hunter-gatherer groups, it would have remained important even as group size increased and decision making became less egalitarian (Seabright, 2010). For further discussion of the importance of community "buy-in," see Boehm (1999); Gibbard (1990, chap. 4); and Kitcher (2011, pp. 96–98).

8. Further complicating matters, notice that with improved information channels comes the possibility of improved channels of *mis*information and the manipulation that would cut against the communication-related benefits suggested in the text. See Sterelny (2012b, pp. 110–111) for discussion.

Conclusion

Recognizing all this is significant. It reveals that practical anxiety can both help *warn* individuals (and groups) that their norms are problematically unclear, and motivate them to *refine* their thinking about what to do as a result. Moreover, because practical anxiety prompts (open-minded) deliberation, reflection, information gathering, and a willingness to explore new solutions, individuals who experience it are more likely to be able to *justify* their actions to others (Ackerman & Fishkin, 2004, chap. 3; Gibbard, 1990, chap. 4; Henrich & Gil-White, 2001). This means that practical anxiety can help facilitate decisions that are (more) interpersonally acceptable—especially to the extent that the resulting investigation brings engagement with the individuals likely to be affected by the decision and those who have influence in the community. But as we saw above, a mechanism of this sort is just what we need in order to explain how widespread norm adherence remained possible in the face of increasingly unclear norms.[9] So the account of practical anxiety we've developed both helps us resolve our puzzle and provides us with a better understanding of how emotions can help secure social stability and accord.[10]

To better draw out practical anxiety's distinctive contribution to the problems associated with norm uncertainty and social cohesion, we can compare it with other emotions that might seem to play a similar role in building and maintaining social accord. Of particular interest for our purposes are shame and conscience—for each has been pointed to as a key

---

9. As Kitcher (2011, pp. 97–98) notes, groups that allowed for revisions to their norms would have been much better equipped to address the difficulties that come with vague, incomplete, and conflict-ridden normative codes.

10. As we have seen (chapter 6), merely experiencing anxiety in the face of (norm) uncertainty does not guarantee the resulting revisions will be for the better. If, say, your anxiety leads you to look to elites and community leaders for guidance, but those individuals recommend self-serving changes, you will tend to revise in ways that will perpetuate the interests of the elites (at the expense of the masses). Sterelny (2012b, pp. 109–112) suggests this sort of duping of low-ranking individuals by elites was common in the transition to large-scale societies. Does this possibility undermine my account of (practical) anxiety's development? I don't think so. Rather, what it reveals is that it will likely be easier to secure social stability than *morally justified* social stability. But that concession meshes with the lessons about the difficulty of securing moral progress that we learned in chapter 6. Also see the discussion of human capacities for "epistemic vigilance" that are employed to protect against being misinformed by others in Sperber, Clément, et al. (2010).

(evolutionarily shaped) mechanism in the development and maintenance of stable social structures.[11]

Though there are interesting differences between shame and conscience,[12] they are alike in that both are understood—in the first place—as aversive affective states that act as correctives to norm violations (broadly construed). In particular, both shame and conscience are principally *backward-looking* emotions: they function as correctives because they implicate one's sense of self in the face of a (potential) norm violation—to feel these emotions is to see what one has done as revealing a personal failure or inadequacy vis-à-vis one's standing in the community. The immediate result of this emotion-induced recognition is appeasement and other reparative/defensive behaviors that aim to restore social accord (and standing) in the wake of a wrong. In short, what makes shame and conscience distinctive as mechanisms of social regulation is the way that their backward-looking orientation allows them to both implicate one's sense of self and engage one's associated desire for social acceptance—a combination that proves to be a powerful force for the production of reparative behaviors and norm internalization.[13]

Seeing that these emotions combine a backward-looking, self-referential perspective with a set of broadly reparative/defensive behaviors is significant in two ways. First, it reveals something about what social structures must be in place for shame and conscience to do what they do. In particular, we see that shame and conscience require that social groups be structured by norms that are (largely) *clear* about what is required/forbidden and what consequences a violation will bring. After all, it's part of the nature of these emotions that they are responses to situations where one sees that one has (likely) done wrong or otherwise violated social expectations—and that presumes clarity in the underlying norms and expectations. Second, we also see that practical anxiety is importantly different. As an emotion you experience in the face of norm uncertainty, it is principally *forward-looking*:

---

11. For further discussion of shame, see Deonna, Rodogno, and Teroni (2011); Fessler (2007); and Maibom (2010). On conscience, see Boehm (2012) and Kitcher (2011).
12. See May (2015, chap. 10) for a discussion of these differences.
13. Recognizing this reveals that my earlier discussion of conscience in the context of Kant and King concerns a more forward-looking version of the affective state that 'conscience' is used to refer to.

it doesn't bring reparative efforts to correct for a wrong already done, but rather engages deliberation, information gathering, and other epistemic efforts aimed at helping one figure out what to do.

Stepping back, this pair of observations reveals that, in shame, conscience, and practical anxiety, we have emotions that contribute—in importantly different ways—to the development and maintenance of social accord. Shame and conscience are tools best suited for situations where there are clear norms. By contrast, practical anxiety brings distinctive resources that help individuals (and groups) manage norm uncertainty.

7.4 Conclusion

This final discussion brings us back to a claim from chapter 1: the dominant focus in moral psychology on backward-looking emotions like shame, guilt, and conscience leaves us with a badly incomplete picture of the role of emotion in moral life. While these emotions are obviously important to our ability to interact with each other as social and moral beings, they are unable to fully explain emotions' contribution to moral/practical decision making and agency. Life is a cascade of uncertainty, and effectively navigating the risks and challenges that arise requires that we be sensitive and responsive to the range of physical, social, and practical dangers uncertainty brings. Anxiety's value lies here. As we have seen throughout part II, anxiety—particularly practical anxiety—is an emotion that is uniquely well suited to helping us recognize and respond to the uncertainties we face. Moreover, the discussion of part I provides us with an empirically informed account of what anxiety is that allows us to understand how it can provide the benefits that it does. Life's anxieties, it turns out, are well suited to answering life's uncertainties.

Acknowledgments

There are many to thank for their contributions to this book and to my development as a philosopher more generally. So I begin at the beginning ...

Thanks go to George Thomas and James Cargile: two of my teachers at the University of Virginia who spurred my interest in philosophy as an undergraduate. While pursuing a master's degree at Arizona State, I benefited from the guidance and encouragement of my thesis director Bernard Kobes as well as from John Devlin—two tremendous mentors.

My most formative philosophical education came during my graduate studies at the University of California, San Diego. I owe much to David Brink for his thoughtful guidance and friendship. In my time at UCSD, I also benefited from the work I did, and conversations I had, with Richard Arneson, Gila Sher, and Jonathan Cohen. My weekly writing group meetings with my fellow graduate students Mike Tiboris and Nina Brewer-Davis were a regular source of insight and encouragement.

Since coming to Washington University in St. Louis, I have benefited from conversations with Anne Margaret Baxley, Eric Brown, John Doris, Brett Hyde, Ron Mallon, Tom Rodebaugh, Gillian Russell, Julia Staffel, Brian Talbot, and Kit Wellman. I'd also like to thank Heidi Maibom and Dave Shoemaker for coming to St. Louis to be part of the manuscript workshop held in March 2016.

I would also like to extend my appreciation to participants in the fall 2015 course on "Philosophical and Moral Psychology": Dylan Doherty, Maria Doulatova, James Gulledge, Rick Shang, Caroline Stone, Melissa Thevenot, and Tom Wysocki. Working through an early version of the book manuscript with this group was tremendously valuable.

Special thanks are due to two of my Washington University colleagues. First, to Lizzie Schechter, with whom I started as junior faculty in the fall of

2011. I have benefited significantly from her advice and comments on two versions of the book manuscript. Second, to Carl Craver, who not only help me see that he was right: the Eagles are superior to the Ramones, but who also did much to sharpen my thinking on the science of anxiety—part I of the book owes much to his contributions and insights.

In writing this book, I have also benefited from fellowships at the Center for the Humanities at Washington University and the Centre for Ethics, Philosophy and Public Affairs at the University of St. Andrews. I am also indebted to the audiences where I had the privilege of presenting portions of the material that went into this book: Georgetown University, KU Leuven, the University of Arizona/Workshop in Normative Ethics, the University of California, San Diego, the University of Colorado, the University of St. Andrews, and the University of Tennessee.

Many others have helped along the way, including Craig Aguile, Caroline Arruda, Nich Baima, Mark Berger, Michael Brownstein, Zac Cogley, Jennifer Corns, Justin D'Arms, Andreas De Block, Michael Deem, Dale Dorsey, Kevin Dorst, Billy Dunaway, Julia Haas, John Haldane, Marta Halina, Dan Haybron, Dan Jacobson, Anne Jeffrey, Dan Kelly, Sarah Kertz, Kathryn Lindeman, Josh May, Tyler Paytas, Christa Peterson, Peter Railton, Grant Ramsey, Kate Schmidt, Nick Schuster, Walter Sinnott-Armstrong, Justin Snedegar, Chandra Sripada, Fabrice Teroni, Mark Timmons, Ian Tully, Stephen White, Erik Wielenberg, Eric Wiland, and David Wong.

Parts of the book build on three previously published or forthcoming articles: "Moral Anxiety and Moral Agency," *Oxford Studies in Normative Ethics, Vol. 5*, Mark Timmons (ed.), Oxford: Oxford University Press, (2015): 171–195, portions incorporated by permission of Oxford University Press; "Anxiety, Normative Uncertainty, and Social Regulation," *Biology & Philosophy* (2016): 1–21, portions incorporated by permission of Springer; and "Emotion, Deliberation, and the Skill Model of Virtuous Agency," *Mind & Language* (forthcoming).

I would also like to thank the MIT Press team, Phil Laughin, Chris Eyer, Anne-Marie Bono, Marcy Ross, Molly Seamans, and Jay McNair as well as Christine Tappolet and Jesse Summers, both of whom revealed themselves as reviewers of the manuscript. Thanks as well to the reviewers who remained anonymous—the manuscript benefited much from their feedback.

Finally, thanks to my parents—Charlie, Jean, and Jim—for helping me get this far. And most importantly, my gratitude goes to my wife Pippin Schupbach for her love and support.

References

Abramowitz, J. S. (2001). Treatment of scrupulous obsessions and compulsions using exposure and response prevention: A case report. *Cognitive and Behavioral Practice*, 8, 79–85.

Abramowitz, J. S. (2008). Scrupulosity. In J. Abramowitz, D. McKay, & S. Taylor (Eds.), *Clinical handbook of obsessive-compulsive disorder and related problems* (pp. 156–175). Baltimore, MD: Johns Hopkins University Press.

Ackerman, B., & Fishkin, J. (2004). *Deliberation day*. New Haven, CT: Yale University Press.

Alheid, G., & Heimer, L. (1988). New perspectives in basal forebrain organization of special relevance for neuropsychiatric disorders. *Neuroscience*, 27, 1–39.

Alpert, R., & Haber, R. N. (1960). Anxiety in academic achievement situations. *Journal of Abnormal and Social Psychology*, 61, 207–215.

Alvarez, R., Chen, G., et al. (2011). Phasic and sustained fear in humans elicits distinct patterns of brain activity. *NeuroImage*, 55, 389–400.

Ammerman, R., & Hersan, M. (1986). Effects of scene manipulation on role-play test behavior. *Journal of Psychopathology and Behavioral Assessment*, 8, 55–67.

Anderson, E. (2014, February 11). Social movements, experiments in living, and moral progress: Case studies from Britain's abolition of slavery. *Lindley Lecture*. Lawrence: University of Kansas.

Anderson, E. (2016). The social epistemology of morality. In M. Brady & M. Fricker (Eds.), *The epistemic life of groups* (pp. 75–94) Oxford: Oxford University Press.

Annas, J. (1993). *The morality of happiness*. Oxford: Oxford University Press.

Annas, J. (2008). The phenomenology of virtue. *Phenomenology and the Cognitive Sciences*, 7, 21–34.

Annas, J. (2011). *Intelligent virtue*. Oxford: Oxford University Press.

Aquino, K., Freeman, D., Reed, A., Felps, W., & Lim, V. K. (2009). Testing a social-cognitive model of moral behavior: The interactive influence of situations and moral identity centrality. *Journal of Personality and Social Psychology*, 97, 123–141.

Aristotle. (1925). *Nicomachean ethics* (D. Ross, Trans.). Oxford: Oxford University Press.

Aronson, E. (1968). Dissonance theory: Prospects and problems. In R. Abelson, E. Aronson, W. McGuire, T. Newcomb, M. Rosenberg, & P. Tannenbaum (Eds.), *Cognitive dissonance theories* (5–76). Skokie, IL: Rand McNally.

Aronson, E. (2008). *The social animal*. New York: Worth/Freeman.

Arpaly, N., & Schroeder, T. (2014). *In praise of desire*. Oxford: Oxford University Press.

Ashcraft, M. H. (2002). Math anxiety: Personal, educational, and cognitive consequences. *Current Directions in Psychological Science*, 11, 181–185.

Avery, S., Clauss, J., et al. (2014). BNST neurocircuitry in humans. *NeuroImage*, 91, 311–323.

Avery, S., Clauss, J., & Blackford, J. (2016). The human BNST: Functional role in anxiety and addiction. *Neuropsychopharmacology Reviews*, 41, 126–141.

Baas, M., De Drue, C., & Nijstad, B. (2008). A meta-analysis of 25 years of mood–creativity research. *Psychological Bulletin*, 134, 779–806.

Baas, J., Grillon, C., et al. (2002). Benzodiazepines have no effect on fear-potentiated startle in humans. *Psychopharmacology*, 161, 233–247.

Bach, D., & Dolan, R. (2012). Knowing how much you don't know: A neural organization of uncertainty estimates. *Nature Reviews Neuroscience*, 13, 572–586.

Bachrach, K., & Zaurta, A. (1985). Coping with a community stressor: The threat of a hazardous waste facility. *Journal of Health and Social Behavior*, 26, 127–141.

Barlow, D. (2001). *Anxiety and its disorders* (2nd ed.). New York: Guilford Press.

Barrett, L. (2006). Are emotions natural kinds? *Perspectives on Psychological Science*, 1, 28–58.

Barrett, L. (2012). Emotions are real. *Emotion (Washington, DC)*, 12, 413–429.

Bastin, C., Harrison, B., et al. (2016). Feelings of shame, embarrassment and guilt and their neural correlates. *Neuroscience and Biobehavioral Reviews*, 71, 455–471.

Baumeister, R., & Tice, D. (1990). Anxiety and social exclusion. *Journal of Social and Clinical Psychology*, 9, 165–195.

Baumeister, R., Vohs, K., DeWall, C., & Zhang, L. (2007). How emotion shapes behavior: Feedback, anticipation, and reflection, rather than direct causation. *Personality and Social Psychology Review*, 11, 167–203.

References

Baxley, A. M. (2010). *Kant's theory of virtue: The value of autocracy*. Cambridge: Cambridge University Press.

Bell, M. (2013). *Hard feelings*. Oxford: Oxford University Press.

Berker, S. (2009). The normative insignificance of neuroscience. *Philosophy & Public Affairs*, 37, 293–329.

Berns, G., Chappelow, J., et al. (2006). Neurobiological substrates of dread. *Science*, 312, 754–758.

Berry, A. (2014). *Unhinged: A memoir of enduring, surviving, and overcoming family mental illness*. Lanham, MD: Rowan & Littlefield.

Bishop, S., Duncan, J., Brett, M., & Lawrence, A. (2004). Prefrontal cortical function and anxiety: Controlling attention to threat-related stimuli. *Nature Neuroscience*, 7, 184–188.

Bishop, S., Duncan, J., & Lawrence, A. (2004). State anxiety modulation of the amygdala response to unattended threat-related stimuli. *Journal of Neuroscience*, 24, 10364–10368.

Blackhart, G., Eckel, L., & Tice, D. (2007). Salivary cortisol in response to acute social rejection and acceptance by peers. *Biological Psychology*, 75, 267–276.

Blanchard, D., & Blanchard, R. (2008). Defensive behaviors, fear, and anxiety. In R. Blanchard, D. Blanchard, G. Griebel, & D. Nutt (Eds.), *Handbook of anxiety and fear* (pp. 63–79). Amsterdam: Academic Press.

Blanchard, D., Hynd, A., et al. (2001). Human defensive behaviors to threat scenarios show parallels to fear- and anxiety-related defense patterns of non-human mammals. *Neuroscience and Biobehavioral Reviews*, 25, 761–770.

Blanchard, R., Griebel, G., Henrie, J., & Blanchard, D. (1997). Differentiation of anxiolytic and panicolytic drugs by effects on rat and mouse defense test batteries. *Neuroscience and Biobehavioral Reviews*, 21, 783–789.

Blanchard, R., Yudko, E., Rodgers, R., & Blanchard, D. (1993). Defense system psychopharmacology: An ethological approach to the pharmacology of fear and anxiety. *Behavioural Brain Research*, 58, 155–165.

Bloomfield, P. (2000). Virtue epistemology and the epistemology of virtue. *Philosophy and Phenomenological Research*, 60, 23–43.

Boehm, C. (1999). *Hierarchy in the forest*. Cambridge, MA: Harvard University Press.

Boehm, C. (2012). *Moral origins*. New York: Basic Books.

Boyd, R. (1991). Realism, anti-foundationalism, and the enthusiasm for natural kinds. *Philosophical Studies*, 61, 127–148.

Boyd, R. (1999). Homeostasis, species, and higher taxa. In R. A. Wilson (Ed.), *Species: New interdisciplinary essays* (pp. 141–185). Cambridge, MA: MIT Press.

Brader, T. (2005). Striking a responsive chord: How political ads motivate and persuade voters by appealing to emotions. *American Journal of Political Science*, 49, 388–405.

Brader, T. (2006). *Campaigning for hearts and minds: How emotional appeals in political ads work*. Chicago: University of Chicago Press.

Brader, T., Valentino, N., & Suhay, E. (2008). What triggers public opposition to immigration? Anxiety, group cues, and immigration threat. *American Journal of Political Science*, 52, 959–978.

Bradley, B., Mogg, K., Falla, S., & Hamilton, L. (1998). Attentional bias for threatening facial expressions in anxiety. *Cognition and Emotion*, 12, 737–753.

Brady, M. (2013). *Emotional insight: The epistemic role of emotional experience*. Oxford: Oxford University Press.

Brennan, T. (2003). Stoic moral psychology. In B. Inwood (Ed.), *Cambridge companion to the Stoics* (pp. 233–256). Cambridge: Cambridge University Press.

Brink, D. (1989). *Moral realism and the foundations of ethics*. Cambridge: Cambridge University Press.

Brink, D., & Nelkin, D. (2013). Fairness and the architecture of responsibility. In D. Shoemaker (Ed.), *Oxford studies in agency and responsibilty* (Vol. 1, pp. 284–313). Oxford: Oxford University Press.

Brosch, T., & Sharma, D. (2005). The role of fear-relevant stimuli in visual search. *Emotion (Washington, DC)*, 5, 360–364.

Brown, E. (n.d.) "Virtue ethics" and the problem of advising fools. Unpublished manuscript.

Brown, L., Tomarken, A., et al. (1996). Individual differences in repressive-defensiveness predict basal salivary cortisol levels. *Journal of Personality and Social Psychology*, 70, 362–371.

Brownstein, M. (2014). Rationalizing flow: Agency in skilled unreflective action. *Philosophical Studies*, 168, 545–568.

Bruch, M. (2001). Shyness and social interaction. In C. Ray & L. Alden (Eds.), *International handbook of social anxiety* (pp. 195–215). New York: Wiley.

Burgio, K., Merluzzi, T., & Pryor, J. (1986). Effects of performance expectancy and self-focused attention on social interaction. *Journal of Personality and Social Psychology*, 50, 1216–1221.

References

Burns, P., & Gimpel, J. (2000). Economic insecurity, prejudicial stereotypes, and public opinion on immigration policy. *Political Science Quarterly*, 115, 201–225.

Cady, E. (1966). *John Woolman: The mind of the Quaker saint*. New York: Washington Square Press.

Calvo, M., & Castillo, M. D. (2001). Bias in predictive inference during reading. *Discourse Processes*, 32, 43–71.

Campbell, R., & Kumar, V. (2012). Moral reasoning on the ground. *Ethics*, 122, 273–312.

Campeau, S., & Davis, M. (1995). Involvement of the central nucleus and basolateral complex of the amygdala in fear conditioning measured with fear-potentiated startle in rats trained concurrently with auditory and visual conditioned stimuli. *Journal of Neuroscience*, 15, 2301–2311.

Cartwright-Hatton, S., Tschernitz, N., & Gomersall, H. (2005). Social anxiety in children. *Behaviour Research and Therapy*, 43, 189–201.

Carver, C., & Scheier, M. (1998). *On the self-regulation of behavior*. Cambridge: Cambridge University Press.

Chen, S., Shechter, D., & Chaiken, S. (1996). Getting at the truth or getting along. *Journal of Personality and Social Psychology*, 71, 262–275.

Cheney, D., & Sayfarth, R. (2007). *Baboon metaphysics*. Chicago: University of Chicago Press.

Christensen, W., Sutton, J., & McIlwain, D. (2015). The sense of agency and its role in strategic control of expert mountain bikers. *Psychology of Consciousness*, 3, 340–353.

Chudek, M., Zhao, W., & Henrich, J. (2013). Culture-gene coevolution, large-scale cooperation, and the shaping of human social psychology. In K. Sterelny, R. Joyce, B. Calcott, & B. Fraser (Eds.), *Cooperation and its evolution* (pp. 425–458). Cambridge, MA: MIT Press.

Cicero. (1927). *Tusculan disputations* (J. King, Ed.). Loeb Classical Library. Cambridge, MA: Harvard University Press.

Cisler, J., Olatunji, B., Feldner, M., & Forsyth, J. (2010). Emotion regulation and the anxiety disorders: An integrative review. *Journal of Psychopathology and Behavioral Assessment*, 32, 68–82.

Clark, D., & Wells, A. (1995). A cognitive model of social phobia. In R. Heimberg, M. Leibowitz, D. Hope, & F. Schneier (Eds.), *Social phobia: Diagnosis, assessment, and treatment* (69–93). New York: Guilford Press.

Coaster, M., Rogers, B., et al. (2011). Variables influencing the neural correlates of perceived risk of physical harm. *Cognitive, Affective & Behavioral Neuroscience*, 11, 494–507.

Cohen, J. (2009). *The red and the real: An essay on color ontology*. Oxford: Oxford University Press.

Colombetti, G. (2014). *The feeling body*. Cambridge, MA: MIT Press.

Confucius. (2007). *The analects of Confucius* (B. Watson, Trans.). New York: Columbia University Press.

Corr, P. (2008). The reinforcement sensitivity theory of personality. In P. Corr & N. McNaughton (Eds.), *The reinforcement sensitivity theory of personality* (pp. 428–507). New York: Cambridge University Press.

Craver, C. (2009). Mechanisms and natural kinds. *Philosophical Psychology*, 22, 575–594.

Csikszentmihalyi, M. (1991). *Flow: The psychology of optimal experience*. New York: Harper Perennial.

Cushman, F. (2013). The role of learning in punishment, prosociality, and human uniqueness. In K. Sterelny, R. Joyce, B. Calcott, & B. Fraser (Eds.), *Cooperation and its evolution* (pp. 333–372). Cambridge, MA: MIT Press.

Cutlip, W., & Leary, M. (1993). Anatomic and physiological bases of social blushing. *Behavioural Neurology*, 6, 181–185.

D'Arms, J., & Jacobson, D. (2000). The moralistic fallacy: On the "appropriateness" of emotions. *Philosophy and Phenomenological Research*, 61, 65–90.

D'Arms, J., & Jacobson, D. (2003). The significance of recalcitrant emotions (or, antiquasijudgmentalism). *Philosophy (London, England)*, 52, 127–145.

D'Arms, J., & Jacobson, D. (2006). Anthropocentric constraints on human value. In R. Shafer-Landau (Ed.), *Oxford studies in metaethics* (Vol. 1, pp. 99–126). Oxford: Oxford University Press.

Davis, M., Walker, D. L., Miles, L., & Grillon, C. (2010). Phasic vs sustained fear in rats and humans: Role of the extended amygdala in fear vs anxiety. *Neuropsychopharmacology*, 35, 105–135.

de Beaune, S. (2004). The invention of technology. *Current Anthropology*, 45, 139–162.

De Drue, C., Baas, M., & Nijstad, B. (2008). Hedonic tone and activation level in the mood–creativity link. *Journal of Personality and Social Psychology*, 94, 739–756.

de Jongh, R., Groenink, L., Van der Gugten, J., & Olivier, B. (2002). Pharmacological validation of the light-enhanced startle paradigm as a putative animal model of anxiety. *Psychopharmacology*, 159, 176–180.

Deonna, J., Rodogno, R., & Teroni, F. (2011). *In defense of shame*. Oxford: Oxford University Press.

DePaulo, B., Kenny, D., et al. (1990). Accuracy of person perception. *Journal of Personality and Social Psychology*, 52, 303–313.

Derakshan, N., Eysenck, M., & Myers, L. (2007). Emotional information processing in repressors: The vigilance–avoidance theory. *Cognition and Emotion*, 21, 1585–1614.

Derryberry, D., & Reed, M. (1997). Motivational and attentional components of personality. In G. Matthews (Ed.), *Cognitive science perspectives on personality and emotion* (pp. 443–473). San Diego, CA: Elsevier.

Derryberry, D., & Reed, M. (2002). Anxiety-related attentional biases and their regulation by attentional control. *Journal of Abnormal Psychology*, 111, 225–236.

de Sousa, R. (1987). *The rationality of emotion*. Cambridge, MA: MIT Press.

Dickson, J., Moberly, N., et al. (2009). Are repressors so special after all? *Journal of Research in Personality*, 43, 386–391.

Dienstbier, R., & Munter, P. (1971). Cheating as a function of the labeling of natural arousal. *Journal of Personality and Social Psychology*, 17, 208–213.

Doris, J. (2002). *Lack of character*. Cambridge: Cambridge University Press.

Doris, J. (2009). Skepticism about persons. *Philosophical Issues*, 19, 57–91.

Doris, J. (2015). *Talking to ourselves*. Oxford: Oxford University Press.

Dreyfus, H., & Dreyfus, S. (2004). Towards a phenomenology of ethical expertise. *Human Studies*, 14, 229–250.

Dutton, D., Clark, R., & Dickins, D. (1997). Personality in captive chimpanzees. *International Journal of Primatology*, 18, 539–552.

Ekman, P. (1971). Universals and cultural differences in facial expressions of emotion. In J. Cole (Ed.), *Nebraska Symposium on Motivation* (pp. 207–282). Lincoln: University of Nebraska Press.

Ekman, P. (1992). An argument for basic emotions. *Cognition and Emotion*, 6, 169–200.

Ekman, P. (1999). Basic emotions. In T. Dalgleish & M. Power (Eds.), *Handbook of cognition and emotion* (pp. 45–60). New York: Wiley.

Ellis, A., & Young, A. (1988). Accounting for delusional misidentifications. *British Journal of Psychiatry*, 157, 239–248.

Endler, N. (1997). Stress, anxiety, and coping. *Canadian Psychology*, 38, 136–153.

Endler, N., Crooks, D., & Parker, J. (1997). The interaction model of anxiety. *Anxiety, Stress, and Coping*, 5, 301–311.

Endler, N., Edwards, J., & Vitelli, R. (1991). *Endler Multidimensional Anxiety Scales*. Los Angeles: Western Psychological Services.

Endler, N., Hunt, J., & Rosenstein, A. (1962). An S-R inventory of anxiousness. *Psychological Monographs*, 76, 1–33.

Endler, N., & Kocovski, N. (2001). State and trait anxiety revisited. *Journal of Anxiety Disorders*, 15, 231–245.

Endler, N., Parker, J., Bagby, R., & Cox, B. (1991). Multidimensionality of state and trait anxiety. *Journal of Personality and Social Psychology*, 60, 919–926.

Enoch, D. (2006). Agency, shmagency: Why normativity won't come from what is constitutive of agency. *Philosophical Review*, 115, 169–198.

Epstein, S. (1972). The nature of anxiety with emphasis upon its relationship to expectancy. In C. Spielberger (Ed.), *Anxiety: Current trends in theory and research* (Vol. 2, 291–337). New York: Academic Press.

Esteves, F., Dimberg, U., & Öhman, A. (1994). Automatically elicited fear. *Cognition and Emotion*, 8, 393–413.

Fahrenberg, J. (1992). Psychophysiology of neuroticism and emotionality. In A. Gale & M. Eysenck (Eds.), *Handbook of individual differences: Biological perspectives*. Chichester, UK: Wiley.

Fessler, D. (2007). From appeasement to conformity. In J. Tracy, R. Robins, & J. Tangney (Eds.), *The self-conscious emotions* (pp. 174–193). New York: Guilford Press.

Festinger, L. (1957). *A theory of cognitive dissonance*. Stanford, CA: Stanford University Press.

Fine, C. (2006). Is the emotional dog wagging its rational tail, or chasing it? *Philosophical Explorations*, 9, 83–98.

Fischer, J. M., & Ravizza, M. (1998). *Responsibility and control*. Cambridge: Cambridge University Press.

Fiske, A. (2000). Complementarity theory. *Personality and Social Psychology Review*, 4, 76–94.

References

Flett, G., Endler, N., & Fairlie, P. (1999). The interaction model of anxiety and the threat of Quebec's separation from Canada. *Journal of Personality and Social Psychology*, 76, 143–150.

Folkman, S., & Lazarus, R. (1985). *Stress, appraisal, & coping*. New York: Springer.

Foot, P. (1978). *Virtues and vices*. Berkeley: University of California Press.

Fossat, P., Bacqué-Cazenave, J., et al. (2014). Comparative behavior: Anxiety-like behavior in crayfish is controlled by serotonin. *Science*, 344, 1239–1297.

Fox, A., Shelton, S., et al. (2008). Trait-like brain activity during adolescence predicts anxious temperament in primates. *PLoS One*, 3.

Fox, E., Russo, R., & Georgiou, G. (2005). Anxiety modulates the degree of attentive resources required to process emotional faces. *Cognitive, Affective & Behavioral Neuroscience*, 5, 396–404.

Frank, R. (1988). *Passions within reason*. New York: Norton.

Frankena, W. (1973). *Ethics* (2nd ed.). New York: Pearson.

Frankfurt, H. (1971). Freedom of the will and the concept of a person. *Journal of Philosophy*, 68, 5–20.

French, P. (2001). *The virtues of vengeance*. Lawrence: University of Kansas Press.

Freud, S. (1926/1959). Inhibition, symptoms, and anxiety. In J. Strachey (Ed.), *The standard edition of the complete psychological works of Sigmund Freud* (Vol. 20). London: Hogarth Press.

Füstös, J., Gramann, K., et al. (2013). On the embodiment of emotion regulation: Interoceptive awareness facilitates reappraisal. *Social Cognitive and Affective Neuroscience*, 8, 911–917.

Gardner, W. L., Gabriel, S., & Lee, A. Y. (1999). "I" value freedom but "we" value relationships: Self-construal priming mirrors cultural differences in judgment. *Psychological Science*, 10, 321–326.

Gewirtz, J., McNish, K., & Davis, M. (1998). Lesions of the bed nucleus of the stria terminalis block sensitization of the acoustic startle reflex produced by repeated stress, but not fear-potentiated startle. *Progress in Neuro-Psychopharmacology & Biological Psychiatry*, 22, 625–648.

Gibbard, A. (1990). *Wise choices, apt feelings*. Cambridge, MA: Harvard University Press.

Gilbert, P. (2001). Evolution and social anxiety. *Psychiatric Clinics of North America*, 24, 723–751.

Goldie, P. (2000). *The emotions*. Oxford: Oxford University Press.

Goldie, P. (2004). Emotion, reason & virtue. In D. Evans & P. Cruse (Eds.), *Emotion, evolution and rationality* (pp. 249–268). Oxford: Oxford University Press.

Goldie, P. (2008). Misleading emotions. In G. Brun, U. Doguoglu, & D. Kuenzle (Eds.), *Epistemology and emotion* (pp. 149–165). Hampshire, UK: Ashgate.

Gorman, J. (2014, June 13). What to do when crawdad grows anxious. *New York Times*. Retrieved from http://www.nytimes.com.

Grant, B., Stinson, F., et al. (2004). Prevalence and co-occurrence of substance use disorders and independent mood and anxiety disorders. *Archives of General Psychiatry*, 61, 807–816.

Graver, M. (2007). *Stoicism and emotion*. Chicago: University of Chicago Press.

Gray, J., & McNaughton, N. (2000). *The neuropsychology of anxiety*. Oxford: Oxford University Press.

Great Britain, Parliament. (1834). Debates in Parliament: Session 1833 on the resolutions and bill for the abolition of slavery in the British colonies. Retrieved from.

Greenberg, J., Pyszczynski, T., & Stine, P. (1985). Social anxiety and anticipation of future interactions as determinants of the favorability of self-presentation. *Journal of Research in Personality*, 19, 1–11.

Greene, J. (2008). The secret joke of Kant's soul. In W. Sinnott-Armstrong (Ed.), *Moral psychology* (Vol. 3, pp. 35–79). Cambridge, MA: MIT Press.

Greene, J., Sommerville, R., et al. (2001). An fMRI investigation of emotional engagement in moral judgment. *Science*, 293, 2105–2108.

Griffiths, P. (1997). *What emotions really are*. Chicago: University of Chicago Press.

Griffiths, P. (2004a). Emotions as natural and normative kinds. *Philosophy of Science*, 71, 901–911.

Griffiths, P. (2004b). Toward a "Machiavellian" theory of emotional appraisal. In D. Evans & P. Cruse (Eds.), *Emotion, evolution and rationality* (pp. 89–105). Oxford: Oxford University Press.

Griffiths, P., & Scarantino, A. (2005). Emotions in the wild: The situated perspective on emotion. In P. Robbins & M. Aydede (Eds.), *Cambridge handbook of situated cognition* (pp. 437–453). Cambridge: Cambridge University Press.

Gross, J. (2015). Emotion regulation: Current status and future prospects. *Psychological Inquiry*, 26, 1–26.

Haidt, J. (2001). The emotional dog and its rational tail. *Psychological Review*, 108, 814–834.

References

Haidt, J., & Bjorklund, F. (2008). Social intuitionists answer six questions about moral psychology. In W. Sinnott-Armstrong (Ed.), *Moral psychology* (Vol. 3, pp. 181–217). Cambridge, MA: MIT Press.

Halberstadt, J., & Green, J. (2008). Carryover effects of analytic thought on preference quality. *Journal of Experimental Social Psychology*, 44, 1199–1203.

Halberstadt, J., & Wilson, T. (2008). Reflections on conscious reflection. In L. Rips & J. Adler (Eds.), *Reasoning: Studies of human inference and its foundations*. Cambridge: Cambridge University Press.

Hanin, Y. (2007). Emotions and athletic performance: Individual zones of functioning model. In D. Smith & M. Bar-Eli (Eds.), *Essential readings in sport and exercise psychology* (pp. 55–73). Champaign, IL: Human Kinetics.

Harbin, A. (2016). *Disorientations and moral life*. Oxford: Oxford University Press.

Harman, G. (1999). Moral philosophy meets social psychology: Virtue ethics and the fundamental attribution error. *Proceedings of the Aristotelian Society*, 99, 315–331.

Harris, P. (1990). Shyness and embarrassment in psychological theory and ordinary language. In W. Crozier (Ed.), *Shyness and embarrassment* (pp. 59–86). New York: Cambridge University Press.

Hatzigeorgiadis, A., & Biddle, S. (2001). Athletes' perceptions of how cognitive interference during competition influences concentration and effort. *Anxiety, Stress, and Coping*, 14, 411–429.

Heerey, E., & Kring, A. (2007). Interpersonal consequences of social anxiety. *Journal of Abnormal Psychology*, 116, 125–134.

Heidegger, M. (1962). *Being and time* (J. Macquarrie & E. Robinson, Trans.). Oxford: Blackwell.

Helm, B. (2001). *Emotional reason*. Cambridge: Cambridge University Press.

Helm, B. (2002). Felt evaluations. *American Philosophical Quarterly*, 39, 13–30.

Hembree, R. (1988). Correlates, causes, effects, and treatment of test anxiety. *Review of Educational Research*, 58, 7–77.

Henrich, J., & Gil-White, F. (2001). The evolution of prestige: Freely conferred deference as a mechanism for enhancing the benefits of cultural transmission. *Evolution and Human Behavior*, 22, 165–196.

Herman, B. (1993). *The practice of moral judgment*. Cambridge, MA: Harvard University Press.

Hieronymi, P. (2014). Reflection and responsibility. *Philosophy & Public Affairs*, 42, 3–41.

Hill, K., & Eaton, W. (1977). The interaction of test anxiety and success-failure experiences in determining children's arithmetic performance. *Developmental Psychology*, 6, 520–528.

Himadi, W., Arkowitz, H., et al. (1980). Minimal dating and its relationship to other problems and general adjustment. *Behavior Therapy*, 11, 345–352.

Hitchcock, J., & Davis, M. (1987). Fear-potentiated startle using an auditory conditioned stimulus. *Physiology & Behavior*, 39, 403–408.

Hitchcock, J., & Davis, M. (1991). The efferent pathway of the amygdala involved in conditioned fear as measured with the fear-potentiated startle paradigm. *Behavioral Neuroscience*, 105, 826–842.

Hoch, P. (1949). *Anxiety*. New York: Grune and Stratton.

Hoffman, K., Gothard, K., et al. (2007). Facial-expression and gaze-selective responses in the monkey amygdala. *Current Biology*, 17, 766–772.

Hofmann, S., Ellard, K., & Siegle, G. (2012). Neurobiological correlates of cognitions in fear and anxiety. *Cognition and Emotion*, 26, 282–299.

Hofmann, S., Korte, K., & Suvak, M. (2009). The upside of being socially anxious. *Journal of Social and Clinical Psychology*, 28, 714–727.

Hofmann, S., & Smits, J. (2008). Cognitive-behavioral therapy for adult anxiety disorders. *Journal of Clinical Psychiatry*, 69, 621–632.

Horton, D. (1943). The function of alcohol in primitive societies: A cross-cultural study. *Quarterly Journal of Studies on Alcohol*, 4, 199–320.

Horwitz, A., & Wakefield, J. (2012). *All we have to fear*. New York: Oxford University Press.

Huddy, L., Feldman, S., & Cassese, E. (2007). On the distinct political effects of anxiety and anger. In W. Neuman, G. Marcus, A. Crigler, & M. MacKuen (Eds.), *The affect effect* (pp. 202–230). Chicago: University of Chicago Press.

Hume, D. (1888). *A treatise of human nature* (L. Selby-Bigge & P. Nidditch, Eds.). Oxford: Oxford University Press.

Hursthouse, R. (1999). *On virtue ethics*. Oxford: Oxford University Press.

Iwata, J., LeDoux, J., et al. (1986). Intrinsic neurons in the amygdala field projected to by the medial geniculate body mediate emotional responses conditioned to acoustic stimuli. *Brain Research*, 383, 195–214.

Izard, C. (1972). Anxiety: A variable combination of interacting fundamental emotions. In C. Spielberger (Ed.), *Anxiety: Current trends in theory and research* (Vol. 1, pp. 55–106). New York: Academic Press.

References

Izard, C. (2007). Basic emotions, natural kinds, emotion schemas, and a new paradigm. *Perspectives on Psychological Science*, 2, 260–280.

Jackson, L., Gaertner, L., & Batson, C. (2016). Can affect disengagement produce moral standard violation? *Self and Identity*, 15, 19–31.

Jacobson, D. (2012). Moral dumbfounding and moral stupefaction. In M. Timmons (Ed.), *Oxford studies in normative ethics* (Vol. 2, pp. 289–315) Oxford: Oxford University Press.

Jacobson, D. (2013). Regret, agency, and error. In D. Shoemaker (Ed.), *Oxford studies in agency & responsibility* (pp. 95–125). Oxford: Oxford University Press.

Jamieson, J., Mendes, W., Blackstock, E., & Schmader, T. (2010). Turning the knots in your stomach into bows: Reappraising arousal improves performance on the GRE. *Journal of Experimental Social Psychology*, 46, 208–212.

Jamieson, J., Mendes, W., & Nock, M. (2013). Improving acute stress responses: The power of reappraisal. *Current Directions in Psychological Science*, 22, 51–56.

Jennings, J., Sparta, D., et al. (2011). Distinct extended amygdala circuits for divergent motivational states. *Nature*, 496, 224–230.

Jones, R., Cox, D., et al. (2015). *Anxiety, nostalgia, and mistrust*. Retrieved from https://www.prri.org/research/survey-anxiety-nostalgia-and-mistrust-findings-from-the-2015-american-values-survey.

Kalin, N., Shelton, S., et al. (2005). Brain regions associated with the expression and contextual regulation of anxiety in primates. *Biological Psychiatry*, 58, 796–804.

Kant, I. (1785/1996). Groundwork of the metaphysics of morals. In M. Gregor & A. Wood (Eds.), *Practical philosophy* (pp. 37–108). Cambridge: Cambridge University Press.

Kant, I. (1797/1996). Metaphysics of morals. In M. Gregor & A. Wood (Eds.), *Practical philosophy* (pp. 353–604). Cambridge: Cambridge University Press.

Kant, I. (1997). *Lectures on ethics*. Cambridge: Cambridge University Press.

Kashdan, T. (2007). Social anxiety spectrum and diminished positive experiences. *Clinical Psychology Review*, 27, 348–365.

Kauppinen, A. (2014). Empathy, emotion regulation, and moral judgment. In H. Maibom (Ed.), *Empathy and morality*. Oxford: Oxford University Press.

Keihl, K., & Hoffman, M. (2011). The criminal psychopath: History, neuroscience, treatment, & economics. *Jurimetrics*, 51, 355–397.

Keller, P. (1999). Converting the unconverted: The effect of inclination and opportunity to discount health-related fear appeals. *Journal of Applied Psychology*, 84, 403–415.

Kelly, D. (2011). *Yuck!: The nature and moral significance of disgust*. Cambridge, MA: MIT Press.

Kendler, K., Zachar, P., & Craver, C. (2011). What kinds of things are psychiatric disorders? *Psychological Medicine*, 41, 1143–1150.

Kennett, J., & Fine, C. (2008). Will the real moral judgment please stand up? *Ethical Theory and Moral Practice*, 12, 77–96.

Kessler, R., Angermeyer, M., et al. (2007). Lifetime prevalence and age-of-onset distributions of mental disorders in the World Health Organization's World Mental Health Survey Initiative. *World Psychiatry: Official Journal of the World Psychiatric Association (WPA)*, 6, 168–176.

Kessler, R., Chiu, W., Demler, O., & Walters, E. (2005). Prevalence, severity, and comorbidity of twelve-month DSM-IV disorders in the National Comorbidity Survey Replication (NCS-R). *Archives of General Psychiatry*, 62, 617–627.

Kierkegaard, S. (1844/2006). *Fear and trembling* (C. S. Evans & S. Walsh, Eds.; S. Walsh, Trans.). Cambridge: Cambridge University Press.

Kim, S.-Y., Adhikari, A., et al. (2013). Diverging neural pathways assemble a behavioural state from separable features in anxiety. *Nature*, 496, 219–223.

Kinder, D., & Kam, C. (2009). *Us against them: Ethnocentric foundations of American public opinion*. Chicago: University of Chicago Press.

King, M. L., Jr. (1967, March 25). State Street speech, Chicago. Retrieved from http://www.jofreeman.com/photos/KingAtChicago.html.

King, M. L., Jr. (1967, April 4). Beyond Vietnam: A time to break silence. Riverside Church, New York City. *American Rhetoric: Online Speech Bank*. Accessed May 8, 2017. http://www.americanrhetoric.com/speeches/mlkatimetobreaksilence.htm.

King, M. L., Jr. (1998). *The autobiography of Martin Luther King, Jr.* (C. Carson, Ed.). New York: Warner Books.

Kitcher, P. (2011). *The ethical project*. Cambridge, MA: Harvard University Press.

Klein, C. (2010). Philosophical issues in neuroimaging. *Philosophy Compass*, 5, 186–198.

Klein, G. (1999). *Sources of power*. Cambridge, MA: MIT Press.

Knauft, B. (1991). Violence and sociality in human evolution. *Anthropological Review*, 32, 391–409.

Knausgaard, K. (2015, January). The terrible beauty of brain surgery. *New York Times Magazine*. Retrieved from http://www.nytimes.com/2016/01/03/magazine/karl-ove-knausgaard-on-the-terrible-beauty-of-brain-surgery.html.

References

Kornblith, H. (1993). *Inductive inference and its natural ground.* Cambridge, MA: MIT Press.

Korsgaard, C. (2009). *Self-constitution.* Oxford: Oxford University Press.

Korsgaard, C. (2010). Does moral action depend on reasoning? *Big Questions,* Templeton Foundation. Retrieved from https://www.templeton.org/reason/.

Kraut, R. (2007). *What is good and why.* Cambridge, MA: Harvard University Press.

Kross, E., & Ayduk, O. (2008). Facilitating adaptive emotional analysis. *Personality and Social Psychology Bulletin,* 34, 924–938.

Kurth, C. (2012). What do our critical practices say about the nature of morality? *Philosophical Studies,* 166, 45–64.

Kurth, C. (2015). Moral anxiety and moral agency. In M. Timmons (Ed.), *Oxford studies in normative ethics* (Vol. 5, pp. 171–195). Oxford: Oxford University Press.

Kurth, C. (2016). Anxiety, normative uncertainty, and social regulation. *Biology & Philosophy,* 31, 1–21.

Kurth, C. (forthcoming a). Anxiety: A case study in the value of negative emotion. In C. Tappolet, F. Teroni, & A. Konzelmann (Eds.), *Shadows of the soul: Philosophical perspectives on negative emotions.* Abingdon, UK: Routledge.

Kurth, C. (forthcoming b). Emotion, deliberation, and the skill model of virtuous agency. *Mind & Language.*

Ladd, J. M., & Lenz, G. S. (2008). Reassessing the role of anxiety in vote choice. *Political Psychology,* 29, 275–296.

Lazarus, R. (1991). *Emotion and adaptation.* New York: Oxford University Press.

Lazarus, R. (1999). *Stress and emotion.* New York: Oxford University Press.

Learner, J., & Tetlock, P. (1999). Accounting for effects of accountability. *Psychological Bulletin,* 125, 255–275.

Leary, M., Knight, P., & Johnson, K. (1987). Social anxiety and dyadic conversation. *Journal of Social and Clinical Psychology,* 5, 34–50.

Leary, M., & Kowalski, L. (1995). *Social anxiety.* New York: Guilford Press.

Leary, M. R., Kowalski, R. M., & Campbell, C. (1988). Self-presentational concerns and social anxiety: The role of generalized impression expectancies. *Journal of Research in Personality,* 22, 308–318.

LeDoux, J. (1996). *The emotional brain.* New York: Simon & Schuster.

LeDoux, J. (2000). The amygdala and emotion: A view through fear. In J. Aggleton (Ed.), *The amygdala* (pp. 289–310). New York: Oxford University Press.

LeDoux, J. (2008). Emotional colouration of consciousness: How feelings come about. In L. Weiskrantz & M. Davies (Eds.), *Frontiers of consciousness* (pp. 69–130). Oxford: Oxford University Press.

LeDoux, J. (2015). *Anxious: Using the brain to understand and treat fear and anxiety.* New York: Viking.

LeDoux, J., Iwata, J., Cicchetti, P., & Reis, D. (1988). Different projections of the central amygdaloid nucleus mediate autonomic and behavioral correlates of conditioned fear. *Journal of Neuroscience*, 8, 2517–2529.

Lee, Y., & Davis, M. (1997a). Role of the hippocampus, bed nucleus of the stria terminalis and amygdala in the excitatory effect of corticotropin releasing hormone on the acoustic startle reflex. *Journal of Neuroscience*, 17, 6434–6446.

Lee, Y., & Davis, M. (1997b). Role of the septum in the excitatory effect of corticotropin releasing (CRH) hormone on the acoustic startle reflex. *Journal of Neuroscience*, 17, 6424–6433.

Leighton, S. (2002). Aristotle's account of anger. *Ratio*, 15, 23–45.

Lelieveld, G., Van Dijk, E., et al. (2011). Disappointed in you. *Journal of Experimental Social Psychology*, 47, 635–641.

Levenson, R. (1999). The intrapersonal function of emotion. *Cognition and Emotion*, 13, 481–504.

Levenson, R., Soto, J., & Pole, N. (2007). Emotion, biology, and culture. In S. Kitayama & D. Cohen (Eds.), *Handbook of cultural psychology* (pp. 780–796). New York: Guilford Press.

Lewis, I., Watson, B., Tay, R., & White, K. (2007). The role of fear appeals in driver safety. *International Journal of Behavioral and Consultation Therapy*, 3, 203–222.

Lewis, M. (2005). Bridging emotion theory and neurobiology through dynamic systems modeling. *Behavioral and Brain Sciences*, 28, 169–245.

Liang, K. C., Melia, K., et al. (1992). Corticotropin-releasing factor: Long-lasting facilitation of the acoustic startle reflex. *Journal of Neuroscience*, 12, 2303–2312.

Mackie, J. L. (1977). *Inventing right and wrong.* New York: Penguin.

MacKuen, M., Wolak, J., et al. (2010). Civil engagements: Resolute partisanship or reflective deliberation. *American Journal of Political Science*, 54, 440–458.

Maibom, H. (2005). Moral unreason: The case of psychopathy. *Mind & Language*, 20, 237–257.

Maibom, H. (2010). The descent of shame. *Philosophy and Phenomenological Research*, 80, 566–594.

References

Maibom, H. (2014). Introduction: (Almost) everything you ever wanted to know about empathy. In H. Maibom (Ed.), *Empathy and Morality* (pp. 1–40). Oxford: Oxford University Press.

Mandela, N. (1994). *Long walk to freedom*. Boston: Back Bay Books.

Marcus, G., MacKuen, M., & Neuman, W. (2011). Parsimony and complexity: Developing and testing theories of affective intelligence. *Political Psychology*, 32, 323–336.

Marcus, G., Neuman, W., & MacKuen, M. (2000). *Affective intelligence and political judgment*. Chicago: University of Chicago Press.

Marks, L., & Gelder, M. (1966). Different ages of onset in varieties of phobias. *American Journal of Psychiatry*, 123, 218–221.

Marks, I., & Nesse, R. (1994). Fear and fitness: An evolutionary analysis of anxiety disorders. *Ethology and Sociobiology*, 15, 247–261.

Marsh, H. (2014). *Do no harm*. New York: St. Martin's Press.

Mathews, A. (1990). Why worry? The cognitive function of anxiety. *Behaviour Research and Therapy*, 28, 455–468.

Mathews, A., Fox, E., Yiend, J., & Calder, A. (2003). The face of fear: Effects of eye gaze and emotion on visual attention. *Visual Cognition*, 10, 823–835.

Matthews, G. (1986). The effects of anxiety on intellectual performance: When and why are they found? *Journal of Research in Personality*, 20, 385–401.

May, L. (2015). *Contingent pacifism*. Cambridge: Cambridge University Press.

McCroskey, J., & Beatty, M. (1984). Communication apprehension and accumulated communication state anxiety experiences. *Communication Monographs*, 51, 79–84.

McDowell, J. (1998). *Mind, value, and reality*. Cambridge, MA: Harvard University Press.

McGuire, J., Langdon, R., et al. (2009). A reanalysis of the personal/impersonal distinction in moral psychology research. *Journal of Experimental Social Psychology*, 45, 577–580.

McMenamin, B., Langeslag, S., et al. (2014). Network organization unfolds over time during periods of anxious anticipation. *Journal of Neuroscience*, 34, 11261–11273.

McNally, R. (2009). Anxiety. In D. Sander & K. Scherer (Eds.), *Oxford companion to emotion and affective sciences*. Oxford: Oxford University Press.

Mennin, D., Heimberg, R., et al. (2008). Is general anxiety disorder an anxiety or mood disorder? *Depression and Anxiety*, 25, 289–299.

Merker, B. (2007). Consciousness without a cerebral cortex. *Behavioral and Brain Sciences*, 30, 63–81.

Michl, P., Meindl, T., et al. (2014). Neurobiological underpinnings of shame and guilt. *SCAN*, 9, 150–157.

Miller, N. (1959). Liberalization of basic S-R concepts: Extensions to conflict behavior, motivation and social learning. In S. Koch (Ed.), *Psychology: A study of a science* (Vol. 2, pp. 196–292). New York: McGraw-Hill.

Miltner, W., Kriechel, S., et al. (2004). Eye movements and behavioral responses to threatening and nonthreatening stimuli during visual search in phobic and non-phobic subjects. *Emotion (Washington, DC)*, 4, 323–339.

Mobbs, D., Yu, R., et al. (2010). Neural activity associated with monitoring the oscillating threat value of a tarantula. *Proceedings of the National Academy of Sciences of the United States of America*, 107, 20582–20586.

Monosov, I. (2017). Anterior cingulate is a source of valence-specific information about value and uncertainty. *Nature Communications*, 8, 1–12.

Moore, G. E. (1903). *Principia ethica*. Cambridge: Cambridge University Press.

Mor, N., & Winquist, J. (2002). Self-focused attention and negative affect: A meta-analysis. *Psychological Bulletin*, 128, 638–662.

Morton, A. (2010). Epistemic emotions. In P. Goldie (Ed.), *Oxford handbook of philosophy of emotion* (pp. 385–400). Oxford: Oxford University Press.

Moyer, K. (1976). *The psychobiology of aggression*. New York: Harper & Row.

Murphy, D. (2005). Can evolution explain insanity? *Biology & Philosophy*, 20, 745–766.

Murphy, D., & Stich, S. (2000). Darwin in the madhouse: Evolutionary psychology and the classification of mental disorders. In P. Carruthers & A. Chamberlain (Eds.), *Evolution and the human mind: Modularity, language and meta-cognition* (pp. 62–92). Cambridge: Cambridge University Press.

Natale, M., Entin, E., & Jaffe, J. (1979). Vocal interruptions in dyadic communication as a function of speech and social anxiety. *Journal of Personality and Social Psychology*, 37, 865–878.

Newman, J., MacCoon, D., et al. (2005). Validating a distinction between primary and secondary psychopathy with measures of Gray's BIS and BAS constructs. *Journal of Abnormal Psychology*, 114, 319–323.

Nichols, S. (2004). *Sentimental rules*. Oxford: Oxford University Press.

Nisbett, R. E., & Wilson, T. D. (1977). Telling more than we can know: Verbal reports on mental processes. *Psychological Review*, 84, 231–259.

Nolen-Hoeksema, S. (2000). The role of rumination in depressive disorders and mixed anxiety/depressive symptoms. *Journal of Abnormal Psychology*, 109, 504–511.

Nussbaum, M. (2001). *Upheavals of thought*. Cambridge: Cambridge University Press.

Oatley, K., Keltner, D., & Jenkins, J. (2006). *Understanding emotions*. Hoboken, NJ: Wiley-Blackwell.

Öhman, A. (2008). Fear and anxiety. In M. Lewis, J. M. Haviland-Jones, & L. F. Barrett (Eds.), *Handbook of emotions* (pp. 127–156). New York: Guilford Press.

Öhman, A., Flykt, A., & Esteves, F. (2001). Emotion drives attention. *Journal of Experimental Psychology: General*, 130, 466–478.

Öhman, A., Lundquist, D., & Esteves, F. (2001). The face in the crowd revisited. *Journal of Personality and Social Psychology*, 80, 381–396.

Öhman, A., & Soares, J. (1993). On the automaticity of phobic fear. *Journal of Abnormal Psychology*, 102, 121–132.

Öhman, A., & Soares, J. (1994). Unconscious anxiety. *Journal of Abnormal Psychology*, 103, 231–240.

Öhman, A., & Soares, J. (1999). Emotional conditioning to masked stimuli. *Journal of Experimental Psychology: General*, 127, 69–82.

Olatunji, B., Abramowitz, J., et al. (2007). Scrupulosity and obsessive-compulsive symptoms: Confirmatory factor analysis and validity of the Penn Inventory of Scrupulosity. *Journal of Anxiety Disorders*, 21, 771–787.

Oler, J., Birn, R., et al. (2012). Evidence for coordinated functional activity within the extended amygdala of non-human and human primates. *NeuroImage*, 61, 1059–1066.

Panksepp, J., & Panksepp, J. (2000). The seven sins of evolutionary psychology. *Evolution & Cognition*, 6, 108–131.

Parra, C., Esteves, F., Flykt, A., & Öhman, A. (1997). Pavlovian conditioning to social stimuli: Backward masking and the dissociation of implicit and explicit cognitive processes. *European Psychologist*, 2, 106–117.

Paul, J. (1980, September). Mutual attraction differs from lust. *L'Osservatore Romano*, weekly edition in English. Retrieved from http://www.ewtn.com/library/papaldoc/jp2tb39.htm.

Peacocke, C. (2004). *The realm of reason*. New York: Oxford University Press.

Perkins, A., & Corr, P. (2006). Reactions to threat and personality: Psychometric differentiation of intensity and direction dimensions of human defensive behavior. *Behavioural Brain Research*, 169, 21–28.

Perkins, A., Ettinger, U., et al. (2009). Effects of lorazepam and citalopram on human defensive reactions: Ethopharmacological differentiation of fear and anxiety. *Journal of Neuroscience*, 29, 12617–12624.

Perkins, A., Leonard, A., et al. (2013). A dose of ruthlessness. *Journal of Experimental Psychology: General*, 142, 612–620.

Phelps, E., O'Connor, K., et al. (2001). Activation of the left amygdala to a cognitive representation of fear. *Nature Neuroscience*, 4, 437–441.

Philips, S., & Steel, R. (2002). Repressive adaptive style in children with chronic illness. *Psychosomatic Medicine*, 64, 34–42.

Pilkonis, P. (1977). The behavioral consequences of shyness. *Journal of Personality*, 45, 596–611.

Pinker, S. (2011). *The better angels of our nature*. New York: Viking.

Pizarro, D., & Bloom, P. (2003). The intelligence of the moral intuitions: Comment on Haidt. *Psychological Review*, 110, 193–196.

Plakias, A. (2013). The good and the gross. *Ethical Theory and Moral Practice*, 16, 261–278.

Plank, G. (2012). *John Woolman's path to the peaceable kingdom*. Philadelphia: University of Pennsylvania Press.

Porter, E. (2016, May 25). We've seen the Trump phenomenon before. *New York Times*. Retrieved from http://www.nytimes.com.

Pratt, M. (1984). Identity: Skin, blood, heart. In E. Bulkin, M. Pratt, & B. Smith (Eds.), *Yours in struggle* (pp. 11–63). Brooklyn, NY: Long Haul Press.

Price, C. (2006). Affect without object. *European Journal of Analytic Philosophy*, 2, 49–68.

Price, J. (2003). Evolutionary aspects of anxiety disorders. *Dialogues in Clinical Neuroscience*, 5, 223–236.

Price, M., & Norman, E. (2008). Intuitive decisions on the fringes of consciousness. *Judgment and Decision Making*, 3, 28–41.

Prinz, J. (2004). *Gut reactions*. Oxford: Oxford University Press.

Prinz, J. (2007). *The emotional construction of morals*. Oxford: Oxford University Press.

Prinz, J. (2011a). Against empathy. *Southern Journal of Philosophy*, 49, 214–233.

Prinz, J. (2011b). Is empathy necessary for morality? In A. Coplan & P. Goldie (Eds.), *Empathy: Psychological and Philosophical Perspectives* (pp. 211–229). Oxford: Oxford University Press.

References

Pultronier, S., Zangrossi, H., & de Barros Viana, M. (2003). Antipanic-like effect of serotonin reuptake inhibitors in the elevated T-maze. *Behavioural Brain Research*, 147, 185–192.

Rachman, S. (2004). *Anxiety*. Hove, East Sussex, UK: Psychology Press.

Raichle, M., & Mintun, M. (2006). Brain work and brain imaging. *Annual Review of Neuroscience*, 29, 449–476.

Railton, P. (1986a). Facts and values. *Philosophical Topics*, 14, 5–31.

Railton, P. (1986b). Moral realism. *Philosophical Review*, 95, 163–197.

Railton, P. (1989). Naturalism and prescriptivity. *Social Philosophy & Policy*, 7, 151–174.

Railton, P. (2009). Practical competence and fluent agency. In D. Sobel & S. Wall (Eds.), *Reasons for action* (pp. 81–115). New York: Cambridge University Press.

Railton, P. (2014). The affective dog and its rational tale: Intuition and attunement. *Ethics*, 124, 813–859.

Rapee, R., Craske, M., et al. (1996). Measurement of perceived control over anxiety-related events. *Behavior Therapy*, 27, 279–293.

Ratcliffe, M. (2008). *Feelings of being*. Oxford: Oxford University Press.

Rawls, J. (1971). *A theory of justice*. Cambridge, MA: Harvard University Press.

Richerson, P., & Boyd, R. (2013). Rethinking paleoanthropology: A world queerer than we supposed. In G. Hatfield & H. Pittman (Eds.), *Evolution of mind, brain, and culture* (pp. 263–302). Philadelphia: University of Pennsylvania Press.

Rietzschel, E., Nijstad, B., & Stroebe, W. (2007). Relative accessibility of domain knowledge and creativity: The effects of knowledge activation on the quantity and quality of generated ideas. *Journal of Experimental Social Psychology*, 43, 933–946.

Rinck, M., Reinecke, A., et al. (2005). Speeded detection and increased distraction in fear of spiders. *Journal of Abnormal Psychology*, 114, 235–248.

Roberts, R. (2003). *Emotions: An essay in aid of moral psychology*. Cambridge: Cambridge University Press.

Roberts, R. (2014). *Emotions in the moral life*. Cambridge: Cambridge University Press.

Rorty, A. (1980). Introduction. In A. Rorty (Ed.), *Explaining emotions* (pp. 1–8). Berkeley: University of California Press.

Rosati, C. (1995). Persons, perspectives, and full information accounts of the good. *Ethics*, 105, 296–325.

Rosati, C. (2006). Personal good. In T. Horgan & M. Timmons (Eds.), *Metaethics after Moore* (pp. 107–132). Oxford: Oxford University Press.

Roskies, A. (2003). Are ethical judgments intrinsically motivational? Lessons from "acquired sociopathy." *Philosophical Psychology*, 16, 51–66.

Rozin, P., Millman, L., & Nemeroff, C. (1986). Operation of the laws of sympathetic magic in disgust and other domains. *Journal of Personality and Social Psychology*, 50, 703–712.

Russell, J. (2003). Core affect and the psychological construction of emotion. *Psychological Review*, 110, 145–172.

Sarkissian, H. (2010). Confucius and the effortless life of virtue. *History of Philosophy Quarterly*, 27, 1–16.

Sartre, P. (1943). *Being and nothingness* (H. Barnes, Trans.). New York: Citadel Press.

Sauer, H. (2011). Social intuitionism and the psychology of moral reasoning. *Philosophy Compass*, 6, 708–721.

Scarantino, A. (2009). Core affect and natural affective kinds. *Philosophy of Science*, 76, 940–957.

Scarantino, A. (2010). Insights and blindspots of the cognitivist theory of emotions. *British Journal for the Philosophy of Science*, 61, 729–768.

Scarantino, A. (2014). The motivational theory of emotions. In J. D'Arms & D. Jacobson (Eds.), *Moral psychology and human agency* (pp. 156–185). Oxford: Oxford University Press.

Scarantino, A., & Griffiths, P. (2011). Don't give up on basic emotions. *Emotion Review*, 3, 1–11.

Schachter, S. (1959). *The psychology of affiliation*. Stanford, CA: Stanford University Press.

Schachter, S., & Latané, B. (1964). Crime, cognition, and the autonomic nervous system. *Nebraska Symposium on Motivation*, 12, 221–275.

Schaffer, J. (1976). Drunkenness and cultural stress. In M. Everett, J. Waddell, & D. Heath (Eds.), *Cross-cultural approaches to the study of alcohol*. The Hague, the Netherlands: Mouton.

Schino, G., Troisi, A., et al. (1991). Measuring anxiety in non-human primates. *Pharmacology, Biochemistry, and Behavior*, 38, 889–891.

Schlund, M., Hudgins, C., et al. (2013). Neuroimaging the temporal dynamics of human avoidance to sustained threat. *Behavioural Brain Research*, 257, 148–155.

Schwartz, B. (2004). *The paradox of choice*. New York: HarperPerennial.

References

Schwartz, N., & Clore, G. (2007). Feelings and phenomenal experiences. In E. T. Higgins & A. Kruglanski (Eds.), *Social psychology: Handbook of basic principles* (2nd ed.). New York: Guilford Press.

Seabright, P. (2010). *The company of strangers*. Princeton, NJ: Princeton University Press.

Seneca. (1995). *Moral and political essays* (J. Cooper & J. Procopé, Eds.). Cambridge: Cambridge University Press.

Shallice, T. (1988). *From neuropsychology to mental structure*. Cambridge: Cambridge University Press.

Shasteen, J., Sasson, N., & Pinkham, A. (2014). Eye tracking the face in the crowed. *PLoS One*, 9.

Sherman, N. (1989). *The fabric of character*. Oxford: Oxford University Press.

Shoemaker, D. (2015). *Responsibility from the margins*. Oxford: Oxford University Press.

Sizer, L. (2006). Toward a computational theory of mood. *British Journal for the Philosophy of Science*, 51, 743–769.

Skeem, J., Kerr, M., et al. (2007). Two subtypes of psychopathic violent offenders that parallel primary and secondary variants. *Journal of Abnormal Psychology*, 116, 359–409.

Slater, M. (2015). Natural kindness. *British Journal for the Philosophy of Science*, 66, 375–411.

Slater, P. (1970). *The pursuit of loneliness*. Boston: Beacon Press.

Slote, M. (2014). *A sentimentalist theory of mind*. Oxford: Oxford University Press.

Smith, D. (2012). *Monkey mind*. New York: Simon & Schuster.

Smith, M. (1994). *The moral problem*. Oxford: Blackwell.

Snell, W. (1989). Willingness to self-disclose to female and male friends as a function of social anxiety and gender. *Personality and Social Psychology Bulletin*, 15, 113–125.

Soares, J., & Öhman, A. (1993a). Backward masking and skin conductance responses after conditioning to non-feared but fear-relevant stimuli in fearful subjects. *Psychophysiology*, 30, 460–466.

Soares, J., & Öhman, A. (1993b). Preattentive processing, preparedness, and phobias. *Behaviour Research and Therapy*, 31, 87–95.

Somerville, L., Wagner, D., et al. (2013). Interactions between transient and sustained neural signals support the generation and regulation of anxious emotion. *Cerebral Cortex*, 23, 49–60.

Somerville, L., Whalen, P., & Kelley, W. (2010). Human bed nucleus of the stria terminalis indexes hypervigilant threat monitoring. *Biological Psychiatry*, 68, 416–424.

Sperber, D., Clément, F., et al. (2010). Epistemic vigilance. *Mind & Language*, 25, 359–393.

Spering, M., Wagener, D., & Funke, J. (2005). The role of emotions in complex problem solving. *Cognition and Emotion*, 19, 1252–1261.

Spielberger, C. (1983). *Manual for the State-Trait Anxiety Inventory (STAI)*. Palo Alto, CA: Consulting Psychologists Press.

Sripada, C., & Stich, S. (2004). Evolution, culture, and the irrationality of the emotions. In D. Evans & P. Cruse (Eds.), *Emotion, evolution and rationality* (pp. 133–158). Oxford: Oxford University Press.

Stanton, E. C. (1898/1993). *Eighty years and more*. Boston: Northeastern University Press.

Sterelny, K. (2012a). *The evolved apprentice*. Cambridge, MA: MIT Press.

Sterelny, K. (2012b). Morality's dark past. *Analyse & Kritik*, 34, 95–115.

Sterelny, K. (2013). Life in interesting times. In K. Sterelny, R. Joyce, B. Calcott, & B. Fraser (Eds.), *Cooperation and its evolution* (pp. 89–108). Cambridge, MA: MIT Press.

Sterelny, K., Joyce, R., Calcott, B., & Fraser, B. (2013). *Cooperation and its evolution*. Cambridge, MA: MIT Press.

Stichter, M. (2011). Virtues, skills and right action. *Ethical Theory and Moral Practice*, 14, 73–86.

Stichter, M. (2016). Practical skills and practical wisdom in virtue. *Australasian Journal of Philosophy*, 94, 435–448.

Stohr, K. (2003). Moral cacophony: When continence is a virtue. *Journal of Ethics*, 7, 339–363.

Stossel, S. (2013). *My age of anxiety*. New York: Knopf.

Straub, T., Mentzel, H., & Miltner, W. (2007). Waiting for spiders: Brain activation during anticipatory anxiety in spider phobics. *NeuroImage*, 37, 1427–1436.

Suhler, C., & Churchland, P. (2009). Control: Conscious and otherwise. *Trends in Cognitive Sciences*, 13, 341–347.

Summers, J., & Sinnott-Armstrong, W. (2015). Scrupulous judgments. In M. Timmons (Ed.), *Oxford studies in normative ethics* (Vol. 5, pp. 129–150). Oxford: Oxford University Press.

Sutton, J. (2007). Batting, habit, and memory. *Sport in Society*, 10, 763–786.

References

Swanton, C. (2003). *Virtue ethics: A pluralistic view*. Oxford: Oxford University Press.

Swerdlow, N., Geyer, M., Vale, W., & Koob, G. (1986). Corticotropin-releasing factor potentiates acoustic startle in rats. *Psychopharmacology*, 88, 147–152.

Tangney, J., & Dearing, R. (2002). *Shame and guilt*. New York: Guilford Press.

Tangney, J., Miller, R., Flicker, L., & Barrow, D. (1996). Are shame, guilt, and embarrassment distinct emotions? *Journal of Personality and Social Psychology*, 70, 1256–1269.

Tappolet, C. (2016). *Emotions, values, and agency*. Oxford: Oxford University Press.

Teixeira, R. C., Zangrossi, H., & Graeff, F. G. (2000). Behavioral effects of acute and chronic imipramine in the elevated T-maze model of anxiety. *Pharmacology, Biochemistry, and Behavior*, 65, 571–576.

Tennie, C., Call, J., & Tomasello, M. (2009). Ratcheting up the ratchet: On the evolution of cumulative culture. *Philosophical Transactions of the Royal Society of London B: Biological Sciences*, 364, 2405–2415.

Teper, R., Segal, Z. V., & Inzlicht, M. (2013). Inside the mindful mind: How mindfulness enhances emotion regulation through improvements in executive control. *Current Directions in Psychological Science*, 22, 449–454.

Thorpe, S., & Brosnan, M. (2007). Does computer anxiety reach levels which conform to DSM IV criteria for specific phobia? *Computers in Human Behavior*, 23, 1258–1272.

Tiberius, V. (2002). Practical reason and the stability standard. *Ethical Theory and Moral Practice*, 5, 339–353.

Tiberius, V. (2008). *The reflective life*. New York: Oxford University Press.

Tiberius, V. (2013). In defense of reflection. *Philosophical Issues*, 23, 223–243.

Tiedens, L., & Linton, S. (2001). Judgment under emotional certainty and uncertainty. *Journal of Social and Personality Psychology*, 81, 973–988.

Tooby, J., & Cosmides, L. (1990). The past explains the present: Emotional adaptations and the structure of ancestral environments. *Ethology and Sociobiology*, 11, 375–424.

Trotter, M., & Endler, N. (1999). An empirical test of the interaction model of anxiety in a competitive equestrian setting. *Personality and Individual Differences*, 48, 285–290.

Trump, D. (2016, November). Donald Trump controversial campaign quotes. *Newsday*. Retrieved from http://www.newsday.com/news/nation/donald-trump-controversial-campaign-quotes-1.11206532.

Twenge, J. (2006). *Generation me: Why today's young Americans are more confident, assertive, entitled—and more miserable than ever before*. New York: Free Press.

Valentino, N., Hutchings, V., Banks, A., & Davis, A. (2008). Is a worried citizen a good citizen? Emotions, political information seeking, and learning via the Internet. *Political Psychology*, 29, 247–273.

Velleman, J. D. (2003). Don't worry, feel guilty. *Royal Institute of Philosophy*, 52(Suppl.), 235–248.

Velleman, J. D. (2008). The way of the wanton. In C. Mackenzie & K. Atkins (Eds.), *Practical identity and narrative agency*. New York: Routledge.

Verhaeghen, P., Joormann, J., & Khan, R. (2005). Why we sing the blues: The relation between self-reflective rumination, mood, and creativity. *Emotion*, 5, 226–232.

Walker, D., & Davis, M. (1997). Anxiogenic effects of high illumination levels assessed with the acoustic startle paradigm. *Biological Psychiatry*, 42, 461–471.

Walker, D., & Davis, M. (2002a). Light enhanced startle. *Psychopharmacology*, 159, 304–310.

Walker, D., & Davis, M. (2002b). Quantifying fear potentiated startle using absolute vs percent increase scoring methods. *Psychopharmacology*, 164, 318–328.

Wallace, R. J. (1994). *Responsibility and the moral sentiments*. Cambridge, MA: Harvard University Press.

Wangelin, B., Bradley, M., et al. (2014). Affective engagement for facial expressions and emotional scenes. *Biological Psychology*, 91, 103–110.

Watson, D. (2005). Rethinking the mood and anxiety disorders. *Journal of Abnormal Psychology*, 114, 522–536.

Watson, G. (1984). Free agency. In G. Watson (Ed.), *Free will*. Oxford: Oxford University Press.

Weeks, J., Rodebagh, T., et al. (2008). "To avoid evaluation, withdraw": Fears of evaluation and depressive cognitions lead to social anxiety and submissive withdrawal. *Cognitive Therapy and Research*, 33, 375–389.

Wegner, D. (2002). *The illusion of conscious will*. Cambridge, MA: MIT Press.

Wells, A. (2000). *Emotional disorders and metacognition: Innovative cognitive therapy*. New York: Wiley.

Whiten, A., Schick, K., & Toth, N. (2009). The evolution and cultural transmission of percussive technology: Integrating evidence from palaeoanthropology and primatology. *Journal of Human Evolution*, 57, 420–435.

References

Wigfield, A., & Eccles, J. (1989). Test anxiety in elementary and secondary school students. *Educational Psychologist*, 23, 159–183.

Williams, B. (1973). Ethical consistency. In *Problems of the self*. Cambridge: Cambridge University Press.

Williams, B. (1981). Moral luck. In *Moral luck*. Cambridge: Cambridge University Press.

Wilson, T. (2002). *Strangers to ourselves*. Cambridge, MA: Harvard University Press.

Wilson, T., & Kraft, D. (1993). Why do I love thee? *Personality and Social Psychology Bulletin*, 19, 409–418.

Wilson, T., & Schooler, J. (1991). Thinking too much. *Journal of Personality and Social Psychology*, 60, 181–192.

Wittchen, H., & Beloch, E. (1996). The impact of social phobia on quality of life. *International Clinical Psychopharmacology*, 11(Suppl. 3), 15–23.

Witte, K., & Allen, M. (2000). A meta-analysis of fear appeals: Implications for effective public health campaigns. *Health Education & Behavior*, 27, 591–615.

Wolf, S. (1990). *Freedom within reason*. New York: Oxford University Press.

Wong, M. (2016). The mood-emotion loop. *Philosophical Studies*, 173, 3061–3080.

Woodman, T., & Hardy, L. (2001). Stress and anxiety. In R. Singer, H. Hausenblas, & C. Jenelle (Eds.), *Handbook of research on sport psychology* (pp. 290–318). New York: Wiley.

Woolman, J. (1774/1952). *The journal and other writings*. London: Dent.

Wringe, B. (2014). The contents of perceptions and the contents of emotion. *Noûs*, 49, 275–297.

Yassa, M., Hazlett, R., et al. (2012). Functional MRI of the amygdala and bed nucleus of the stria terminalis during conditions of uncertainty in generalized anxiety disorder. *Journal of Psychiatric Research*, 46, 1045–1052.

Zeidner, M. (1998). *Test anxiety: The state of the art*. New York: Plenum Press.

Zeidner, M., & Matthews, G. (2005). Evaluation anxiety: Current theory and research. In A. Elliot & C. Dweck (Eds.), *Personality and individual differences* (Vol. 16, pp. 459–476). New York: Guilford Publications.

Zeidner, M., & Matthews, G. (2011). *Anxiety 101*. New York: Springer.

Zeier, J., & Newman, J. (2013). Feature-based attention and conflict monitoring in criminal offenders. *Journal of Abnormal Psychology*, 122, 797–806.

Index

Abolition movement, 4–5, 185–188
Abramowitz, J., 78–79, 125n22, 199
Affect program, 7–8, 14–15, 22–26, 62–65, 83–88, 90–92, 94–95
Affect program features (APFs), 62–65, 83–88
Affirmative action, 74–75, 90, 165–166
Allen, W., 16, 111, 116
Alzheimer's example, 5, 15–16, 132–134, 142, 164–166, 170
Amygdala, central nucleus of, 40–46, 48–49, 63
Anger, 24, 62, 66, 74–75, 76–77, 91n29, 103–104, 106, 110–111, 116, 124, 126–130, 134–136, 137, 165–166, 191–192, 192n4, 208n2
Annas, J., 3, 4, 104, 127n24, 142, 153–164, 167, 170, 172, 199–200
Antideliberationist challenge, 146–147, 147–153, 155, 166–181
Anxiety
  and accuracy motivation, 70, 98–99, 121–122, 166–169, 192–197
  affect program, 6–8, 14–15, 22–26, 47–59, 62–65, 66, 71, 80–83, 85–86, 87–88, 91, 94–98, 199
  as aretically valuable, 5, 6, 16, 104–105, 126–134, 135, 136, 139–140, 145
  as conscious state, 12, 49–50, 58–59, 92–97
  and ego-defensive motivation, 70, 166–169
  as emotion versus mood versus feeling, 9–11
  facial expression, lack of, 53–54
  formal object of, 107 (*see also* Fittingness conditions)
  as forward-looking emotion, 1–2, 11, 63, 141, 201, 214–215
  functionally integrated inputs and outputs, 25, 56–57, 67–72, 98–99, 116, 164
  as intrinsically valuable, 6, 104, 126, 134–136
  neural circuitry of (*see* Amygdala, central nucleus of; Bed nucleus of the stria terminalis [BNST])
  as pancultural phenomenon, 53–54
  role in learning and development, 113–116
  and self-defense motivation, 70
  trait versus state, 8–9
Anxiety disorders, 11, 26–27, 77–79, 84n20, 111, 117–121
Aristotle, 127n24, 128,
Arpaly, N., 128, 131, 146, 149n7, 177n36
Attentional biases, 35–38

Barlow, D., 4, 112
Baxley, A., 127n24

Bed nucleus of the stria teminalis (BNST), 40–46, 49, 59, 63, 65, 71, 80–83
Bell, M., 105, 134n34
Boehm, C., 206, 207, 208, 209, 214n11
Boyd, R., 30–31
Brader, T., 77n12, 189–190, 191–192, 196, 197, 200
Brink, D., 148, 201n10

Category. See Kind, natural; Projectability
Cognitive-behavioral therapy (CBT), 199–200
Cognitive dissonance, 14, 28n7, 64–65
Cognitive processing. See also Metacognition
    multi-level, 12, 24, 25n3, 48–50, 51–53, 53n30, 55, 57–59, 72, 77, 79–80, 85, 92–97, 147–153
    type 1 and type 2, 12n11, 151, 159n22, 178
Confabulation, 143, 151–152, 172–173, 180
Conscience, 140–141, 180–181, 186, 195–196, 213–215
Cooperation, 206–209, 211–215
Craver, C., 27, 84n20
Creativity, 4, 114, 114n11, 122
Csikszentmihalyi, M., 112n10, 114, 155
Cultural-cognitive model, 56, 57, 61, 92–93
Curiosity, 65n4, 131

D'Arms, J., 105, 106, 107–109, 108n7, 131n30
Deliberation. See Cognitive processing
de Sousa, R., 106–107, 109
Dinner party example, 97, 165
Disgust, 7, 25, 55, 95, 95n33, 110–112, 117, 124–5, 199, 208n2
Doris, J., 16–17, 79n15, 146–147, 150–152, 154n16. See also Antideliberationist challenge

Dreyfus, H. and Dreyfus, S., 153n15, 155n18, 156, 159n21, 164, 172–173
Duke of Wellington, 187–188, 190, 198

Ekman, P., 22–23, 24–25, 47, 53–55, 62
Embarrassment, 28n7, 63n1, 186, 194n7
Emotion (anxiety) cultivation, 98–99, 136–137, 169–171, 197–200. See also Reappraisal of emotion
Empathy, 193–194
Endler, N., 8, 68, 72–73, 197
Environmental anxiety, 15, 62, 67–68, 68–83, 87, 90, 91, 98–99, 105, 109–110, 125, 205–207, 211
Envy, 105, 107–108, 110
Euthanasia example, 132–134
Existential anxiety, 1, 14, 27, 84–86, 87, 91
Extended amygdala complex (EAC), 34–35, 40, 45, 51, 63. See also Amygdala, central nucleus of; Bed nucleus of the stria teminalis (BNST))
Fear, 7n3, 10, 11, 14–15, 21, 26, 28, 31, 32–47, 54–56, 62–63, 86n22, 91n29, 93n30, 95n33, 106–107, 110, 116, 124, 140n41, 166, 207–210
Feelings, 9–11, 85
Fessler, D., 25–26, 214n11
Fine, C., 146n2, 148, 152, 153n14, 153n15
Firefighters, 163–164
Fittingness conditions, 109–110, 132–133
Fittingness objection, 105–109
Foot, P., 104n1, 142, 153n15, 162n26
Frank, R., 66n5, 207–208, 208n2, 211
Frankena, W., 134–135
Freud, S., 88n26

Gala example, 92–97, 118
Goldie, P., 9n6, 29, 29n8, 55, 57, 110n8
GRE test, 123–124, 170, 200n9

Index

Griffiths, P., 14, 24, 25, 27, 30–31, 47, 53, 55, 59, 62, 66n5, 84n20, 86n22, 88, 140n42
Guilt, 1, 11, 70, 86n22, 113, 133–134, 141n43, 161, 161n23, 186–187, 196, 215

Haidt, J., 16, 17, 146, 150n10, 150–152, 152n12
Helm, B., 106, 107n6, 129n28
Herman, B., 179–181, 196
Hoch, P., 27–28
Horwitz, A., 12, 27n5, 84n20, 112n10, 119–121
Humility, 131
Hursthouse, R., 3, 104n1, 127n24, 142, 153n15

Immigration, 188–191, 196, 197
Izard, C., 23n2, 54, 95, 95n33

Jacobson, D., 105, 106, 107–109, 108n7, 131n30, 133–134, 152n12, 153n14, 161n23
Jamieson, J., 122, 123–124, 170

Kant, I., 3, 4, 104–105, 110, 126, 127n24, 135–136, 140–141, 179–181, 196, 214n13
Kelly, D., 24, 95n33, 117, 199
Kennett, J., 148, 152
Kierkegaard, S., 14, 27, 84–86
Kind, natural, 26–55, 61–65, 90–99. *See also* Projectability
King, M. L., Jr., 184, 186–187, 190, 194–197, 198, 200, 214n13
Kitcher, P., 184n1, 185, 193, 206, 207–210, 212n7, 213n9
Klein, G., 163–164
Korsgaard, C., 104n2, 115n12, 146n2, 147n4, 148

LeDoux, J., 11, 12, 12n11, 35, 41n20, 42, 50, 53, 56n33, 84–85, 92

Levenson, R., 7–8, 22–25, 93, 95, 98n34
Lust, 105, 107–108

MacKuen, M., 74–75, 75n11, 77, 90, 112, 114, 165, 168, 192n4, 196, 197
Maibom, H., 70n6, 79n15, 214n11
Mandela, N., 5, 15, 67
Marsh, H., 3, 15, 67, 162n25
McDowell, J., 3, 4, 104n1, 142, 147n4, 177
Metacognition, 6, 114–116, 193–194, 211–215
Metaethics, 201n10
Misattribution, emotion, 89, 113
Moods, 6–7, 9–11, 85, 128n18
Moral anxiety, 4–6, 88–90
Moral concern, 126–137, 141, 193, 201
Moral progress, 6, 17–18, 183–201

Naturalism, 12–13, 130–131
Nelkin, D., 148

Öhman, A., 12, 23n2, 25, 32n12, 33–37, 51, 56–57, 78
Oldowan toolmakers, 157–159

Paradigm scenario, 107, 109
Performance anxiety, 3–4, 14, 69, 81, 86–88, 103, 121–124, 169–170. *See also* Social anxiety
Perkins, A., 37–38, 73, 89, 113
Practical anxiety, 1–2, 6, 13–17, 67–73, 74–77, 78–79, 81–83, 88–90, 91, 98–99, 105, 109–110, 114–115, 124–125, 126–143, 145–147, 164–182, 183–201, 205, 209–215
Prinz, J., 9n6, 16, 32n11, 55, 95, 95n33, 106, 108n7, 146, 150n10, 194n6
Projectability (minimal, robust), 30–32. *See also* Kind, natural
Psychopathy, 113
Public service announcements (PSAs), 200

Punishment anxiety, 15, 67–74, 77–79, 81, 86–88, 90–91, 92–97, 98–99, 109–110, 121–122, 125–126, 164–165, 169, 205, 207–209

Railton, P., 13n12, 115n12, 135–136, 137n36, 149n7, 153n15, 155n18, 164, 172–173
Reappraisal of emotion, 123–124, 170, 198, 198n8, 200n9
Refugee case, 161–168
Regress of practical judgment, problem of, 149–150, 176–178
Regret, 11n8, 133, 160–161, 161n23
Repressor phenomenon, 25n3, 49–50, 58–59, 97
Roberts, R., 55, 63, 66, 107–108, 137
Rules of moral salience (RMS), 179–181, 196
Rumination, 46, 92–97, 117–118, 122, 169

Scarantino, A., 27n6, 30, 53, 106n4, 140n42
Schroeder, T., 128, 131, 146, 149n7, 177n36
Scrupulosity, 27, 78–79, 125n22, 199. *See also* Anxiety disorders
Seeding model, 157–158
Shame, 1, 11, 14, 26, 28n7, 63–64, 70n6, 186, 194n7, 196, 208n2, 213–215
Sherman, N., 199–200
Situationism, 154n16
Skill model of virtuous agency, 153–164, 171–173
Social anxiety, 2–4, 64n2, 73–74, 86–88, 121–122, 164–169
Somerville, L., 43n23, 81
Standard deliberationist model (SDM), 145–153
Sterelny, K., 157–158, 206–207, 207, 209n3, 210, 212n8, 213n10

Stoics, 103–104, 137–140, 141
Stossel, S., 2, 111, 116, 118–119

Tiberius, V., 115n12, 146n2, 148–150, 152n13, 153n15, 171, 174–179
Trump, D., 188

Uncertainty, 6–9, 65n4, 68, 69–70, 177n36

Valentino, N., 76–77, 112, 114, 166, 168, 192n4, 196
Velleman, J.D., 88n26, 141n43, 153n15, 164, 172–173
Vietnam War, 186–187, 194–196

Wakefield, J., 12, 27n5, 84n20, 112n10, 119–121
Williams, B., 133, 133n33, 161n23
Wilson, T., 151–152, 170–171
Woolman, J., 4, 15–16, 17, 67, 184–186, 190–194, 196–200
Worry, 10, 14, 26–27, 45–46, 92–97, 103, 116, 117–118, 119, 121–123, 169–170

Xanax objection, 130–134